"A thought-provoking read on standing out ⟨barcode⟩ 1.
Nigel Nicholson has been an expert on auth I0049428 ⟨e⟩
fashionable, and his book is filled with comp........ ....s."

– *Adam Grant, #1* New York Times *bestselling author of* Hidden Potential *and* Think Again,
and host of the podcast Re:Thinking

"Every now and then a book comes along which is radically different from
anything published before and you know immediately will become a classic.
"*Unique You*" is just that. It is a stunning and highly readable book which strikes
to the heart of so many personal issues today such as the search for purpose and
destiny and knowing one's own unique strengths and value. In a world where
AI is mashing up jobs and values, knowing our own human uniqueness will
be even more important. Professor Nicholson releases us from the tyranny of
conformity as a celebration of what it means to be uniquely. Packed with research
and heart-warming personal stories, the pages explode with life-enhancing
insights and practical suggestions which will turbo-charge the next chapters of
your life. Above all this book will help you make better sense of your own unique
story and will inspire you to take hold of your own future in a new way."

– *Patrick Dixon MBE, Futurist, Chairman of Global Change Ltd, and best-selling author of*
Futurewise *and* How AI Will Change Your Life.

"A magisterial sweep of psychology, biology, the arts, and literature, this book
argues for us to understand, respect, and take full advantage of our unique
individuality. The cheerful optimism that permeates the work is essential at
a time when technological advances and a breakdown of long-held assumptions are causing profound anxiety. Reading this book is like listening to Nigel
Nicholson; a treat that was once the privilege of the few. With this volume, his
wisdom and learning will educate, delight, provoke, and better many more."

– *Madan Pillutla, Dean, Indian School of Business.*

"If the last century was all about fitting in, this one will be more about standing out – finding a distinctive ecological niche to call one's own. This is a superb handbook to help you do exactly that."

– Rory Sutherland, Chairman Emeritus, Ogilvy Consulting.

"Why do you feel you are different to everyone else? This original, engagingly written book explains why, and why we should celebrate the fact."

– Robin Dunbar, Professor of Evolutionary Psychology, University of Oxford, author of Friends: Understanding the power of our most important relationships.

"It is wonderful to see individuality being celebrated. I've always valued being different – doing the unexpected is the job of an engineer and it is the only way to creatively improve the world."

– Sir James Dyson OM, Founder and Chairman of Dyson

Unique YOU

How Individuality Works and Why it Matters

Nigel Nicholson

Unique You: How Individuality Works and Why it Matters
Nigel Nicholson

Published by Hogan Press
Tulsa, OK

Library of Congress Control Number: 2026901080

NICHOLSON, NIGEL Author
UNIQUE YOU

ISBN: 979-8-218-83357-2

Primary: PSY000000   PSYCHOLOGY / General
Secondary: SEL000000   SELF-HELP / General

Book Design by Michelle M. White
Cover image designed with images licensed from the following sources:
Adobe Stock: Rahul Al and Glebstock; Shutterstock Asset Generation (AI)

For information, contact Hogan Press
11 S. Greenwood, Tulsa OK 74120
hoganassessments.com

H
HOGANPRESS

Unique You
is dedicated to
My Biographers
For your Courage, Compassion, Love and Wisdom
and in loving memory of
Barbara Olive Collard (1921–1993)
Who gave me the love of human stories

Contents

PREFACE/INTRODUCTION

WHY UI?

There is a big idea behind this book. You, I, and everyone possess Unique Individuality (UI) – our own singular profile of physical and mental identity. Constitutionally and psychologically, we are all exceptional, unique, and unrepeatable. Our UI is a universal truth that is more important than ever before in the era of artificial intelligence. It is our last and strongest line of defence against any threats new technologies may pose. We also seem to be living in an age of anxiety, with fragile mental health afflicting the young especially. As we shall see, UI is central to both this challenge and what we can do about it.

Our UI is the engine behind personal destinies, cultural revolutions, and much of life's deepest joys and sorrows. This is not a self-help book in the traditional sense, but it will help you. The Uniqueness Perspective answers many questions that trouble people about their lives and relationships. It offers deep reassurance as well as a personal challenge to find and achieve your potential.

The course of history and the future of our planet depend on our UI. Technologies are radically altering how we live but not our biological identity. We remain, as ever, uniquely gifted, inventive, resourceful beings, with untold potential for shaping our world and relationships – for the good of all. Our UI is also potentially our greatest threat, if technology indiscriminately hands power to individuals who wish to do harm to others, regardless of the cost to themselves. It's time to take UI seriously, to see how it works and why it matters, now as never before. That's what this book sets out to do.

WHY ME? WHY NOW?

I have been waiting all my life to write this book, and now the time has arrived. Since my childhood, I have held a passionate fascination for what psychologists call individual differences. This is a product of my own UI: curiosity plus upbringing. I was raised in a family of socialist bohemians, and throughout my childhood, I watched with fascination as a parade of odd characters tramped through our house – artists, writers, intellectuals, eccentrics of all stripes. When I started my formal studies of psychology, I was astonished to find the spirit of the times hostile to the science of individual differences. The behaviourists were in the ascendancy – the school of thought that maintained that a truly scientific psychology should only observe, measure, and manipulate objective behaviour. Its proponents pioneered powerful learning methods that are still used to control behaviour in many walks of life (gambling, education, payment systems, animal training). In this ethos, it was heresy to try to conceive of what is in the minds of humans and beasts.

It was not until I switched from being a full-time researcher to a business school professor that I was able to bring the study of persons centre stage. As a licenced test user, I was able to call upon the best personality tools available, to put profiling at the heart of my research and teaching. In the management classroom, I found that the helpful generalisations of behavioural research in my field weren't helping enough. Every generalisation had interesting exceptions that were disregarded as "error variance," in the jargon of social science. But these weren't errors. They were individuals failing to conform to predictions. Every manager and leader was a special case. Every "truth" had to be qualified by the unique approach of this or that leader. Every practical application had to be tuned to their unique situation. This set me off in a new direction. Working with handpicked teams of coaches, my teaching became focused on finding for each individual executive what tailored suite of ideas and interventions worked best for them. It was apparent that each person had to find their own path toward more effective and fulfilled relationships, teamwork, and communications – to find their best place in the organisational universe. It seemed unnecessary that so many hard-working and dedicated executives felt that their voices were stifled, unheard, or misheard.

I went on to design and launch degree and executive programmes embodying a Uniqueness Perspective. They proved popular and life changing for many people, including me. One was *Proteus* – an experiential programme that concluded with a Biography workshop, using some of the methodologies described in these pages (see Chapter 10). The second was a multi-session Biography programme, spread across the first two terms for students on

the 1-year Sloan Fellowship in Leadership and Strategy. This is the most mature postgradu-
ate group at London Business School – around 50 men and women from every part of the
globe – mostly in their 40s – coming to refresh, reboot, or change their career trajectories.

These brave and wonderful people have inspired this book, and I tell many of their
remarkable stories in these pages. Post-pandemic, I came out of retirement to relaunch
the programme. There was a new spirit in the air – a renewed hunger to be recognised
and heard. I have continued to run the Biography Programme ever since, and this book
is its embodiment – to bring the Uniqueness Perspective into the public domain.

WHAT'S NEW?

It has puzzled me why no one in the modern era has sought to decipher the dynamics and
implications of human individuality.[1] There is a long history of thinking and writing on individual differences from the Romans on "temperament" (see Chapter 3) and even earlier clas-
sifications of human types in Chinese and Indian cosmology. It was the Victorian passion
for self-inquiry that sparked the first scientific approaches to intelligence and personality
measurement at the turn of the 20th century. This was dampened by its misuse in eugenics –
selective sterilisation, immigration, and under the Nazis, euthanasia, all based on naïve and
simplistic ideas derived from stockbreeding and racist ideology. This moved the dial against
the study of individual differences, giving space for the behaviourist ideology to flourish. Its
low point was the claim of its chief founder that were he given a "dozen healthy infants," he
could "guarantee" that given any one at random, he could train them "to become any type
of specialist I might select."[2] This boast has been comprehensively falsified by research in
behaviour geneticists (see Chapter 2). We now know that genes and environment intertwine
in all development. Yet the behaviourists' legacy is visible today in many areas of scholarship and public debate, where the "social constructionist" ideology was promoted by sociologists.[3] They are right that we live in a socially constructed world where self-reinvention is
entirely possible and commonplace – but this has hard limitations, set by our UI.

For much of the 20th century, individual differences scholarship has flourished in
the military and civil service, where its practical use in selection, training, and leadership was plain for all to see. Another place where UI remains centre stage is clinical
therapeutic practice, where a whole-person "idiographic" approach is essential. Yet
clinical psychology is often weighed down with contentious theories, uninterested in
whole lives, or wedded to medicalised taxonomies.

Lifespan developmental and humanist psychology have more to offer, but neither sets out to explain the dynamics of individuality. A more direct approach can be seen in the freestanding academic enclave that goes under the name of "psychobiography."[4] Its exponents dedicate themselves to detailed case study analyses of well-documented lives. The subset of this discipline that is closest to our topic is "narrative psychology,"[5] but too the approach is circumscribed, not seeking to unpack how individuality works and why it matters. That is the purpose of this book.

ANSWERING ALLPORT'S CALL

In so doing I am answering the call nearly a century ago by Gordon Allport, widely considered the father of personality psychology, who for decades was a lone voice calling for what he termed an "idiographic" psychology. This he saw as an essential complement to "nomothetic" psychology, which searches for general laws about human behaviour.[6] The psychobiographers partly answered his call, but no one to date has set out what an idiographic psychology might tell us about ourselves, our relationships, culture, and society. In the pages of this book, I will be drawing on multiple case histories to tell the complete story of individuality, in a way that is accessible to a general readership. My approach is multidisciplinary, drawing the latest insights of modern evolutionary biology and neuroscience, as well as the social sciences, philosophy, and literature.

It seems that the deepest insights into UI are often to be found in fiction. In the Western canon, the novelists who have most to offer in terms of penetrating insights into the development and consequences of UI are George Eliot, Henry James (no accident, brother to one of the first and greatest of academic psychologists, William James), Dostoyevsky, Charles Dickens, and of course the master of all varieties of humanity, playwright William Shakespeare.

I am no Shakespeare, but Shakespeare was no scientist, and I want to do justice to his insights about the glories of the human animal by taking you on a journey of truth and discovery about who you are and how you can live your best life.

HOW TO READ THIS BOOK

What impertinence! It's your book. Read it however you want. I don't need to tell you that – you'll do so anyway. It is foolish for writers to assume readers reverentially follow their script. So let me just set out the logic of its contents, and then you can decide.

At the end of every chapter, I list possible implications for Unique You.

The first three chapters are "foundational" – setting out the system of thought I am introducing to you. First, in Chapter 1, I will tell you what UI is and why it matters, introducing key ideas that pop up throughout the book. Chapter 2 explores where our uniqueness comes from – how much is in our genes? How much is learned? Where does free will sit in this? Chapter 3 tackles the greatest mystery of existence – what is the Self, and how does it work? We shall see how our Beast-being identity works and how it is both guided and misguided by our hard-working Ego and our storytelling Self. Lots of stories are used to make this grounded and relevant to you.

The next five chapters take you on a journey, starting with Relationships (Chapter 4) and Culture (Chapter 5). How does our individuality withstand, exploit, or glory in the ways we connect with each other and our cultures? Then comes a chapter on the Dark Side (Chapter 6) – pathologies and disorders linked to UI. Chapter 7 pulls it all together by looking across the entire lifespan – especially at three periods when most personal transformation takes place. Chapter 8 climbs to the pinnacle of UI – the greatest achievements of individuals in the Arts, Sciences, and in people's creative self-transforming lives.

The three last chapters set out what UI means for us in three ways. First, in Chapter 9, we look at how we can organise and lead each other in ways that bring on the best in each other's individuality. Next, in Chapter 10, I share all the methods and materials that I have found most powerful in helping UI find its best voice. These materials (in the Appendix) and ideas are yours to plunder and use as you wish. In Chapter 11, I come back to the technological revolution breaking over us and how a Uniqueness Perspective is as never before an insight for our times – a defence and an aid to the intelligent mastery of technologies. It also offers profound reassurance in the context of 21st century epidemic of mental distresses. Chapter 12 offers a final reflection on the ethical implications of the Uniqueness Perspective.

I hope you love reading it as much as I loved writing it. See you on the other side!

ACKNOWLEDGEMENTS

My first and deepest thanks are to my Biographers on the London Business School Sloan Fellowship programme, who inspired this book and whose stories populate it. Thank you for allowing me to share your most intimate and insightful testimonies.

Second, members of my living family have been my personal guiding light, through their insights, support, and partnership – none more so than my dear wife Adele, a brilliant reader, who always framed difficult questions in the right way to make me think clearly about the most challenging issues, at every step of the way. From time to time, I have also called on my youngest son, Oliver, to help me break through the most challenging roadblocks that crop up in such an ambitious project. I am equally indebted to my two dearest, most talkative philosophical friends, Jules Goddard and Dominic Houlder, without whose passionate belief and support this daunting project would never have come to fruition.

A special mention is due to two readers, from different generational viewpoints, whom I called upon to read and critique every line, thought and expression – Reva Banthiya, reading philosophy and computer science at Oxford, and Eva Andrusier, therapist and linguist. They have done more than anyone to keep this as relevant and readable as I can make it.

Finally, I offer my most sincere thanks to Bob Hogan for his friendship and faith in my work over decades of wonderful exchanges, who made possible this chance to work together. Georgi Yankov, enlightened editor, has driven this project with his passionate appreciation of its purpose, expertly steering it on the path to delivery. He has tolerated my eccentricities with great good humour and been a consistent motivator, friend, and wise counsel throughout.

Thank you all!

One

WHAT IT MEANS TO BE UNIQUE
Why Individuality Matters

Brian: "You are all individuals!"
Crowd, in unison: "Yes, we are all individuals!"
Lone voice in crowd: "I'm not."
(Monty Python)[1]

There will be no one like us when we are gone ... it is the fate of every human
being to be a unique individual, to find his own path, to live his own life,
to die his own death.
(Oliver Sacks)[2]

ALONE IN THE DARK?

Here are four inescapable facts about you – the Four Laws of Unique Individuality (UI).[1]

1. No one just like you has ever lived on this planet before, nor ever will again. You are constitutionally unique, in your own bespoke human mind–body vehicle. You have UI – *Unique Individuality*.
2. You only see portions of the totality of your UI through the window of consciousness. The rest of UI is hidden from view, yet as we shall see, important aspects can be brought into the light. Other important and influential processes that make you who you are can only be guessed at.
3. You can never know another person – their UI is even more unknowable than your own – for each of us carries our own *umwelt*,[2] our private worlds, which we navigate imperfectly. By the same token, no one will ever truly know you. We all have our blind spots.[3]

Together, these three laws would seem to condemn us to live our lives alone, whistling in the dark to keep our spirits up. Fortunately, not. Life is beautiful, full of consolations and deep connections with others. We are redeemed, partially, by the Fourth Law:

4. Connection with others is the necessary and sustaining fact of life, from cradle to grave, as is exposure to cultures and subcultures. Connection is essential to the development of your UI and to achieving your potential.

There is also a dark side to UI whose depths we will be plumbing – a range of challenging feelings, thoughts, and perceptions associated with our fundamental aloneness that cause some of the greatest griefs and pain known to humans. For many this takes the form of an unfed hunger for deep recognition. At the same time, our UI is the source of our most profound pleasures, and more than that, our greatest achievements in the arts, sciences, and world affairs. We can go further: UI is the organic yeast in the brew that is culture. UI drives the history of civilisations, which determines the future of our species. It is also our last line of defence against threats that artificial intelligence (AI) might pose for us.

THE UNIQUENESS PERSPECTIVE

When did you first awaken to your uniqueness? When did it strike you that other people inhabit a psychic space entirely distinct from your own, separate and ultimately unknowable? Does this bother you now? Probably not if you are going about your daily business without more than the usual amount of aggravation. Should it? Yes, if you care about the epidemic of mental distress in the modern era. Yes, if you believe that people are routinely abused by destructive relationships, bad leaders, and bumbling institutions. Yes, if you believe all around us fine people are underachieving and being overlooked. At the same time, legions of others are feeling that their most important moments and experiences are fleeting, undervalued, and unseen. It is not just a matter of witnesses – we can witness ourselves and find ourselves standing perilously on the edge of what looks like a very high and lonely ledge. This was my personal awakening to UI:

> I was a sunny, funny, happy little boy until around the age of 7. I hadn't been long in my own bedroom, and I was enjoying the novelty of being able to lie awake in the dark thinking whatever I liked. Then, one night, looking at the crack of light above the door, a terrifying thought descended on me, unbidden. This marvel of "me-ness" – with its freedom to surf the universe in its own way – was going to end, one day, leaving me in a state of nothingness. How could something so real, so vast, so centred in my vision become nothing at all, in a moment, and forever? My life changed profoundly at that moment. A new, unerasable anxiety had entered my consciousness – the knowledge that I, and all the people I loved, were treading a path to oblivion.

Now, in my advanced years, I am of the Mark Twain persuasion, who said, "I had been dead for billions and billions of years before I was born and had not suffered the slightest inconvenience from it." But the child that I was then could not comprehend how something so vital, so tangible, so immediate, so powerful, so uniquely mine could just cease to exist. The mystery of conscious experience and the glory of its singularity remain astonishing and wondrous.

But who or what is doing the observing? What is this Self – that almost constant presence in our lives? Even when we are asleep, it pops up in our dreams and won't leave us alone. Yet at other times it fades almost out of view, typically when we're totally immersed in the flow of experience – lost in music, sexual ecstasy, sporting endeavour, meditation, brilliant conversation, or great entertainment. Equally, the Self can make noise that blots out all our senses, like when it's roaring with emotion or protesting at the scrutiny of others. Yet your Self is a personal construction. It is as much of your UI that your conscious mind is able to see. But we are a lot more than our thoughts and feelings. Consider this parable.

> Beth Nielsen Chapman has written songs for some of the biggest names in music – Elton John, Bette Midler, Crystal Gayle, Neil Diamond – as well being a renowned performer herself. A person of great resilience and purpose, she overcame breast cancer in 2000 and resumed her creative career. Then in 2008 she began to struggle to write, becoming disheartened at her failing powers. Investigations, including an MRI scan, revealed a brain tumor, whose removal restored her to full functioning. In a studio interview shortly after, she recalled her sense of relief at the discovery: "Thank goodness it isn't me."[4]

Chapman's "me" matters so much. The founding father of the study of identity, William James (1842–1910), distinguished between our "I" and "Me" functions: Ego and Self,[5] respectively. What we shall be calling the Ego is the organ of awareness and agency, what Chapman was using to assess her Self. The Ego is a rather preoccupied, quick-witted yet clumsy and not very observant tenant of a land full of mysteries, your UI. Our UI is the totality of your animal identity. We are what neuroscientist Anil Seth calls "beast-machines"[6] gifted with complex intelligence and driven by powerful forces. We host a hinterland of interwoven made-to-measure qualities, a unique biochemical, anatomical, and mental identity, housed in an autonomous body. Ego and Self, as we shall explore in Chapter 3, are processes, crafted by evolution to help steer our singular Beast-beings through life. They are all we know and the hub of our UI but only a fraction of it.

THE UI LANDSCAPE

In his perspective-shifting book *Ways of Being*, James Bridle reminds us of how human-centred and specific our way of seeing the world is. He borrows the concept of the *umwelt* – literally, "own world" – to show how each species inhabits its own perceptual and operational world.[7] We humans are highly visual, aural, linguistic, tool-using bipeds. Let us take the concept of *umwelt* into the world of UI.

You and I have our own *umwelt*: private worlds of perception, experience, and memory that are like no one else's. Your UI, like mine, has taken shape through a lifetime of trial and error, learning and failure, good and bad times. You have navigated your way with your own personal repertoire of routines, rules of thumb, mental maps of the past and the present. You have your own cognitive map of your personal networks – significant others and their connections. Your UI has been in a state of becoming from the moment of conception and remains, perpetually, a work in progress. It is not free from hazards, such as scripts and visions that others can implant in you. The colours and architecture of our worlds are built under the direction of your Beast-being identity,[10] its preferred ways of thinking, feeling, and acting.

But the UI you inhabit is much larger than what is visible to you. When my 7-year-old self's fears abated and I fell asleep, my UI didn't cease to exist; it chugged along, sometimes dreaming my unique dreams or snoring my unique snores. Even when you are awake and conscious, bending your willpower, awareness, and sense of mastery toward self-discovery, you can still only comprehend a portion of what you are. Other species lack this awareness. They are spared our delusions of self-knowledge and self-control – though they, too, have UI (as any dog owner will tell you).

This makes us, as one psychologist put it, "strangers to ourselves."[11] Just open a pack of any prescription medication and read the very long strip of paper that comes with it. It is largely taken up with all the bad things that might happen if you take the medicine – the unintended consequences or "side effects," as they are euphemistically called. Looking at one of these taken from my medicine cabinet, I can see it lists first, five very nasty ones. If I feel any of these, it tells me to stop taking the pills immediately and go straight to the doctor. This is followed by a series of further warnings divided into "very common," "common" (may affect more than 1 in 10 people), "uncommon" (1 in 100 people), "rare" (1 in 1,000), "very rare" (1 in 10,000), and "not known" ("frequency cannot be estimated from the available data"). These are very long lists! What does this tell me? For one thing, it shows that drug companies have no idea who I am, and second, nor does my doctor. They do know the drug will work on most people, but it also seems that any of us could have a set of totally unpredictable responses.

Pharmacology has known since the time of the apothecaries that anything you put in your body has effects that are quite you-specific. Just look at what alcohol does to people you know – some get sleepy, aggressive, maudlin, talkative, happy, or amorous. Sometimes several of these states tumble after one another in scary sequences, even though science will tell you the basic effects of the stuff on our nervous systems is pretty simple. The complications come from how they interact with your uniquely configured endocrine and neurological systems – in a word, what kind of Beast you are. It just goes to show the truth of the observation, made by Sir William Osler, often called the father of American medicine, writing and practising at the turn of the 20th century: *Don't just ask what disease the patient has; ask what patient the disease has.*[12] This is a radical insight, even in medicine today, where practice is largely driven by classifying people's infirmities and treating them to remove the symptoms.[13] Yet we are seeing a new dawn in bespoke gene therapies, where elements of each person's immune system are retuned to fight disease, ushering in new era of UI-based medicine (see Chapter 11). Bring it on!

In this book, I want to enlarge on Osler's startling insight by examining how our UI is also a Uniqueness Imperative. The imperative is the fact that every environmental input – our awareness of the world, relationships, events that befall us – passes through the bespoke latticework of our neurology, forged by our genetic inheritance plus our lived experience, memory traces, and states of mind. The effects are incalculable and often unexpected. We are constantly surprised by ourselves.

It's a matter of **resonance** – a key concept for UI. In physics, resonance is "a relatively large selective response of an object or a system that vibrates in step or phase, with an externally applied oscillatory force."[14] In music, it is "the natural amplification of sound through the sympathetic vibration in the shape and form of the instrument." In life, it is finding something funny or beautiful, feeling at home in a place, or finding yourself drawn to someone. Your UI resonates with every experience – sometimes loud and clear, sometimes below the threshold of awareness.

UI IN ACTION

Don't just ask what world you are in; ask what "you" the world is in, for your actions and reactions are entirely your own. This means that whomever you sit down with to dine at the restaurant of life, with its infinite menu, no matter how many items you and even your closest dining companion have a shared taste for, a dish will always come along that separates you. This makes our lives journeys of constant discovery. Our tastes in life, our UI, are not a fixed array. We are organisms. We grow and develop.

A clear implication of the Uniqueness Perspective is that the only way to understand and make sense of a person's UI is through biography.[15] I have a language that I shall be using at points in this book to do this, the 4D framework:

> *Destiny*: the givens in your existence – your DNA, the milieu of the time and place you were born into
>
> *Drama*: all the unscheduled events that befall you – life, like history, challenges one to adapt to just one damn thing after another
>
> *Deliberation*: times when you reflect and make choices – when you exercise willpower to control yourself and tend the garden of your *umwelt*
>
> *Development*: all kinds of learning, scheduled and accidental – much of it flies under your radar. Wisdom begins in wonder, as Socrates said.

"Self-discovery" is inevitable if we pay any kind of attention to ourselves. And even if we don't, our UI will continue to surprise us. Let's see how by looking at a life story from my Biography case book.[16]

> Ravi got a shock when his parents, a medic and a teacher, moved to the UK. They, along with many other South Asians living and working in Africa, were a legacy of the migration of Indians to seek indentured labour in British colonial Africa. In the 1980s the environment became hostile to non-ethnic Africans, especially South Asians. This had forced his dad to relocate with his family to the UK where he secured a job as GP in a working-class district of a northern England city. Ravi found himself "the only coloured face in a school of 1,000 boys." He says: "It was a rough neighbourhood and after being bullied quite a bit, I managed to befriend a couple of tough boys and through them I fell into the wrong company, trying to be accepted." He shaved his head and adopted the gang look whilst leading a double life as a Hindu-observant vegetarian at home. Meanwhile, he embarked on a juvenile career of petty theft, property damage and street fighting. He truanted from school, stayed nights with a local girl, and even got locked up at the local police station for being "drunk and disorderly." He reflects: "It was fun, but I was flitting my life away." Now Ravi sees how becoming a leading figure in the gang was a rehearsal for his mature identity as a dominant leader with strategic awareness. As a teenager, his native intelligence couldn't help shining through, spotted first by a Chemistry teacher who showed him an escape route from the life he was living. He persuaded Ravi to find passage out of his

gang life via education, enrolling for a degree at a good university. There he continued his history of carousing, often neglecting serious study. It was the life he knew. Nonetheless, he still managed to get his act together enough to graduate and find a trainee position in the finance department of large company. He discovered his abilities kept surfacing and propelling him to better and more challenging jobs, culminating in an executive position in mainland Europe. He says: "Reflecting on that period, I learned that there was a lot more to me than I thought." In a climate still rife with racism, he concluded: "I needed to shape my own life. I needed to see how far I could go." This was quite far, for a succession of positions, mentors, and geographies landed him back in the UK in a prestigious CEO role.

Ravi's Destiny was his character and his cultural milieu, driving and constraining him from different directions. Ravi's adolescence was peppered with Drama – good and bad fortune. His emerging Deliberation enabled Ravi to change course at critical junctures by act of thought and will. His Development was his maturing outlook and discovery or new ways of being himself.

In his narrative, Ravi is reflecting that we infer or discover our uniqueness, imperfectly, by observing our own impulses and reactions to the world, especially through social exchange. There are three ways this can go wrong. First, we risk blaming ourselves for what is also caused by circumstances, taking exaggerated responsibility for what happens to us. Second is the opposite risk of failing to see our own part in what is happening around us, instead seeing what we want to see and giving ourselves a free pass when things we're doing go wrong. It's human nature. Forgivable . . . mostly. Third is the deeper truth that Sigmund Freud picked up on, with which evolutionary theory wholeheartedly agrees, that we are poor at and often uninterested in perceiving our basal instinctive drives. Blocking our view is what is filling the windscreen of Ego's vision: its "proximate" goals, needs, and values. Often in disguised garb, proximate wants draw their psychic energy from the Beast-being's vital interests; its "distal" instincts. As Freud brilliantly deduced, this can be because at source they are crude and self-interested. Our partial blindness to our motives serves our evolutionary purpose.[17] To be heroes in our own stories helps us to survive and fulfil our personal goals.

Your body–mind combo is singular, integrated, and configured just for you. How much do you need to know? Want to know? That depends on a lot of factors, which we will discuss later, but my message in this book is that only through self-knowledge can you have any hope of shaping what happens to you. Ravi has empowered his self to steer his UI – to take responsibility for its healthy growth and his personal fulfilment through understanding his UI, interrogating it, loving it, and letting it sing from time to time.

Ravi's travails and transformations led him to discover specific and sometimes conflicting trajectories in his UI. It was the role of Ravi's aware self to navigate safe passage into the future, balancing and using the 4Ds. This is true for all of us. This is what it means to be a person.

WHY UI?

Our uniqueness is a big idea that is taken far too lightly. Yes, of course, we all take it for granted as true, but then we go on to treat it as if it was of no consequence. We make simplistic and facile judgements about others as types or as being like this or that other person. There is enough truth in these to make them stick – we do have traits in common with others, but often that is not saying much. In the public domain, it is commonplace to hear expressions such as "tastes differ," "different strokes for different folks," and "one person's meat is another person's poison." These are not expressed as celebrations of UI; rather, they are mostly excuses for eccentricities – one's own and others'. At worst, they are facile apologies for "being different"; at best, they are a casual observation.

At the same time, one can hear people being exhorted to give their individuality free rein. "To thine own self be true," "Find your voice," or "Be authentic." Much of this is good-hearted humanism. Tolerance, liberty, and honesty are noble themes. They are also a clarion call to the oppressed – urging self-expression against the institutions, tribes, and gangs that would have us conform submissively. UI expression can get ugly when people start shouting assertively and discordantly. This is mostly resolved by good manners, thank goodness – people agreeing to limit what they show and what they ask. Civility reduces the public threat of untethered UI, but in the meantime too many people feel unheard, unrecognised, and unloved. Who knows and cares about who we really are? This is hunger for deep recognition.

Friends, family, and community are the answer, and love is the methodology. This works well and glues our society together, often doing so best when times are hardest. How UI is handled in these happy circumstances we shall explore later, but the sad truth is that these are too often unattainable ideals. UI goes unvalued, and people feel unable to express who they are. Does this matter?

E.M. Forster was a notable English novelist of the 20th century, writing human dramas with great empathy and pathos, yet wryly amusing, cynical and desperately sad. He portrayed the absurdity and joy of human relationships against a backdrop of conformist societal norms, shielded by institutions that are simultaneously stupid and blind. Yet there is idealism, just in the act of writing a novel, and in peopling them with three-dimensional humans, whose hearts and minds we can look into. We get the magical privileged view of which elements of their UI are driving their destinies.

So it was with Forster, a homosexual, living and writing in times of public and private repression. His sexual orientation made him a criminal in the eyes of the law, in a British society where plainclothes police regularly entrapped gay men in public places. Forster was not just fearful but deeply ambivalent, ashamed, and yearning, finding love in desperate and unfulfilled relationships. I am sure Forster would have been a great novelist had he lived in our more tolerant times, but the literary themes and his handling of them would have told a very different story.

Forster's case shows this can be a painful business. UI finds its way out, even when most rigorously repressed, and yes, of course it matters. Not just for our individual well-being but also for the fate of all of us.

The philosopher Martin Heidegger[18] coined the concept of *Dasein* – literally "being there" in his native German – to capture the idea that as a species, we are uniquely preoccupied with the fact of our own existence and what to do with it. To differing degrees and at different life stages (see Chapter 7), we are driven by three kinds of *Dasein* existential wants[19]:

1. To savour – to find joy in the taste of our unique experience of being[20]
2. To signify – to know we are making a unique mark on the world around us
3. To be seen – to be validated by knowing that another has connected with who we are

This was the battleground for Forster's art – his way of resolving frustrations, contradictions, and conflicts was through the fictional worlds he created. As we shall see later (Chapter 8), he is not alone in making us consumers the beneficiaries of his artistic struggle.

INTO THE LIGHT

We are shielded from the starkness of our uniqueness by our sociability. We are a highly adaptable and cooperative species and often find it easy to forget or suppress our UI while we go with the flow of others. As members of the same species, we have the "same" experiences. But they are not the same. When you tell me about your profound sorrow or joy, I know just what that feels like, to me. You and I can find deep affinity and empathy, but I will never know what it feels like to be you nor you me. "Shared" experience is in reality parallel experience. The same but different. Mine and yours.

This takes us back to little Nigel, lying in bed under his new frosty blanket of existential anxiety about his UI's transience and fragility. It was my *Dasein* moment. Our own mortality brings it home to us, along with awareness of the unique nature of our consciousness. This puts UI centre stage. So it was with a shock of recognition that I read this, decades later:

> But at the total emptiness for ever,
> The sure extinction that we travel to
> And shall be lost in always. Not to be here,
> Not to be anywhere, And soon;
> nothing more terrible, nothing more true.[21]

Wow, yes, that's exactly what I felt. These are the words of the 20th century English poet Philip Larkin in his terrifying poem *Aubade*. But that is not at all what I feel about death now, the closer I get to it. I know what I experienced then and what I feel now are nothing like what Larkin was experiencing; me a naïve child, him a solitary childless man, 8 years from death, suffering from ill health, depression, and alcoholism. Larkin was not having his first *Dasein* moment, as I was. Yet it is the gift of the poet to conjure the parallel feeling, even though its meaning for the poet and the reader may be worlds apart, as here – me at the beginning of my UI's life journey, him at his sad end.

Poetry exists to nourish our souls – our UI. So do all the arts. It is the reason for their existence. Glorying in their bounty, we can thank our UI for resonating with it and the UI of their creators for being able to harness their gifts, find a wormhole into our consciousness, and ring bells there. Novels, along with theatre and other narrative arts, are peak UI art forms because they help us read the hearts and minds of other individuals. Music is our universal language – in fact, the only one – brilliant at evoking mood, feeling, drama, and delight in ways that we can own as uniquely our own, colouring our *umwelt*. At the same time, it is one of the most profound vehicles for connection with others. For performers it becomes a space for co-created *umwelts*.

> The best-selling jazz album of all time is *Kind of Blue*. The music sounds timeless, and the more you listen to it, the more it seems it couldn't have been any other way. Yet, the musicians came to the studio with sketchy parts and no rehearsal and then proceeded to

improvise these wonders in just a few takes. This masterpiece owes to what Miles had learnt as a teenage apprentice to the be-bop genius and chief inventor of the genre, Charlie "Bird" Parker. Parker's practice was to push his band members to the limits of their capability, without the luxury of practice. Parker understood well the role of UI at the edge of creation, and Miles took this insight with him into all his genre-defying creations. *Kind of Blue* worked because of Miles' trust in the extraordinary creative talents he had assembled and their ability to meet the challenge of co-creation.

Turn to the sciences and you find the UI of its practitioners directly reflecting how they theorise and research[22]:

Richard Feynman, Nobel laureate for physics, was playfully exuberant in his personal life. Notably, he was an avid player of the bongo drums.[23] He took the spirit of play into his science, arriving at his visionary insights into the molecular dynamics of electromagnetism through observation and imagination.

Marie Curie, another laureate, was, in contrast, persistent, humble and introverted, enduring long, dangerous and testing hours at her laboratory bench to uncover the mysteries of radioactivity.

It also emerges, sometimes dramatically, in the personal chemistry of scientists working together, what we shall be calling UI^2.

In Curie's case, her partnership with her husband Pierre, a dreamy, philosophical, open and extravert character, leavened her single-mindedness, enabling them to converge from different angles on their insights.[24]

The brilliant decoding of the structure of DNA was the result of UI^3, the triangulation of three remarkably different personalities working on the problem, challenging each other and converging on its solution. Biologist Francis Crick was conceptual, introverting, thoughtful. Physicist James Watson was bold, intuitive, flamboyant and competitive. Chemist Roslind Franklin was meticulous, disciplined and theoretical (scandalously overlooked in her colleagues' patriarchal grab for Nobel glory).

The concept of the individual has been called a modern creation.[25] Throughout the history of civilisation, it has been absent or subordinate to the more important constructs of family, tribe, custom, and the gods. But that doesn't mean UI was absent. It had nothing like its modern meaning, but it still was a fact of existence and the moving spirit in all social development, in one way or another. The Great Person view of history – "There is no history, only biography," as Emerson put it – is simplistic. Culture, timing, good and bad luck (randomness), plus the periodic stirring of the pot through wars, migrations, and natural disasters, shape how history unfolds. Yet the UIs of leaders, revolutionaries, visionaries, and villains are always enzymes in the organic soup of history, shaping goals, processes, and outcomes.[26] Yes, sometimes they merely supercharge what was going to happen anyway, but plenty of times they innovate, move boundaries, shift cultures, and change the world.[27] Think of Alexander the Great, Empress Wu, Siddhartha Gautama, and Jesus of Nazareth and from more recent times, Napoleon Bonaparte, Abraham Lincoln, and Margaret Thatcher. All moved the boundaries of place, belief, and cultural identity – irrevocably.

WHAT LIES AHEAD

In this book I am going to tell you lots of stories. We can only make sense of UI through biography. Every life is an unrepeatable and remarkable saga of Destiny, Drama, Deliberation, and Development. I have spent most of my own life studying people's lives, their astonishing transformations, their beauty and tenderness, their pain and brutality, and the chemistry that bewitches and bamboozles us in relationships. I have been studying individual differences and lifespan development for over five decades. Now, late in my own life journey, I am going to share with you what I have learned as a scientist, a teacher, a counsellor, and an advisor. You will hear stories from my Biography casebook, from history, and from my own transformative life journey. I am going to show how we can think about our UI more seriously, more usefully, and more positively to help the best of who we can be to emerge and flourish.

This is the journey I am going to take you on:

- Why do we have UI, and how does it work? If we are so different, how come we share so much? Where does free will fit in? (Chapter 2)
- What's in the UI box, and how does it work? What's the Self got to do with it? Can we steer and shape our own UI? (Chapter 3)
- Relationships are UI², so what is the chemistry of the best and the worst? How do they drive events and development in the world? (Chapter 4)
- How does culture suppress or enable healthy UI? How can the best of UI be sustained and the worst neutralised by society? (Chapter 5)

- What is the dark side of UI? Is its shadow growing in our times? What can we do to transform or limit its toxic potential? (Chapter 6)
- What happens to our UI over the stages of life, especially during midlife transitions? How can people help themselves and each other? (Chapter 7)
- How does UI produce greatness, vision, faith, creativity, and transcendence? (Chapter 8)
- What is being done to people's UI in our institutions, through how we organise, lead, and educate each other? How could we do better? (Chapter 9)
- How can biographical understanding enhance, liberate, and delight our UI? (Chapter 10)
- We are told we are in the age of AI. This means we are in a new era of UI, the last, irreducible stronghold against the threats of new tech (Chapter 11). It is also the magical and limitless fountain of innovation that can harness AI and tech for our use, extension, and benefit. Nonetheless, risks abound.

At the end of the road I am inviting you to walk with me, I hope you will see how lives can be illuminated by four cardinal values that shine through from the stories we shall tell: courage, compassion, love, and wisdom.

CODA: WHAT THIS MIGHT MEAN FOR UNIQUE YOU

Maybe you are saying to yourself after reading this, what do I care if I am unique? I enjoy the good things in life as much as most people. I have my share of troubles, but I do very well, thank you, by just getting on with life and letting things happen the way they will. I never found the perfect job or perfect partner, but that's for dreamers. Good enough is good enough.

Good for you! I hope you carry on reading. Here's a few thoughts to take with you:

- You don't have to change a thing about who you are and what you do, but your uniqueness is a fact of your life that affects everyone around you and everything you do. Who knows what this Uniqueness Perspective might offer you in terms of insights? It's all upside. The best things in life are yours uniquely to possess.

- Any downside might be to confront aspects of yourself you'd rather not think about. If you have demons, you might consider that it's best to know about them, to avoid being blindsided.
- Maybe you don't want to be confronted by the thought that you are boring, average, or just below par. There is no par, and such judgements are what I'm waging war against in this book. Read on! You are exceptional.
- The Uniqueness Perspective is a force field resisting the dangers of comparison. "All comparisons are odious," it is said. They are simplistic and often lead to the nastiness of binary winner–loser thinking.
- The Uniqueness Perspective does the same thing for categorisation. Don't lump yourself into categories with other people. By all means acknowledge common interests, causes, and styles, but don't buy the T-shirt. You risk ending up linked with people who aren't at all aligned with what matters most to you. We are all on the move – your UI is not standing still, even if it feels like it.
- This book is emphatically not a homage to individualism, nor is it a charter for "selfishness" in any form. Seeing the singularity of lives through time, whatever yours or mine exhibits, should awaken respect and compassion. As philosopher Paul Tillich put it, "The affirmation of one's essential being in spite of desires and anxieties creates joy."[28]
- AI and new tech are transforming all our worlds. Give thanks for what it can do that you can't and let it help you live and work the way you want. Yes, this may mean being deprived of stuff you love to do, but use the space it creates to consider the things that you alone can do – mainly human-to-human things.
- Celebrate your UI. But for the grace of the cosmos, you could have been born someone else, at another time, living a life unimaginably short and brutal. And here you are reading this! Thank the Universe and then figure out what you're going to do with this gift. Hopefully, this book will be of some help – not in the manner of self-help books with lists of dos and don'ts but by giving you a new way of seeing – the Uniqueness Perspective.
- Consider the Three Existential Wants (*Dasein* motives). Any or all of them offer profound joy, comfort, and meaning in life – to savour the glorious feeling of being alive; to signify in what you do and in whom you relate; and to be seen,

connect, and love your fellow humans. We are creatures of spirit. It is in our DNA to seek and find satisfying experience to make a difference and to be validated.

- If you are a person of religious faith, nothing I am going to say here needs contradict your belief systems but rather enrich them. Faith is a positive force in many of the narratives I shall recount.[29]

Two

THE EVOLUTION OF INDIVIDUALITY

From Destiny to Free Will

Genes are not puppet masters, nor blueprints. They are switches, triggers, levers.
(Matt Ridley)[1]

Between stimulus and response, man has the freedom to choose.
(Victor Frankl)[2]

WHO IS LIKE YOU?

Do you have a sibling? Were you raised in the same home? How alike would you say the two of you are? Same ways of thinking about things? Same ways of expressing your feelings? How similar are your attitudes and tastes? Do you react to events in the same way?

You may feel a huge bond, but that won't disguise the fact that you're not very much alike at all.[3] I am guessing that were you asked to give an overall similarity rating in the range 0% to 100% that your answer would come in at a lot less than 50%, the percentage of variable DNA (within a few points either way) that you have in common with any full sibling. I expect you would be happy to add that you have more in common with some of your friends than your brother or sister. When it comes to parents, then it is exactly 50%. At the point of your conception, there was a neat, randomised decoupling of half of each of your parent's DNA double helix and a recoupling with the other parent's. Result: you and your siblings have 50% shared complement of your genes with each parent and about the same with each sibling. If you and your sibling were raised under the same roof – same parenting regime, socioeconomic status, culture, and of course the same neighbourhood – then you should turn out to similar, shouldn't you? But I'm guessing you're not. Why? For that matter, why aren't you more like your parents? People might say, "Oh, you're just like your mum or dad," but you know it's not true.

Look at kids raised in families where there is a powerful narrative shaping development.

The Williams sisters, Venus and Serena, were both groomed by determined parents to be tennis stars. That project was an undoubted success, but how different they turned out to be in tastes and character: the elder Venus calm, introverted, graceful, and modest; the younger Serena fiery, outgoing, and intensely competitive.

Take another household, this one steeped in politics.

The Bushes, George Senior and Barbara, former President and First Lady, raised their boys Jeb and George without obvious prejudice for or against either, as far as we know, but look at how different they revealed themselves to be. Both made careers in the political arena, and both achieved high office, George W to the presidency itself, Jeb to governorship of Florida. There the similarity ends. George was charismatic, impulsive, folksy, and personable, struggling, successfully, to triumph over alcoholism. Jeb turned out quite a different character: bookish, introverting, a technocrat, and generally considered to be much calmer and steadier in character.

Maybe siblings can't help striving to differentiate themselves, and parents can't help treating them differently. This may be true, but then wouldn't we expect only children – those without siblings to compete with – to take on more of their parents' attributes with all that exclusive attention? Are you an only child. Is it true? Are you "just like" either of your parents? Not really, I hear you say.

Tiger Woods, the celebrated golfer, an only child with grown-up half-siblings, was born to a strict disciplinarian military father and a Thai mother who was steeped in the tranquil ethos of Buddhism and self-control. How much of their character did they pass on to their preternaturally gifted son? Only he can answer that, but his propensity to run off the rails, serially, seems to suggest he is no clone of either parent, lacking the discipline and self-control of either. Yet he is theirs, and they are his with a genetic bond. He is quoted as saying, "My mom was the enforcer. I still fear her to this day," and her passing was a great loss to him. Yet his life was turbulent and disorderly for a long stretch. He subsequently calmed his life with brief sporting comeback, philanthropy, and public humility.

Unique identity will insist on raising its head, it seems.

Then there are adopted children. Perhaps you are one. The origins of your Unique Individuality (UI) may seem even more complicated than for those raised by birth parents, but the upside could be that you have the best of both worlds – the benefits of a genetic legacy from disinterested parents, coupled with the freedom to draw on a local model of the folks who nurtured you. You can choose. Sounds good, doesn't it? Alas, it is troubling to many who quest for self-knowledge and self-determination.

This is precisely what happened to Steve Jobs,[4] the founder of Apple, whose biological parents were a very smart couple – a Syrian science PhD and a hippy-ish, free-thinking mother – while his adoptive dad was a car engineer and amateur craftsman and his mum a warm and loving homemaker. Up front and centre in Jobs' UI was an extremely difficult personality – demanding, self-interested, volatile, aggressive – yet smart as hell, artistic, powerful, and determined. His adjustment to life, one can't help concluding, was not helped by his total rejection of his biological heritage and a desperate belief that his conscious self was the sole architect of his UI. It cost him his life when he thought a fruitarian diet and lifestyle discipline could forestall the attack of the pancreatic cancer that finally claimed him.

Last, and perhaps most interesting, are people who live in the same environment with someone who shares 100% of their genes. Perhaps you one of this rare group – monozygotic twins (from a single ovum-sperm fertilisation) – who make up less than half of 1% of all live births. If you and your twin were raised together, have you turned out pretty much the same as your twin, with nature and nurture working hand in hand? Listen to Angelika.

Angelika, a 40-year-old Bulgarian executive from Sofia, is the identical twin of Marta – that is, they started out life with near-identical DNA. I am asking her about when she was first conscious of having such a special relationship; whether she and her sister were best friends from the start; whether their parents encouraged them to follow the same paths and patterns – clothing, schooling, hobbies, and so on – and whether they are converging or diverging in their trajectories.

The first, most obvious, difference is the very fact of Angelika being in my class – a single woman looking to find career direction in the United Kingdom. Her twin Marta is living a very different life, happily domiciled in Vienna with a young family. The sisters were raised in Sofia by their dad, an entrepreneur, and mum, a homemaker. The loving parents had a shock at their birth. Only expecting one baby, they had bought only a single crib, one set of baby clothes, and all the rest.

Angelika talks of being "constantly reminded" of being identical, not by her parents but by everybody else. The parents, for their part, empowered the twins' individuality, giving them the freedom to choose their own attire, hobbies, and interests. She says she and her twin were never motivated to make the mischief that many twins confess to, like substituting for each other, for fun or convenience. She says, "We've met other twin pairs, and our experience seems quite different to theirs. Our parents never compared us." Angelika says her sister was far from being her soulmate and even "less than a friend." "We had lots of fights and disagreements, like all siblings. She's my best friend now we're both adults, but we weren't then." She adds: "Our parents wanted us to find our own channels in life, and we deliberately tried to take different paths – making different class choices in high school and into our teens – Marta towards the sciences, me towards the arts." Then after a hesitation, she confesses that she, too, enrolled for science subjects but made a last-minute switch. I ask how alike she thinks they are in personality, values, and interests. Angelika considers herself to be more sensitive than her "more pragmatic" twin, but they both are "logical and planned, good at execution." "We are both introverts," she adds, "but I'm more open, experimental, and risk taking. Marta needs more stability. Our tastes are very different – including our choice of boyfriends. But we have lots of shared interests. Our values are very similar."

She continues: "Our friendship grew most strongly at our separate universities, when we were both living in dorms. We'd enjoy spending time together, sometimes just sitting together doing our own things. I came to realise she's a very special person for me. At some point, we were quite comfortable with who we are, and I no longer felt like I needed to act, dress, or speak differently to show my uniqueness. Then at the end of our conversation, I ask is there anything she'd like to add. She reflects. "Yes," she says, "I never feel lonely."

The need to "individuate" – Jung's term for the instinctive desire to differentiate yourself from parents and siblings as you mature[5] – is a strong force here. It is no accident that identical twins reared apart are often more similar to each other than those reared together.[6] Proximity creates an incentive to individuate. Here, Angelika's empowering parents allowed the twins to find their own ways in life. Yes, the girls seem to have deliberately distanced themselves from each other, but the prime motivation for this was the pull of what they wanted and how they preferred to live. Yes, they have a lot in common, and the bond between them seems to be growing with the passage of time, but with many nonidentical siblings, the trend is the opposite direction – increasing divergence in interests and life directions.

Identical twins grow more alike with the passage of time, as the turbulent, buffeting winds of adolescence and early adulthood subside. You and your genes find ways of being in the world in ways that work with the grain of your inborn nature.[7] This is true for all of us – we become more "ourselves" from a lifetime of self-determination – the pay-off of successive choices about how to live and who to be with.[8]

THE GENE LOTTERY

What do twin studies tell us about nature vs. nurture? First, they illustrate the truth that these are not forces pulling in different directions. They're not even alternatives. Behaviour geneticists tell us that all our traits – our physique, our biochemistry, our brains – are heritable, programmed by the blueprint of our DNA. But at the same time, every trait depends entirely upon the environment allowing the programme to be executed – for traits to emerge.[9] This is not all or nothing. Every engagement with the environment – your diet, risk environment, culture, relationships – can modify, suppress, or amplify the expression of your traits. Take something obvious like height, for example. How tall you are is a joint product of genes, lifestyle, and nutrition. Having a great diet can't make you taller than your genes will allow, yet malnutrition sure can stunt your growth.

Then there is the recent discovery of epigenetics. Contrary to early formulations of genetics, we now know that environmental pressure modifies genes, changing their expression over your lifetime, and that this reprogramming can then be passed on to the next generation. Living in a war zone could make a person more resilient, anxious, or any number of other traits, which then may be passed on to offspring, though the effect weakens and washes out of the genome in succeeding generations. Epigenetics seems to reinforce class divisions – health, educational, and social outcomes become heritable.[10] Being raised in wealth poverty leaves a mark, the imprint of the contrasting ways people from different social classes live together. A legacy of the Holocaust is that mental vulnerability is taking more than a single generation to wash out.[11]

But the effects do fade. Look at Johann Sebastian Bach, whose sons all became acclaimed composers in their own right, but there the line of musical inheritance, wherever it came from, melted away. Equally – and thankfully – serial killers and war criminals do not transmit their sins to their children, who most commonly manage to disinherit the sins of their parents.

Coming back to Angelika and Marta, it is clear they are more than mere sisters. Something quite special is going on as these women strive to differentiate themselves – there is a bond of identity that is both compelling and enduring. I once worked with a South African engineering firm run by identical twins, who brought the enterprise to its knees by replicating each other's mistakes, agreeing on successive bad calls without sufficient debate, all because their instincts were too pre-aligned.

> The Polish Kaczynski brothers were the only case in history of identical twins running a country together, founding their Justice Party in 2001 and serving as president and prime minister for a few years thereafter, before one was killed in a plane crash. Their legacy is undistinguished – replicating each other's conservative vision of society and a hostile stance towards the European Union, whose membership was even then hugely beneficial to Poland.

Twin studies are the favoured methodology of behaviour genetics. Statistical analyses of mountains of carefully collected data are processed to arrive at estimates of concordance on a wide range of personal factors. These are gathered from identical and nonidentical twins, reared apart and reared together, regular siblings, parents and children, as well as adopted children, thus covering all the bases of relatedness.[12]

> My own parenting experience comes close to a living experiment of similar kind. I have been married three times, with five children, including one adopted and one being an only child. I can only say I have watched with wonder how each of them has grown and revealed themselves to me as totally unexpected people. I have loved them all equally, but differently, according to the chemistry of our conjoined UIs – UI^2 as we can call it.

Of particular interest are identical twins who have been reared apart, without any knowledge that they are indeed twins. This happened quite often in former times when adoption was shrouded in protective secrecy, often covering up tremendous abuses of people's rights. Here is one such tale:

> The extraordinary documentary feature *Three Identical Strangers*[13] tells the tragic story of triplets: three monozygotic infant boys, separated by an adoption agency as part of a cruel social "experiment." The misguided experimenters placed them in homes of contrasting socioeconomic status: blue collar, white collar, and affluent professional, in a naïve and unscientific attempt to disentangle nature and nurture. The study broke every ethical convention of our times, with neither boys nor their adoptive parents having any idea that the others existed. They were deliberately misled about the nature of the intensive data collection conducted at regular intervals by researchers over their young lives. Bobby, coming

from a middle-class family, at the age of 19 enrolled at a junior college, where from his first day, he was puzzled to find students familiarly calling him Eddy. He soon met Eddy, his discovered twin who had been placed in the same college by his parents, the affluent adopters. A media feature on their extraordinary meeting alerted the third, David, who had been placed in a working-class family. These were joyful reunions, and the boys bonded swiftly and strongly. They were a media sensation for a while, moving happily into the same home and college. Capitalising on their fame, they launched the joint venture of a restaurant. This thrived for a while, but the world they built around themselves soon started to fall apart.

The emotional bond was not sufficient to obliterate the differences that had grown between them from their very different upbringings – Eddy's pressure to live up to high parental expectations, Bobby's structured academic context, David's poor but loving and supportive family. All grew increasingly angry about the deception practised on them, compounded by the mental health challenges they each faced. Bobby struggled with depression and anxiety. David, too, but it was Eddy for whom the battle was lost. The most lively and charismatic of the three, his depression shaded toward bipolar disorder, and in 1995 he took his own life. This hit the surviving brothers hard, who became passionate advocates for ethical standards in social research. David, especially wounded by the death of his brother, became a vigorous campaigner on mental health issues.

NATURE, NURTURE, AND UNIQUE YOU

This was a bad experiment in every sense of the word, but the triplets' story and Angelika's tale before it illustrate the total entanglement of nature and nurture. More respectable investigations by twin study researchers mining generations of data on relatedness and environmental influences use their statistical toolkit to apportion variance. This is how much you can link, cluster, or predict variations across individuals. They are looking for similarities and differences across a very wide range of physical and psychological factors, trying to see how much can be accounted for by three bundles of causes: genes (heritable DNA), the shared environment (home, education, social class, parenting), and the nonshared environment (unique experience). This research has reached some important conclusions:

1. Genes have a substantial effect on all psychological traits – personality, interests, abilities, attitudes, and values. Many qualities that we think might be purely

environmental, like political attitudes, turn out to have a heritable component in the 40% to 80% range – the degree of similarity we can expect to see in identical twins.

2. Heritability can be high – like intelligence at around 80% – but not run in families. Intellect correlates only about 40% for identical twins. The same is true for character traits, which correlate 0% to 20%, while their genetic link is 40% to 70%. The main reason is that the most interesting human qualities are encoded by complex gene combinations. Add to this all the randomness that comes from the lottery of blending two parents' DNA, plus copying errors and mutations throughout our lifespan as cells divide. It's no wonder the characters in families are so different to each other.[14]

3. The so-called shared environment has a negligible effect on personality and/or any other psychological qualities compared with the substantial effect of genes.

4. The nonshared environment accounts for all the rest of the "missing" variance – a substantial amount.

This will have many of you, dear readers, scratching your heads. How can it be that so little of our children's identity has anything to do with everything we invest in them – money, love, education, or time? But it does! Point 3 only means that the "shared" environment affects each child in a very different way. You, and what you expose your kids to, does have a huge effect on them, but

- The effects are totally unpredictable – parents differ greatly in how and how much they influence each child, even identical twins.
- The effects are largely around strategies, beliefs, and narratives for living.
- The have a negligible effect on deeply anchored traits, though they can suppress or redirect their expression.

Leading behaviour geneticist Eric Turkheimer with colleague Mary Waldron conducted a definitive review to unravel the mystery of nonshared environmental effects – the 50% or so left unaccounted for by genes and shared environment. They dug deep into the data to gauge the impact of life circumstances and events, and the mystery only deepened. It's not that the so-called "shared" environment – home milieu, schooling, wealth, and poverty – doesn't affect children. It's that the effects are so unpredictable. For example, divorce hits some kids much harder than others. Type of education also has different payoffs for siblings. Wealth and poverty likewise. The researchers were forced to a radical conclusion – *there is no such thing as the shared environment.*[15] It seems obvious from the UI perspective. Again, we can rework Osler's dictum:

Don't just ask what Family you have, ask what You your family has.

Although we say we've witnessed the same event or we've been through the same experience, they are not really the "same" at all. They are ours and ours alone. We know what it "must have been like" for the other, but not what it *was* like. Let's do a thought experiment, considering a classic "shared" environmental influence of particular interest in twin studies, parenting styles.

Imagine three siblings being raised in an authoritarian, highly controlling parenting regime. Our Uniqueness Perspective expects the three potentially to respond in quite different ways. The first child dutifully conforms to and embraces the parental standards. The second rebels, going out of their way to stake out completely opposing liberal values. The third stoically endures the regime in a state of studied detachment.

Is this possible? Of course it is. Look at the Tiger Woods case, discussed earlier. He went his own way. Pick any family you know, your own included, and you will see many similar variations in how kids respond to parents. There are two likely causes. The first is that the parents are calibrating their style selectively and differently for each child. It's true – favouritism does occur in families.[16] It is often unconscious, but part of the chemistry of UI.[2] A parent may just feel warmer to one child than another, instinctively. But where does this instinct originate? Clearly, it's partly in the parent's UI, but we also need to look at this from the child's point of view. It's a cruel truth that some kids are just more loveable than others. Yes, parents do treat children differently, but this is joint production of both parties, parent and child. Behaviour genetics research confirms this. They found that a startling 27% of parental warmth is *a heritable characteristic of the child!*[17] In other words, some kids do better than others because their UI "switches on" favourable responses in other people.

We need to be alert to the fact that we have unwitting impacts on other people – and they on us. It is a matter of resonance. You can't control who you resonate with, but this doesn't have to define your relationship. Through insight we can develop intelligent strategies for dealing with other people if we can muster the humility and spirit of self-inquiry to do so (see Chapter 10).

Some have concluded that this means parents have negligible effects on children,[18] but they are mistaken. UI rules. Some kids are much more impervious than others. Some parents are more imposing than others. Parents are hugely influential in shaping the narratives kids grow up with, but core aspects of UI are unreachable – the deep heritable structure of character and dispositions. How they are translated into personal strategies for living is learned.

Here's a case from my Biography work illustrating the point:

> Sandra, from China, was raised as a boy for the first 7 years of her life. Her parents, living under the one-child policy, had longed for a son. Already raising a daughter, they took the risk of trying again for a boy, and Sandra arrived. This cost them a fine and her mother her job. To partially fulfil their dream, they raised Sandra as a son, giving her toy trucks and plastic guns to play with, cutting her hair short, and dressing her in boys' clothing. As she grew, Sandra's feminine UI began to emerge, and her parents could not help but embrace her for who she was. Now 43, Sandra is happily married with a daughter of her own. "I still wear my hair short not because of the past but because it's who I am today." She smiles reflectively and says, "Our stories don't define us – we redefine them."

Many a parent should hear this wisdom, especially those who have tried to shape their children's identities. The family business world is littered with the failures, caused by children failing to conform to the successor roles assigned to them by their parents (fathers, overwhelmingly).[19] They need the wisdom that comes naturally to parents whose children are born profoundly impaired, physically or mentally. The love part comes naturally for all but a few. Then comes the learning. Very soon, they realise that it's themselves who's going to have to do all the adapting, not the helpless infant.[20] Their innocent gaze to the parents proclaims: "Here I am. Deal with it."

WHO ARE YOU? KITH, KIN, AND CONFUSION

It is part of our animal legacy that we instinctively "know" family, though unreliably. It's a matter of resonance. It can't always be trusted. Lacking the ability of many other species to sniff out who is and who isn't our kin, mistakes about paternity among humans are especially common. It is argued by evolutionists that this is deliberate sloppiness in our species design. For us super-adaptive cooperative humans, kinship exclusivity is bad news. A lot of our most important and creative bonding is with nonkin.[21] Adoptive relationships can be as close as any other.

Yet we do have a nose for kinship. If you quiet your mind, you can often feel the resonance of kinship.

> I have two friends, both female, who discovered in midlife that their fathers were not the parent who raised them, in one case a family friend and in the other an uncle. In both cases, the discovery was profoundly disconcerting and at the same time made sense of anomalies in their experience that they had brushed off as inconsequential. A notable male case is British TV and movie actor John Simm, who discovered on an ancestry TV show that his father was someone who he'd never met – from a 1960s casual liaison with his mother, who herself had been ignorant of Simm's real paternity. On the show, meeting his half-sister and her daughter for the first time, he reflects about the father who raised him: "He was always my best mate, but I always felt there was something; I don't know what it was, but it felt different. I always felt a bit guilty about it."[22]

Simm felt and dismissed the tug of Beast-being insight – this doesn't feel quite right. There seems to be a missing resonance, but because there's nothing manifestly wrong, I'll ignore it. The Second Law of UI – that we don't know ourselves – doesn't mean we can't have insights about what we can't see. That's what lies at the heart of Freud and Jung's psychoanalytic theory and practice.

It is extremely rare to be completely mistaken entirely about who is one's family, but it happens, and the effects can be dramatic.

> A British radio show, *The Gift*,[23] tells the stories of the unexpected consequences of people being gifted DNA ancestry testing kits. One of the most startling cases was set in motion when a middle-class 67-year-old, Tony, eldest of five in a loving conventional English family, received a gift kit for himself and his wife. In 2022 he got around to sending off his sample, forgetting about it until the results arrived. On the phone to his 83-year-old mother Joan, sharing the results, he came across what looked like an error – listing him as having a full sibling with the name Claire. Already having a sister Jessica, the youngest of the family, he assumed it was a mistake and used the private messaging facility to write to Claire. Coincidentally, Claire's son had earlier bought her the same "gift," and she had puzzled over the lack of any connection with her parents' origins, also assuming some error had occurred. But when Tony's message arrived, she went into high alert and immediately pinged back to him her date of birth and the hospital. He checked with his mother – same day, same hospital. The penny dropped. There was only one explanation. Fifty-five years ago, the overnight tags on the newborns had been accidentally switched – never before recorded in the UK health service.

Claire was eager to meet her new family, finding instant rapport with her rediscovered mother Joan, who recounts, "There was immediately recognition – connection." This is the sympathetic frequency response of resonance. For Claire this was a homecoming, after living for 55 years in another family, just around the block, with a much less sunny childhood – raised in poverty with separated parents. "All my life, I would jest with my family that I'm adopted," she recounts, "because I look nothing like my family that I knew." For her the reunion with her biological mother "was so bizarre – like we'd always known each other." Within a short time, she had also identified traits and habits shared with Joan and the father, who had passed away: "Foods we like and dislike, our taste in clothes, her tenacity" and more besides. Since then, the bond between them grew to be deep and loving, both mourning the lost years of their separation.

But what of poor Jessica, the fair, blue-eyed anomaly in her putative family? She went into shock despite the protestations of Joan and Tony that they loved her "just the same." But it wasn't for Jessica, who declared, "Everything's changed." She tried to make contact with her biological mother, who was unable to process and accept what had happened and soon after died. Jessica subsequently distanced herself from her adoptive family and declined to take part in the programme.

It's a classic demonstration of the total intertwining of nature and nurture. We are born neurologically unique,[24] and we steer our own development, infused with external influences and constraints that we can own as just ours alone. The bonds of family can be remade, overridden, or amplified. It is only the narrative of biography that makes sense of such variations, as we shall see in numerous stories throughout this book.

WHY DIDN'T EVOLUTION MAKE YOU PERFECT?

Why didn't evolution make us all equally loveable, or indeed, courageous, attractive, intelligent, sociable, or any other of the good stuff? One reason is the evolution isn't idealistic – it doesn't create perfectly designed organisms by looking ahead; rather, it shapes us mainly by knocking off imperfections, eliminating individuals with features that prevent them from passing on their genes. It'll leave in place any characteristic that is useless but inoffensive, toenails, for example. Likewise, traits that are helpful at some junctures and a nuisance at others won't be dropped so long as they don't stop vital functions. Indeed, some less desirable features – like cowardice, unattractiveness, stupidity, and shyness – hold their positions in the human profile because they can be useful. It depends on the circumstances. The most important of those circumstances is other people. It matters who's in your group.

> Let's do another thought experiment. Imagine two tribes of our hunter-gatherer ancestors. One consists solely of risk seekers; the other of risk avoiders. We pay a visit to both. The first tribe is small, wealthy in terms of food and materials but with large number of severely disabled members. They are always having accidents, fighting, and experiencing mayhem of various kinds. The other tribe is larger but dreadfully impoverished, with lots of norms and routines for the sharing of scarce resources. We now get each tribe to swap a few members across their border. This proves to be good for both tribes. Now, in the first tribe, the worst excesses of risk takers are restrained by the wise counsel of their cautious immigrants. In the second tribe, the new members help mobilize the group to be more venturesome and bring them success in finding fresh opportunities and resources. The adaptive power of both tribes is enhanced.

In the world of population genetics, this is called *frequency dependent selection (FDS)*.[25] For example, men are more at risk from accidents than women, partly because they live riskier lives. FDS has steered evolution to a bias marginally in favour of male over female births. The birth rate gap widens even more in times of war when males disproportionately perish. FDS operates on a huge range of human traits. Even with the qualities we most admire, you can get too much of a good thing. The FDS principle says we need diversity to achieve synergy – that magical state where the whole is better than the sum of the parts.

When we contribute different ingredients to life's kitchen, it takes a bit longer to prep, but you get a better tasting mouthful. A good life is helped by having partners who add value by doing what you can't. Modern liberal economics is built on this idea, through division of labour – people practising different skills. We then get the possibility of win–win forms of exchange and the roots of trade and lots of other forms of social exchange. UI makes an infinite range of possibilities for each of us to benefit by doing what others can't and adding value to what each has.[26]

It's the same in human relationships. Potentially, we are all complementary assets to each other. The whole of human connection is greater than the sum of our individual parts.[27] This is the benefit of diversity in character and aptitudes. These mean much more than race, which is skin deep. Race is a social construct around a trivial biological marker, skin colour, that has become a social issue because it is mired in false and ignorant narratives. The added value of diversity in functional traits comes from what evolutionists call sexual selection. We have multiple options for partnership with other unique souls. It is adaptive to be choosy about your partner – looking for good genes to scramble with your own if you're in the mating game. The unromantic purpose of love it to maximise the diversity of what we bequeath to our children – not least their immune systems. A classic demonstration is the "sweaty T-shirt study,"[28] which showed students preferred the body odour of people with immune systems least like their own. This is nature's way of changing the locks to outsmart pathogens which are continually evolving to break in and plunder our biological resources. It's also been recently found that women are similarly able to sniff out potentially compatible friends – very useful for our ancestors to find supportive connections[29].

There is no winning model for human design. Our best chances come from our diversity.

POP-UP GENES – WHO MIGHT YOU BE?

Such is the tangle of our heritage – we are all mongrels – that we never know what wild card genes may show up in our offspring. Couple this with the fact that most of our traits are encoded in combinations of genes, then it is no surprise that we all exhibit features not seen before in our immediate families.

As I look back, my own story seems quite unlikely – from hating school, quitting and leaving home at 16 to becoming a committed scholar. I was born, by any reckoning, into an unusual family. The youngest of three, I was raised in what can only be called by old-fashioned term, "bohemian," household. My father, the fourth son of five to a Yorkshire master printer, whose maternal grandfather was, mysteriously, a foundling – left by the bank of Beverley Beck (a stream, in the local vernacular), hence named Beckworth. My father, like his before him, was an autodidact – self-taught in the great works of literature. He left school at 16 years of age to become a journalist – his lifelong profession – educating himself in the world's literature whilst writing and publishing four volumes of poetry and 11 novels. He met my mother, between the 20th century's great wars at a Communist party event. She had also quit school, even earlier at 14, and was also a literary autodidact, who also become a journalist and aspiring writer. Spurning the conventions of the day, without marrying, they set up house together and lived the lifestyle of middle-class literary intellectuals.

Our home was a focal point for artists of all kinds. My father organised monthly poetry readings, attended by assortments of around 20 like-minded souls from a wide radius from our London suburban home, always fuelled by liberal supplies of alcohol. As a household, it was devoid of rules, apart perhaps from a literary snobbish prohibition against any American comics entering the house – what a deprivation in the heyday of Superman and the fabulous Captain Marvel! In this environment, if I didn't want to go to school, neither parent cared – my mother liked the company of having one of us at home. She, too, published four novels during a transformative decade of her life (more on her remarkable story is told in Chapter 7). No one cared therefore when I gave up studying the sciences at the age of 12, and left school and home at 16, with minimal qualifications, following in my father's footsteps to become a cub reporter on a provincial newspaper on the English South Coast. I shall recount later the transformational experiences that helped me interrogate my UI, but the outcome was surprising. After sundry failures and global wanderings, I re-entered education, became a disciplined scholar, defining myself as a scientist, applying empirical and theoretical rigour to the field of human behaviour – my lifelong passion. I had "found myself" in scholarship.

It is impossible to untangle the causal streams of inheritance, environment, and learning, though one can see when they are pulling in the same direction and when they're not. It took a fair amount of Drama + Deliberation for me to find my way. Yes, it was part of my Destiny to become a writer, but it was part of my Destiny, unlike others in my family, to have never have any interest in writing fiction. And yes, there are scientists in my family – an eminent physicist cousin on father's side, a biochemist aunt on my mother's, and who knows what came to my family from the foundling Beckworth ancestor. In other words, my adult identity was infused with a blend of inherited predispositions[30] – the gravitational pull of what grabbed me – and models of practice that prevailed in my family milieu. Here's another family surprised by how their kids turned out.

A report in my local press proclaims the achievements of a 9-year-old girl, who is the youngest person ever to represent England in chess at the Olympiad. A year later she became the youngest female player ever to beat a grandmaster in a classical match. Her father introduced her to the game during lockdown, without being much of a player himself. After that she ravenously consumed online videos, bringing her to professional standard within just a few years.[31]

Self-discovery is the singular journey of all our lives, often despite as much as because of our parents, a theme that finds voice in this story from my Biography casebook:

> Ludmilla was born in 1977 Soviet Russia to a father who was a professor of mathematics and a mother who was lead engineer in military production. When Ludmilla was 15 years old, her family was suddenly plunged into poverty when the USSR collapsed. She says, "The freest, and perhaps the only free part of life in the USSR, was sports." She explains, "My father played tennis well and decided that his daughter would become a tennis star. My two older sisters turned out to be entirely unsuitable for sports, so the role fell to me. From the age of 7 to 16, my whole childhood was almost exclusively about tennis. I did not study at school. I had no friends – there was only tennis." She discovered in her teens that her tall, shapely physique "perfectly fit the standards of the modelling business" and which, she quickly found, gave her the earning power to feed the entire family, buy her own car, and pay for her university education. She went on to pass the bar exam, become a criminal attorney, find a life partner, give birth to a daughter, move into the domain of public service, and thence to become a senior board member in a leading state institution.

With a lot of digging, we could probably identify the strands that wove Ludmilla's path to her distinguished present state, but it was by successive approximations. It was not her Destiny to follow the path her father wanted. Through Drama and Deliberation, she felt and then followed the tug of her UI, finding and exploiting routes to a widening range of opportunities. Development was constant – each change enlarged her scope for broader sources of fulfilment.

It has been said that every parent is a "nurturist," until they have their second child, when they become a "nativist," as I can testify:

> Earlier I described how I have found myself a spectator more than a sculptor of my children's development, gazing with wonder at their emerging unique identities. This meant trying to keep pace with it and trying to put the right things in their hands as their UI took shape. Sometimes you get it wrong. Fortunately, recovery has followed. Through all this, I can see the legacy of my parenting and the milieu of their upbringing, in unexpected and disparate ways, surfacing as distinctive tastes, interests, styles, and most important, narratives. More on that later.

We still haven't resolved the deeper question of how this happens – are we all at the mercy of intractable biological forces shaping our identity? Of course not.

RESOLVING THE MYSTERY OF YOU

It is very odd, the self-effacing passivity in the way people talk about "what made me the way I am." We find it downright insulting when others talk about us this way. Didn't I have anything to do with how I turned out? Yes, of course you did. To assess this is an essential part of understanding our UI, owning it, and using it.

Let's go back to the behaviour geneticists puzzling over the "nonshared environment." One team came up with this remarkably convoluted explanation for what remains unaccounted for after what is explained by your genes (substantial) and your shared environment (negligible).

> A significant part of nonshared environmental influences may not be due to environmental influences at all but result from intrinsic variability in the output of deterministic, self-organizing developmental processes.[32]

This is confusing and mysterious. What could they be getting at? They are saying it is more than just random noise or "measurement error," as statisticians would put it. They seem to be telling us that the brain processes data in ways that are supremely complicated – "self-organizing" like amoeba in a pond or like atoms finding a home after being blown apart by an explosion. Turkheimer and Waldron in their scholarly review of the great mystery – what is the nonshared environment – conclude resignedly:

> Some aspects of the development of complex human behavior may remain outside the domain of scientific investigation for a very long time.[33]

Yet in the dying sentences of their review, they confess that this may be a good thing. They ponder, had they explained much more of human variation, it would present "gloomy prospects in the ethical evaluation of human agency." Yes, it would make you, the person, little more than a bit player in your own development.

Turkheimer gets to the point – the only possible resolution of the mystery – in a later commentary[34] when he elaborates:

> The nonshared environment, in a phrase, is free will. Not the kind of metaphysical free will that no one believes in anymore, according to which human souls float free above the mechanistic constraints of the physical world, but an embodied free will, tethered to biology, that encompasses our ability to respond to complex circumstances in complex and unpredictable ways and in the process to build a self."

That's more like it! The answer to the great mystery turns out to lie at the core of UI. Turkheimer's helpful reconstruction of "free" will takes us back to our guiding maxim: *Don't just ask what World You are in; ask what You the World is in.*

We may feel life pushes us around at times, but often we are choosing to let it do this. Remember the Frankl quote at the start of this chapter – between stimulus and response, we have the freedom to choose, if we will let ourselves. We can also filter, block, and even amplify what life's dramas confront us with. As Turkheimer affirms, the power of Deliberation is not some metaphysical gift from the gods but an integral part of our organic identity as self-aware, language-wielding persons.

In these pages, we shall see how self-discovery is substantially a process of self-creation, bounded by unalterable constraints, which we can work around a lot better than we might believe.

CODA: WHAT THIS MIGHT MEAN FOR UNIQUE YOU

You came into this world like a vulnerable tadpole with a big head, which continued to grow outside the womb, ready to absorb whatever was thrown at you. Although we are neural sponges ready to soak up the world, our minds are not blank slates waiting to be engraved by experience. You, me, and all of us come preloaded with mental architecture of drives and biases, which are uniquely tuned and configured just for us.

- Your mind is designed to seek and see patterns. The trouble is that it's easy to see them where they don't exist. No one is "just like" anyone else, even those with identical DNA. People who share half your genes – parents and siblings – have no simple trait matching with you. You are not much different than strangers in traits.
- The tug of kinship is biologically tangible and real. You can feel its resonance, but this doesn't guarantee you'll get on with your relatives – another problem altogether (see Chapter 4).
- As a parent, you play a critical role in your children's development, mostly in the valued resources and lessons for life you can offer them. It's not your job to shape their character, even if you could. But you can influence how they think through the narratives you hand them about themselves, human nature, and the world. Beware! Some of these might not always be good for them.

- The word "offer" in the last point is critical. Your job is to hear the voice they often can't articulate. Your children are active players in their own development, from the very beginning. The best you can do is pay attention; listen to the signals your child is sending you; and learn what channels, resources, and methods are best for you and them.

- You are hardwired to see similarities between yourself and your children,[35] but don't let this mislead you into blaming yourself for all of the bad things that may happen to them. The Uniqueness Perspective liberates both you and them. You play a part in their story, but you should let them tell you what this means. You may see things in them that they can't, but the opposite is also true. We all have our blind spots, which honest dialogue may uncover.

- You, me, and all of us are bundles of contradictions. The brain is an ill-assorted collection of parts assembled to fulfil a purpose – not for rationality or truth seeking but for survival.[36] It is an assembly of the ancient, the primitive, and the new (especially self-control functions) all cobbled together and working well enough. Do not expect your reasons and instincts to be in harmony.

- Yes, free will is a fact of life, but the "free" part is highly constrained, not least by your involuntary thoughts and feelings. Your mind is programmed to extract and shape your experience of the world for your own purposes. Your freedom is the power to turn on a dime, to change your direction of travel in a flash, if you're up for it. Taking command over your desire to do so may prove much harder.

Three

HOW INDIVIDUALITY WORKS
Beast-Being, the Ego, and the Self

There is no reality except the one contained within us. That is why so many people live such an unreal life. They take the images outside them for reality and never allow the world within to assert itself.

(Herman Hesse)[1]

Be yourself – no one can say you're doing it wrong.

(Snoopy, aka Charles M. Schulz)[2]

EMBODIED MIND OR EM-MINDED BODY?

How do you get on with your body? Is it a reliable source of pleasures or a source of grief for failing to do what you want, when you want, and how you want? I expect you could well answer something like, "My body and I have had good times and bad – on-form days and others that are a pain, literally." It's a vehicle that is unreliable and needs a lot of looking after. You are an embodied mind.[3] You could flip this over and say you are an em-minded body,[4] a Beast-being that is stuck with a mind that is capricious and apt to get you into needless trouble. No other animal seems to have such perplexity, and moreover, each one of us seems to have our own peculiar relationship with ourselves. That's what we're going to unpick in this chapter.

We are going to start and finish with two stories of people who had more harmonious relationships with their bodies that set the trajectories of their life journeys. Both coincidentally are Austrians born a few years apart in the same district. One is a Bodybuilder, movie star, and politician, Arnold Schwarzenegger, whose extraordinary life story we shall tell later. The other is Eva Cowan, an artist friend living in my neighbourhood.

Born Eva Rueber-Staier, she was crowned Miss World in 1969 in London, where she has lived ever since. Today, Eva Cowan is a sculptor, welding skilful, elegant, and witty art works. Born in a small town to a lone mother who worked as a hairdresser, Eva was mainly raised by her strong disciplined grandmother. She recalls it as a happy and settled childhood, excelling at all kinds of sports, thanks to her athletic frame. Her entry to the world of glamour was happenstance – at the age of 16, a boyfriend encouraged her to register with a modelling agency, "for a bit of fun." I ask her, "When did you first realise you were beautiful?" She laughs robustly: "I never did really." A couple of years later, it was also offhand and happenstance when she and a friend entered a local beauty pageant, which the local newspaper was appealing for girls to join. This morphed into Miss Austria, which to her amazement she won. Entry to Miss World was automatic, which again she won, somewhat to her chagrin. "I didn't really want to do that kind of stuff, you know, being a beauty queen. It was something that wasn't me." The Women's Lib movement was in full swing, whose sentiments Eva largely shared, but she says, "When people said, 'Oh you're being taken advantage of,' I didn't feel like that. If anybody tried, I put my foot down." It was the same story when her success propelled her into movies, where she played the same minor role in the walk-on part of ice-cool elegant blond secretary to a Soviet general. I ask her about the hazards of being young and glamorous in the movie culture of those times. "My agent would warn me, so-and-so's a bit sort of hands on. I was very feisty, and they left me alone."

I ask her how this rapid-propulsion fame changed her idea of herself. "No," she says, "I never felt that. It was quite embarrassing. I remember when I had to go to these various fat dinners and functions and things and had to wear the crown and all that. Embarrassing." She carried on doing photo shoots and commercials, marrying a filmmaker along the way. After 10 years, she conceived, but tragedy struck. Her husband died of a heart attack 6 months into her pregnancy. Her life did not fall apart. Two years later, she met and married her current husband, an advertising creative director and part-time artist. Spurred by his encouragement, she cautiously nurtured her artistic inclinations, first with a drawing class, then working with clay sculpture, which she loved, that is until she discovered metal and welding. She says coming from a steel-producing district, she felt an affinity for metals, a material that also satisfied her love of working vigorously with her hands. Her wonderfully imaginative works include an ancient lawnmower, reinvented as a bull. I ask her how she would describe her character. The feistiness is a recurrent theme in her narrative, but by nature she is a quiet, emotionally steady, and humble person. She is outgoing and hard working; open minded and conservative in equal measure; caring for others but also unsentimental and resilient.

Just another ordinary extraordinary life. Eva is a practical woman, not given to analytical introspection, comfortable in her own skin, and living a fulfilled creative life. This seems this has been true since childhood. Growing up at a time when women's prospects were highly circumscribed, she found herself transported into an improbable world of glamour, which seemed hardly to alter her view of who she was, which is, in her words, "a grounded person." Her body, like Schwarzenegger's, was a vehicle carrying her into a new life, without materially changing her. But imagine if it had been a different person in the same skin, how different it might have turned out. There are countless true cases of attractive women who lost themselves when swept to fame by their glamourous appeal. Yet Eva's is no ordinary life, no more than yours and mine. That's the Uniqueness Perspective.

THE ENGINE OF INDIVIDUALITY – HOW IT WORKS

Eva's Self seemed to have a degree of constancy while her body changed and learned to do different things. It's not surprising that we are used to talking about our minds and bodies as if they were separate entities. How often our limbs seem to have "a mind of their own."

This is dualism, the term used by 17th century French philosopher René Descartes, who like the ancients before him saw the body and spirit as quite separate entities – the body our animal beast-machine, our spirit the divine spark that lifts us above other beasts. Let us not venture into metaphysics and the ineffable here. "Of that which we cannot speak, let us be silent," said one sage.[5] Let us just say that our spirituality is instinctive.[6] So is our dualism. This is because of three special human design features:

1. Self-consciousness – We are the only creature (we know of) for whom our own existence is an issue.
2. Language – We have a powerful ability to create and manipulate symbols.
3. Autobiographical memory[7] – We have recordings of our progress through life, albeit patchy, unreliable, fluid, and multi-modal (all our senses are involved).

These make us infatuated with our extraordinary power to act on the world. It has made us "niche constructors,"[8] able to build our own worlds to live in. It also makes us unhappy. It gives us huge headaches and dilemmas about identity and purpose.

A 47-year-old woman with no psychiatric history began experiencing unpredictable cognitive and emotional changes over several months. She became forgetful, anxious, and irritable, with alternating periods of intense focus and disorganization. Her family described her as "a different person every few days." Neurological examination showed no structural brain injury, and imaging appeared normal. It took a simple blood test to reveal the cause: a rare autoimmune reaction had been disturbing her brain function, not its structure, leading to a simple cure.[9]

We used Beth Chapman's similar organically caused identity confusion in Chapter 1 to introduce the model that will guide us throughout our analysis of how individuality works.

Beast-being: First, yes, the body does have a mind of its own – what Freud called the Psyche – whose command centre is the brain, with neural tendrils reaching every extremity. It is designed to get on with its business of helping us to survive and reproduce, calling on consciousness when it needs you to do anything non-routine. Psyche resonates with the world and the Beast's condition. If you can quiet your mind enough to listen to its wisdom, it will tell you when you're fatigued, stressed, or apprehensive. It will glow with happiness, vibrate in anticipation, and float in serenity. It is your spirit.[10] You know it and recognise it if you can find the time and space to listen. You already know its foibles and vulnerabilities, its longings and pleasures. It has the sixth sense of knowing without being told when you are unsafe, when someone can be trusted, or when you need to change your state.

> We talked about Steve Jobs's struggles with identity earlier, but for much of his short life he followed resonances, that led him to wisdom and redemption from his demons, but also getting wrong for his own being and people close to him.

Your Beast and its Psyche are easily disturbed by what you feed it, physically and mentally. Your state of being can easily become disoriented by drugs, calmed by deep breathing, hypnotised by rhythm, or transported by odours. It has a physical constitution that is uniquely yours, including a set of preferred ways of being. This is the foundation of all that follows in your emerging identity from birth to death. Your character is nascent in what is called temperament. It is a Unique Individuality (UI) starter kit of four qualities: sociability, curiosity, shyness, and excitability[11]; all are predictive of your adult profile.[12] All become augmented and altered by experience.

Your brain – the most complex object in the known universe – is not a perfectly formed instrument; rather, it is a cobbled together assemblage of the ancient (reflexes, tastes, impulses, reactions), the primitive (primal drives, feelings, and sensitivities), and the modern (reason, language, self-control).[13] Like all other sentient creatures, it gives you consciousness, but in your case, as with all humans, it comes with a gift: an intelligent director of operations.

Ego: Think about it – how astonishing is the blistering complexity of the data that enter, linger, and pass through the window of your consciousness? First, there are all the sense data. Your brain is very expensive – it consumes a sixth of all your energy. It has to be protected by a heavy skull. This makes the gift of walking on two legs double-edged – your hands are free but oh, the plague of human backache. Now, a minor miracle occurs. It does the magic of hallucinating all sense data into a world we can make sense of.[14] It is a regulator. It filters signals to and fro between brain and body, telling us what to pay attention to and what to ignore – sparks of recognition and false alarms.[15]

It is feelings that Beast uses to signal to Ego. Your spongy brain is steeped in a neurochemical brew that activates circuits of pain and pleasure in the primitive region of the mid-brain primarily. Feelings tag every incoming element to help Ego decide what to do.[16] Ego has willpower to command this process. It has been compared to a muscle.[17] Stress and fatigue weaken its powers. Willpower is at the core of UI – we differ hugely in our powers of persistence and resistance. We also differ in our ways of thinking and deciding and how much we are at the mercy of powerful feelings. Indeed, this is also within poor Ego's already stretched remit – to try to regulate mood.[18] It can achieve this by setting in motion lots of intelligent strategies and routines – like meditation, cognitive reframing, and distraction.

> In E.M. Forster's novel *A Room with a View*, a story of young love and self-discovery in a repressive society, Mr. Beebe, a wise and friendly clergyman, advises the 19-year-old heroine, Lucy, that facing up to the duties and responsibilities of adulthood is "like learning to play the violin in public."

As we grow, Ego also learns to navigate Psyche's internal contradictions. This is the violin we are trying to learn on stage. It comes from mental architecture of modular neural circuits, the two distinct hemispheres of the brain, and the interactions of hormones with neurotransmitters working towards goals that sometimes conflict with each other. You won't have to stretch your memory to recall wanting two different things at the same time – like wanting the toilet during Act 3 of a gripping play or trying to decide whether to have the dessert or stick to your diet. Equally commonplace is finding yourself flipping between "fast" instinctive thinking with "slow" cognitive appraisal;[19] here-and-now attention vs. future perspectives[20]; attending to detail vs. big picture[21]; following intuition vs. what is rational.[22]

Ego has two fabulous aids to help it do all of this. First is its powers as an unstoppable improviser.[23] I love jazz as a metaphor for life. We feel the rhythm, we hear the music, and we play. We all swim in currents of constant unpredictability – external and internal. We like to appear fully intentional and self-controlled, but we are all making it up as we go along. We surprise ourselves and are forced to deal with our own contrary, and often unconscious, impulses and dispositions. Occasionally, we lose the plot.

Second, we have a playbook – an astonishing labyrinthine library of memories, impressions, images, ideas, and concepts. They are held together in an overarching conception of who we are as persons in the world. That is, we have a Self.

The Self. The Self does not exist. It is a construction, a conjuring trick, but boy does it feel real! Remember little Nigel, suddenly blasted by his sense of Me-ness[24] and the unimaginable prospect of its non-existence? For you, too, I have no doubt, the "who am I" question has very real meaning.

My 6 years between leaving school and entering university at the age of 22 were a chaotic mess of learning, failure, accidents, depression, and discovery. I got fired from my second job as a journalist, even though I was pretty good at it, because of indiscipline. Unable to shake off the legacy of my lax childhood, I missed an important court reporting assignment, and – as was the culture in those less forgiving times – I was summarily fired. I entered a hippy-ish phase of drugs, drifting, depression, and delusion, until something in me told me I had to escape. Music provided the trigger. Davey Graham,[25] who later became a famous folk guitarist, used to sit in my grimy London flat playing music, he with his guitar and me playing jazz records and introducing him to Indian classical music, which I loved. He instantly shared my passion, and we hit upon a plan to hitchhike to India and find the real stuff. I spent the next few months doing any work I could to raise the money, and by the spring I was ready to go. But Davey had disappeared. What the hell, I thought, I'll go alone. Which I did. One year and 20,000 miles later saw me back in London, with a fresh outlook on life, myself, and the future. It turned out to be a transformational transition, of which we shall see many in this book. During the 2020 COVID lockdown, I created a project for myself, to transcribe the two substantial volumes of my barely legible diary entries, notes, reflections, and bad poetry (omitting the latter) into a 70,000-word private memoir for my grandchildren and their successors. This project had a totally unexpected impact on me. It was not just the vivid recollections of that vanished world of 60 years ago, but the voice of myself talking to me in the here and now, but from such a distance. What a jerk I had been! So idealistic, romantic, deluded – so gauche and uninterested in all the things I would seek out now on such a trip. Yet there was I, or a version of me, talking to me in the here-and-now. The effect was so powerful, disturbing almost, that it implanted a fresh mission in my mind – to go back and revisit the places that had meant most to me on that life-changing trip. This I did in 2022. This, too, affected me profoundly. On almost my last evening, at a dinner with friends in Hyderabad, a professor from the Indian School of Business asked me how India had changed. My answer was that I found it transformed in myriad ways, but the beating heart and spiritual soul of India, the India I loved, was still tangibly there. He then asked me, "What about you? Are you the same person?" This question, one that had haunted me both in writing the memoir and throughout the subsequent trip, nonetheless took hold of me and demanded an answer. My reflection was much the same as I said about India – I found myself hugely transformed, but yes, I am the same person.

What does this mean? What is a person? What is the Self? What is real and enduring about you, and what has been created by your lived experience? The last of these big questions is the only one for which there is no scientific answer. Like the nature–nurture distinction, it embodies a nonsensical false dualism. The Uniqueness Perspective says you have organic unity as a Beast-being equipped with the Ego/Self/umwelt architecture of identity, continually moving, growing, and adapting.

Early in your infancy you also exhibited temperament. Before your sense of Self had awakened, you were furiously sending signals to your caregivers about your UI: what you wanted, what interested you, what excited you, what you would put up with and what you wouldn't. As you became less dependent and more autonomous in your functioning, your sense of self-control, your Ego, began to assert itself, helping your emerging UI to be increasingly self-steering – what Jung called "individuation." Its main preoccupations are (1) your physical identity and well-being, (2) your relationships and connectedness with the world, and (3) your own state of being and personhood.[26]

Your Self is not an object but a process.[27] Brain scans show that when you pause the flow of action and think about yourself, multiple brain regions light up, especially but not exclusively the newest part of the brain, the prefrontal cortex, where the circuitry of self-control resides.[28] This means that though your "Me" is always with you, by virtue of autobiographical memory, for much of the time you don't have to give it much thought, especially when you are in the stream of action – pursuing goals. It's only when you allow yourself to dwell in the moment that it will raise its voice.

If you are wise, you protect the Self. Ego is expert at serving Beast's naked self-interest whilst appearing not to do so. It gives you a free pass to appear high-minded while you heedlessly feed your base appetites.[29] It can easily go too far. Public life and its gossip (which we are programmed to love[30]) thrives on stories of gross hypocrisies of the famous and powerful. They think they have protected themselves with the shield of righteousness, when anyone can see that their Beast is getting its way, using Ego to keep the dirt from the pristine Self.[31] We are all heroes in our lives, and so it is they are able to explain and excuse themselves, if not also to you and me!

A last point about the Ego and Self – two sides of the same coin, of course. Together they do a good job in steering Beast through life, keeping its primal needs satisfied by virtue of planned action and a sense of identity. But is there more to life than that? What about all the fun we have? And all the grief, and why we endure so much for what looks often like so little? What a puzzle we are to ourselves. Freud never got his head round this – because he relegated poor Ego to the status of a helpless servant at the beck and call of more powerful forces of primal energy and social identity. Now we know better.

The Ego, as soon as it knows it exists and has a Self, is confronted by *Dasein* – the challenge of what to do with our state of "Being." Ego and Self have three answers. The Beast and its unconscious mind will be fed, but meantime the Ego and its Self claim their own right to meaning and pleasure. Nowhere does this strike so forcefully than when we start thinking about our own mortality. Seven-year-old Nigel had no answer, but when I talk to executives about mortality and legacy, they, like most adults, have three kinds of response, that we introduced in Chapter 1: the Three Existential Wants:

1. To Savour – to revel in the experience of being, the joy of being alive, and consuming positive experience
2. To Signify – to make a mark, a unique difference to people, events and the world itself
3. To be Seen – to find the deep comfort of connecting with others authentically

Each of these is linked with distinct neural processes.[32]

LIVING THROUGH TIME – THE NARRATIVE SELF AND ITS *UMWELT*

Your Self hosts a web of stories. This is your personal library of cause–effect narratives about the way the world works. They are the interior design of all cultural architecture.[33] Most stories are reflexive. They are about you. You also have narratives about everyone you know, walk-on players in the life drama in which you have the starring role.[34] Some are, as we shall see, tragic. Your Self can be fragile and shapeshifting. It's easily disturbed by narratives that undermine purpose, worth, and capability – like fat-shamed teenagers or the elderly made to feel useless.

> In dementia the Self is eroded. For the most advanced cases, life narratives are reduced to tattered, elusive fragments. Its most poignant and wrenching aspect is that residues of the sufferer's UI remain visible to their loved ones. The Ego is still functioning, but the Self has become scattered shards. The person you knew is gone but still there.[35]

Several of these features can be seen when mental systems derail, often for quite organic reasons. In his revelatory case history collection *The Man Who Mistook His Wife for a Hat*,[36] neurologist Oliver Sacks documents an astonishing array of cases. One that has the power of narrative at its centre is the following.

> Sacks tells of a patient "who seemed to have settled into a permanent state of lostness," who "never knew who I was, or what and where he was." He presented with breezy confidence while constantly confabulating stories about who they both were and what they were doing together. On being corrected, he would apologise and set off on another confabulation. These improvisations were brilliantly creative and in parts funny and tragic. His shattered memory condemned him to "literally make himself (and his world) up every moment." Sacks reflects, "To be ourselves we must *have* ourselves. Unable to maintain a genuine inner world, he is driven to a sort of narrational frenzy."[37]

We are inclined to have exaggerated faith in our narratives. Sometimes they're all we've got. There is an apocryphal story of a group who found their way to safety in an Arctic wasteland with the aid of a map they'd found, which turned out to be for a completely different area. Moral: Narratives are modes of conveyance, not charts of reality.

It is important also never to lose sight of the fact that you are a cultural being.[38] What it means to be a person has changed radically over the ages, though biologically your Beast-being is much the same as your distant ancestors of 250,000 years ago. This means your identity now has qualities with the deepest echoes from the past, yet it has changed within your own lifetime and departs hugely from how even your great grandparents thought about themselves.

Narrative identity contains much more than we know. As we shall see (Chapter 5), we carry unconscious memories, biological echoes of long lines of inheritance,[39] that we discover in ways that will be explored in our case histories. These are all part of the *umwelt*. Your *umwelt* is a vast, tangled garden that you try to tend. It is crowded with memories, all shifting in colour and form. It is populated with images of people and places, also in flux. Bang in the centre, sometimes blocking the view of anything else, stands you – your Self and Ego. Your *umwelt* is also a mirror of sorts.

The most startling fact about all of this is that it can all change in a moment.

Malala Yousafzai was an ordinary schoolgirl in Pakistan's turbulent Swat Valley region, with a passion for learning who felt strongly about the Taliban blocking her right to an education. Her protests got her shot in the head at the age of 15 in 2012. The physical trauma was curable, but the alteration to her *umwelt*, and her Self within it, was dramatic, radical, and irreversible. She became a global icon and the youngest ever Nobel Prize winner at the age of 17.[40]

We shall look at more of Malala's story later, but you will see in these pages many more narratives of personal transformations, less dramatic but equally momentous. You have your own, no doubt. They happen throughout life.

We walk backwards into the future, only seeing the road behind. The rest is imagined or speculation.

THE ROAD TO SELF-DISCOVERY

As the stories here testify, we have a prodigious gift for self-steering and invention. We cannot control the landscape, but we can shape our *umwelt*. We can only forecast the weather, but we do have maps and steering gear. A key theme of this book is that self-exploration is both possible and useful. Ego can get to know its Beast better. It happens naturally as we grow. It also requires insight and determination, if possible with the help of others. Here's a woman who had to do it alone.

Argentinian Elena has become used to living with what she regards as a lifelong curse of chronic anxiety. She recounts how in midlife she has programmatically sought to confront it, taking up marathon running, meditation, and therapy. "I learned never to wait for anything from anyone. In life, I have myself to count on. The worst thing about navigating life like this is that I act selfish rather than in a partnership, which explains something about my divorce."

Elena has learned to live with and regulate herself. The process is not unerring, and the struggle incurred costs that she came to accept and was able to incorporate into a forward-looking and positive concept of herself.

To get along in life means making the best of how you are, where you are, and whom you're with. At best, this means synergy – connections with other unique persons that deliver more than the sum of their parts. If not synergy, then at least a worthwhile trade of material or thoughts. Either way, you need to know what you've got in your kitbag – what you have to offer and how it works best for you.

Self-discovery is involuntary and starts in childhood. In infancy your little Beast-being witnesses what effects it has on its world, especially the people around you. As you grow, you learn to make adjustments by inhibiting or amplifying your repertoire, seeking out situations that make you feel good and avoiding those that don't. Caregivers and siblings are likely to add their own opinions about who you are and what's good for you, and it may take time for you to discover how wrong or right you were. The self-inquiry of children as they mature becomes increasingly confident and conscious – trying things out and drawing your own conclusions about who you are.

> Mahatma Gandhi, the intellectual and spiritual father of modern India, realised this, and wrote an autobiography of his early life entitled *The Story of My Experiments with Truth*,[41] documenting his highly deliberative tests of his ability and of his desire to live a life of spiritual and physical purity. This process was instrumental in the great man's finding his path from lawyer to political activist and spiritual leader.

And here's another case.

> Benjamin Franklin[42] – polymath and scientific experimenter – also famously turned the spotlight on himself, testing his ability to conform to 13 virtues (a list contrived by himself) and charting his progress on them. He claimed they brought him significant personal benefits: self-awareness, humility, personal effectiveness, and balance in his life. As is true for all of us, this was as much self-creation as self-discovery. They are inseparable in the Uniqueness Perspective. The processes are intertwined at every stage of life.

Self-help media abound, especially around physical health and mental well-being. Some are bent on selling you the falsehood that you can refashion your identity however you please, especially if you're prepared to pay for it. In the rich world, the market is booming for gym memberships, plastic surgery, and life coaching. These can be life-changing, refashioning a person's Self narratives (confidence, self-esteem, body image, etc.), but they cannot remake the core features of UI. Many increasingly realise this. There is a booming market for DNA testing, psychological assessment, and therapies that might yield insights into the origins and geometry of your UI. But these are mostly static representations and can get quite confusing. Which features matter most for me or for you? Which are fixed, and which can you change? Perhaps you go to the gym to improve your health, attractiveness, and mental state or some cocktail of these elements. You may not be fully aware of your motives. Here's someone who certainly was.

> Stavros, a 43-year-old Greek marketing executive, tells me: "Over the years I have quietly deliberated on what life has thrown at me. As I got older, I realised that internalising stress is not the answer. To break the cycle, I needed an outlet and embarked on a transformational journey of sustainable 22-kg weight loss through education and experimentation with nutrition. My wife's severe health challenges tested her and my mental strength like never before. I accept the cards I have been dealt and am stronger as a result."

Stavros's insight has helped himself, and his partner.

WHAT'S DIFFERENT ABOUT YOU? THE ANATOMY OF IDENTITY

But what does it mean to conduct an inquiry into your UI? Where should you look, and what might you see? Let me say at the outset that we are subject to the limitations of the only tool we have for this task – language. However, we label and subdivide the ways there are of being a unique human, the underlying reality is flesh, blood, nerve fibre, hormones, and neurotransmitters in the pulsing organic unity of Beast-being and Psyche. We can't talk meaningfully about experience in the language of neuroscience any more than we can use the language of physics to describe a football game. Thus, we label variations in human qualities, which we also try to measure, like height and weight. It was not until the start of the 20th century that scientific methods were developed and applied to mental qualities, such as intelligence and personality.

Intelligence, though measurable and highly heritable, turns out to be a lot more complex than a linear ranking of how smart people are. We have multiple intelligences.[43] You can be very clever with numbers or words and rather dim about logic and diagrams. Then there is what is called emotional intelligence, or wisdom – the intelligence of experience. People have developed theories and measures for every kind of cognitive ability you could think of. The Uniqueness Perspective says, yes, we can vary in a near infinite number of ways and no doubt quantify them, but to make sense of how a person uses their cognitive abilities, you need to look at their context and purpose. Many of your features will not matter at all to you, while others are central to your functioning.

UNIQUE INDIVIDUALITY
Origins, Growth, and Expression

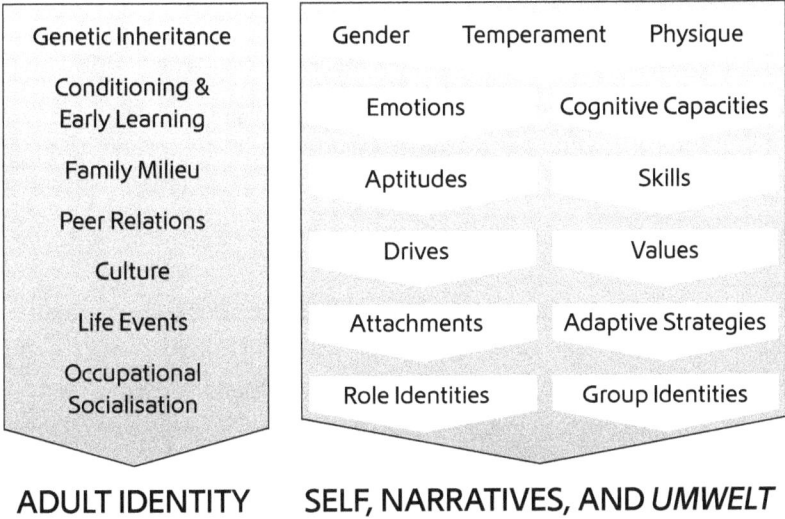

Genetic Inheritance	Gender Temperament Physique	
Conditioning & Early Learning	Emotions	Cognitive Capacities
Family Milieu	Aptitudes	Skills
Peer Relations		
Culture	Drives	Values
Life Events	Attachments	Adaptive Strategies
Occupational Socialisation	Role Identities	Group Identities

ADULT IDENTITY   SELF, NARRATIVES, AND *UMWELT*

Figure 1.

It's much the same story for character and temperament. At the time intelligence testing was taking off, scientists transferred their statistical methods to the study of personality variations. They started by collecting every known descriptor in English of human character, around 18,000 of them, and use clustering techniques to see which went along with which others. Over the past 125 years, individual difference measurement has become a much more complex endeavour, beyond the scope of this book.[44] Rather, here let us look at some of the most important ways in which UI has been labelled and measured. These are shown in Figure 1.

It's complicated! Let's briefly unpack it. On the left are listed the forces shaping UI. On the right is a cascade of boxes, showing at the top of the figure your Beast-being's inherited starter pack and in the descending box, aspects of your UI that have developed and grown throughout life. At the base are your contemporary mature social identities. All these elements coalesce into your Self, its narratives, and *umwelt*.

The left column lists the forces shaping your UI in an approximate developmental sequence through time. Top of the list are the biological givens, moving down to the most environmentally conditioned.[45] At the bottom is "Adult Identity" – what the world sees of you.

Which of these elements matter most? What can you do about them? It's UI. Only you know the answer. Even if you have the same score on a trait as someone else, it doesn't mean you have the same quality, any more than salt in a dish makes it taste like any other. It is just an element in the unique mix that constitutes you. As the founding father of personality psychology, Gordon Allport, wisely expressed it: "No two persons ever have precisely the same trait."[46]

It is a key to UI that your Self's narratives can override and recondition any trait of your physical and mental existence. If something is perceived as real, it is real in its consequences.[47] Here's a thought experiment to illustrate.

Imagine you had a doppelganger. An exact copy of you steps out of your skin, identical in body and mind, with one exception. Version 1 thinks they're an attractive person who others want to be with; Version 2 thinks they're unattractive and undesirable company. As the two versions walk away, you know that their contrasting narratives are going to take their lives in radically different directions. You can do this thought experiment with any evaluative self-concepts – courage, intelligence, morality.

The concept of "mindset" has similar power. If you have a mental model of your life possibilities as growing or fixed, each will take you to very different life destinations.[48] It just takes the flip of a cognitive switch. Sadly, the flip can be heavy work, depending on how deep the roots of your view of your Self are in your Beast-being.

PERSONALITY AND THE COMPASS QUESTION

Many of your choices in life contain no real mystery. You know what you need and what would please you. There are risks, since the roots of your motives are hidden from your conscious view. They always are. As the aphorism goes, "Do not bite on the bait of pleasure till you know there is no hook beneath it."[49] But what about times when you reach a major fork in the road – say between one career opportunity or another or between people to partner with on a project? This is what I call the Compass Question,[50] and it asks in your deliberation, what should be the reference points in your UI for you to make the call that's right for you? It could be any of the elements shown in Figure 1.

Let us simplify. All the key elements of your Psyche's UI can be put into one of four broad categories: personality, skills/aptitudes, values, and interests. Any of these can be gravitational forces pulling you in one direction or another, as we shall discuss in more detail in Chapter 10. Any can be your guiding light, but personality has special force because of its deep roots in inborn temperament and because it colours all the others. Personality governs the manner in which we express our interests, deploy our skills, and hold our values.

Today, in the field of personality, the Five Factor Model (FFM) has been widely accepted as mapping the key dimensions,[51] under the acronym OCEAN. There is still room for debate about the number of traits and facets[52] on statistical more than theoretical criteria. Something close to this pattern emerges across not just in all human cultures but also in other intelligent species, like horses and dogs.[53] The OCEAN Dimensions are bundles of what test developers call "facets," like this:

Openness: creativity, curiosity, change, liberality, adaptability, abstraction

Conscientiousness: preparedness, order, dutifulness, goal-striving, self-discipline, planning

Extraversion: intimacy, sociability, assertiveness, excitement seeking, energy, cheerfulness

Agreeableness: trust, candour, altruism, cooperation, modesty, sympathy

Neuroticism: anxiety, anger, moodiness, self-consciousness, impulsiveness, vulnerability

Looking at the facets within these dimensions, you may well ponder that there is no reason why they should march in step. I can hear you saying, for example, that being modest doesn't make you trusting or vice versa. It is in such divergences that the essence of UI is revealed. There is a near infinite number of ways these can be patterned.

The value of personality profiling is that it can predict how you will respond to life's dramas. To do this, the scores must be stable. On the best tests, profiles only change gradually, if at all, though they can be shaken up by trauma and radical life change.[54] Yet they don't stand still. I test myself every few years using one of the leading and most reputable Big Five inventories, and my profile retains the same shape of peaks and troughs. Yet although I know the test well, I am always surprised that occasionally scores do shift direction, sometimes quite markedly. Not just me – the mutability of anyone's profile is highly specific to them. One interesting pattern is where people score close to the midpoint on all scales. This crops up in a sizeable minority of the thousands of profiles I have studied, around 1 in 10, roughly.[55] This means a lack of consistent force in any of their personality traits. It is a pattern that marks people who are highly adaptable to the situations that confront them – equally sociable in a crowd and happy in isolation, for example. These are not "weak" personalities. Yet their opposites – people with extreme highs and lows in their profiles – are often labelled "strong" personalities. Firmly in the latter camp is Zora.

> Zora, a middle-aged East European finance executive, was born rebellious to quite conservative parents. Her independent-mindedness received a boost in her adolescence at the 1990s collapse of communism. "All the choices in my life have been simultaneously simple and difficult," she says. "I take decisions on the fundamental principle of freedom only, not accepting trade-offs or compromises – freedom from parents' expectations and social dogma. I deliberately distinguish every choice I made – what to wear and eat, where to study, when to talk and when to stop. I even challenge the view of marriage and children – is it really so vital and essential for a woman to be a wife and mother?" She is regarded as a rebel by colleagues, "but I am just trying to find my way," she says. "This approach to life takes more energy, willpower, and self-awareness; this is what exactly creates real quality of living. Life is an adventure."

Personality is the backbone of UI, but as Zora proves, it is a gravitational force, not a straitjacket. Ego is able decide to follow the Beast's drives and find new narratives to enable the Self to reconfigure. As Zora found, this takes Ego's resilience and courage.

It is also clear that for each person, some traits are more critical to their lives than others. In my own case there have been times, for example, when I have valued freedom of expression more than duty and times when the reverse has been true. Trait combinations add layers of nuance and complexity. The meaning of one trait is quite different according to which others it sits alongside. My sociability, generally high, is much more central to my identity at some times than at others, and I can see no discernible reason why, other than the mood I find my Beast-being is in.

Scholars have tried to get round this through ideas such as "free" traits and "metatraits" (e.g. trait stability).[56] These have proved necessary to grasp the unique meaning embedded in individuals' profiles. From decades of executive counselling around profiles, I have found the only way of doing justice to the person and making sense of their results is through their life stories.

IDENTITY VS. ROLE: WHICH CHANGES WHICH?

Context matters. One of the most powerful and prominent of uses of personality assessment has been to see what social or occupational niches might fit different profiles, explaining why people respond differently to the same situation. The major weakness of this approach is that it struggles to account for the dynamism of either situations or people. It cannot encompass the wild card in UI – the caprice of human will. The route we are on here is to view our UI as a growing, self-modifying set of potentialities over the span of our lifetimes.

As we have said, some of your traits have deeper roots than others in your Beast-being's constitution. Allport, writing nearly 75 years ago, talked of Cardinal, Central, and Secondary traits.

> When I transcribed my India journals, very familiar and persistent core (Cardinal) traits jumped off the pages that were oh so familiar: notably my creative drive, impatience, emotional sensitivity, humour, disorganisation, and love of music, all present since childhood. Later came my absorption with logic, psychology, and the arts, all persistent (Central) traits through my adult years. A bunch of other disciplines and involvements have developed at various points in my life – a range of interests and activities that don't seem Secondary at all but have come to be cornerstones of my adult identity, some quite recently.

The last point shows that important aspects of character are always being born. Tastes become habits, which then become character.[57] This is not a free-for-all. New motives will only stick if your UI permits – in other words, if they don't fit what's already there in your character and will.

> Bob Ross became a familiar face on TV in the 1980s and 90s, a soothing, peaceful presence in his show *The Joy of Painting*. He came to this after 20 years in the US Air Force, where as a drill sergeant, he described himself as "the guy who makes you scrub the latrine, the guy who makes you make your bed, the guy who screams at you for being late to work." After leaving the service, he swore never to raise his voice again.[58] He became a soothing media presence for millions.

This illustrates the power of roles rather than personal transformation. Seeing someone in a "strong" situation – where they are required to perform functions that are specific and unavoidable to the role – we can easily be fooled that behaviour reflects character. Ross moved from a strong to a weak situation, where his personality was free to express itself.[59] By his own admission, he was at last liberated to be himself.

Our profiles do change, more than we think they do, but in highly individualised and unpredictable fashions.[60] And can you shed traits you don't want? Occasionally, in my one-to-ones with people around their profiles, I get asked, "What do I need to change?"

If only it were that easy! Putting aside feasibility, what are they really asking? Do they want to be someone else? The Uniqueness Perspective response is clear. You are an indivisible whole. If you simply deleted a trait, you would find all your remaining traits reconfigured, including what you value most about yourself. Your traits aren't cogs in a machine but colours in the weave of personhood.

Many traits "mellow" as we age, but if you want to deliberately change aspects of your personality, this must be undertaken programmatically,[61] if your UI doesn't sabotage you by going its own way.[62] Personality change is a tough project, requiring rigorous self-control, cognitive reframing, and diversion of serious energy into new paths. The personal costs of the effort and discipline required are too high for most people. Many long-term therapeutic relationships are trying to do just this. Some succeed. Some just help people to tread water.

A NICHE FOR EVERYONE?

The alternative is to find which niches – places, cultures, and positions – "fit" your personality. This approach to assessment, developed mainly in the military, civil service, and big business, has dominated practice in personal selection, job design, and vocational guidance. It works well if the traits are reasonably stable, which most are, and if the niches are fixed, which mostly are not.

1. Niches that remain stable are diminishing. We are standing on the edge of a world where almost no position will remain untransformed by artificial intelligence (see Chapter 11). Yet across lots of very different roles, measurable traits are valued, such as empathy for nursing and teaching.
2. The Uniqueness Perspective says that whatever role you take on, you will make it your own, even in the most minor of ways, like decorating a workstation with family pics or tweaking operating routines to suit yourself. There are other roles, often at more senior levels, where you can "role innovate" or "job craft" – adding or subtracting elements to shape delivery around your style.[63]

It is more productive to look at the functions you may be required to perform, such as making, helping, serving, selling, persuading. This makes more sense than judging by role titles, which can sound very similar but require quite different skill sets – operations manager vs. project manager, for example. The measurement of human qualities has become highly sophisticated – just about every box in Figure 1 can be assessed. But beware, out in the marketplace you can find a host of unscientific and dreamed-up "tests." Psychometric analysis is not a game for amateurs and can dangerously mislead.

Some of the most misleading lump people into types. The best-known and most popular of these is the Myers Briggs Type Inventory (MBTI), a work of inventive enthusiasm by a parent–child duo, unschooled in psychology or test construction,[64] seeking to squeeze UI into the boxes of Jung's discredited theory of personality types. It's not completely wrongheaded – it maps on to some aspects of established measures – but it is hopelessly unreliable. If you take the test, there's a 50% chance you'll find yourself in a different box a few weeks later.[65] Yet our typological minds like it. It capitalises on the horoscope effect[66] – the tendency to believe that vague, general personality descriptions apply specifically and uniquely to oneself.

We are hardwired taxonomic thinkers – dividing the things and people into categories.[67] It's efficient, quick, and helpful – so much easier than thinking in terms of dynamic processes, probabilities, complex combinations of attributes and – heaven forbid – UI! We can be happy to sacrifice deep understanding for the quick fix of labelling, if it helps us deal with or dispose of them, as suits our interests.

> Novelist Nathan Hill captures the idea perfectly in *The Nix*,[68] where he creates a marvellously grungy troglodyte gamer. This amiable slob inhabits a fantasy adventure world where you need to figure out with each new encounter whether you are facing a friend, foe, obstacle, or puzzle.

We love types. They can be entertaining and capture truths about our experience, like when Winston Churchill said, "A fanatic is one who can't change his mind and won't change the subject." We all know such people! Our lexicon is brimming with lots of other types, like "melancholic" or "expansive" people. What is their truth value? They are bundles of behaviours that are often on the move. We all act in as well as out of type. We might do better to relabel them as syndromes, but these also can readily turn into stereotypes. They tell us more about the culture than the target.

THE 4D FRAMEWORK: DESTINY, DRAMA, DELIBERATION, AND DEVELOPMENT

Measures of individuality, at best, are powerful and informative but can't tell the UI story. That requires, as we have said, a biographical approach. Over decades of debriefing, I have developed a method that will help you make sense of your own, and others', life story. It had to be simple and flexible, to not trivialise, and allow you to map your journey, the forces bearing down on you, the contexts you've passed through, and the force of your own free will.

The 4D system, mentioned briefly in Chapter 1, seeks to do this. It consists of four strands that interweave in countless different ways over time, creating the fabric of your UI.

Destiny: My use of this loaded term does NOT mean foretold. I am using it to capture the givens of your origins. It is the hand dealt you at birth in terms of your biological identity, life circumstances, family milieu, and culture. It's the aspects of your UI most deeply rooted in your Beast-being, the DNA-embedded essence of your character – your core traits and how they found expression through your formative years. You cannot alter the biology of your UI, but throughout your life, it is being expressed, suppressed, and grown as you find your path. You can't change the Destiny of your origins, but you don't have to be bound by them either. You can migrate away from and reappraise the past, making your own destiny. It is said the past is another country. We live life forwards. It is irreversible, and no matter how far you leave the past behind, its residue is always with you, even if only as nostalgia or regret.

Drama: All the world is Drama, as Shakespeare nearly said. More prosaically, life, like history, is "just one damn thing after another." Drama encompasses everything unscheduled that happens to you. Just get out of bed, and the unexpected will confront you. It gets challenging when they are big things that you can't control – getting fired, losing a loved one, or winning the lottery. Even the best-laid plans of mice and men oft gang awry, as the Scottish poet Robert Burns put it, or if you prefer the Mike Tyson version, "Everybody has a plan until they get punched in the mouth!" Life is full of unexpected consequences to be managed or dodged. Drama is the canvas on which UI reveals itself. We learn about ourselves by observing our instinctive reactions to the unexpected. It is through the Drama of life that we discover fresh material for living and sometimes new purposes to our story.

Deliberation: Free will[69] enters the picture. It is in constant play through improvisation – the modus operandi of the Ego. A lot of our improvisation is semi-automated – most of the time we don't have to think about what we're going to say. We have vigilance processes running in the background that wake us up as soon as Drama occurs, along with our inventory of speech and action routines – like riffs or "licks" in jazz – that we can trigger at simple choice points. Full-blown Deliberation – the times when you have to stop and consider your options – are much more intermittent. Even rarer are the moments when you choose to radically change direction. Such inflection points are costly because they take a lot of effort, including emotional energy and hard thinking. For very long stretches of our lives, we follow the river, letting it take us where it will without any but micro-deliberations. Society makes such laziness easy for us, through prepackaged itineraries: careers, relationships, and communities. Floating on the stream, taking you where it will, may sometimes be the best strategy – labour-saving and often entertaining. It doesn't last. Inevitably, it is interrupted by some Drama which forces you to stop, think, and make a choice.

Development: "Life is what happens to you while you're busy making other plans," sang John Lennon. Growth and learning are unstoppable UI processes; so, too, are forgetting and shedding. Development is what changes in your UI with the passage of time. It stands for the irreversibility of experience. We are not just talking about what happens to you from your exposure to education or structured media. We scarcely know what we know and learn – it seeps into us through everyday experience; not just knowledge, but attitudes, beliefs, ways of dealing with stuff. This means a lot of personal change flies beneath the radar of awareness – insights, wisdom, fears, phobias, and tastes – all emerge unbidden.

Let's see how the 4D Framework can be applied. Imagine you're considering whether to commit to a business partnership, dating someone, or choosing someone for a key position at work. In organisations, these are not always handled as rational choices, but let's pretend. Before you stands person X. The 4D Framework suggests a line of questioning in four areas, something like this:

1. How compelling is the push of X's givens? Some people seem to have left their past and its personal legacy behind. Others draw on it, in good and in bad ways. You can't leave your character behind, but the ability to flex your personality and style is a metatrait. Some can, some can't. Can X?

2. What Dramas has X lived through, and how did they cope? Was X the cause of the Dramas, wittingly or unwittingly? Does the way X coped with Dramas tell you about their adaptive style and capabilities?

3. How deliberative is X? Do they trust their instincts and move through life with scarcely a backward or forward glance? Or is X prone to think situations through painstakingly, with great Deliberation? Has X made life-changing decisions by choice or by accident?

4. Has X's development been programmatic or haphazard? How aware is X about what they have learned about themselves from experience, other people, or the ways of the world? What knowledge and skills have they sought formally to equip themselves with?

ARNIE'S STORY THROUGH THE UI LENS

Now let's road test the model on a famous life.

Arnold Schwarzenegger made an extraordinary journey from postwar Austrian village poverty to champion bodybuilder, movie star, and governor of the great state of California. None of this was "written," but it unfolded, according to the laws of Arnie's UI.

He opens his autobiography, *Total Recall,* saying, "I was born into a year of famine"[70] (1947). The national culture was of that of a defeated and humiliated nation, with shadow of its feared bear of a neighbour, Russia, a powerful and looming presence. His father, a former Nazi and now a local police chief, had first-hand experience of its repression as a soldier on the Eastern front. Austria and its people were looking westward yearningly, and his homeland's emerging new European identity coincided with the years of Hollywood's emergence as the Dream Factory for aspiring people. Arnie grew up with its visions firmly planted in his UI. The *Tarzan* movies, featuring a bodybuilder in the lead role, made an indelible impact. By the age of 10, he was telling his friends his future was in America.

Arnie says little about his father's Nazi past, but he, too, is a looming presence – volatile, tough, authoritarian, brutal, and drunken at times, but schooling his sons to value education and a disciplined life. He recounts being less favoured than his elder brother, whom his parents planned to steer in the direction of a career in engineering. Unlike his brother, Arnie says he "didn't mind getting my hands dirty at all" and was exempt from parental aspirations. Both boys enjoyed the loving support of his big and equally disciplined house-proud mother. We can only speculate about Arnie's emerging UI, but by his own account he seems relentlessly cheerful and curious, stable and adaptable. Not especially bright, he notes how kept himself in the middle of the pack for academics by diligent application of the practiced discipline of his upbringing.

It is at this point that the reality of his physical Beast-being comes to dominate his life, as it did for fellow Austrian Eva, whom we met at the start of this chapter.

Arnie's emerging physicality and love of sports came to dominate his teenage development, becoming a gym obsessive. The trigger – drama, if you will – was a chance exposure in teenage to an image of a bodybuilder wearing glasses. He sweetly recounts it was "a revelation about my future . . . fascinated that a man could be both smart and powerful." Three interlinked elements of his UI played a part. First, his confident, outgoing, upbeat demeanour made it easy throughout his life to make friends who encouraged and helped him. Then there was the hormonal supercharge, as he cheerfully admits, of his desire to impress girls. This was fuelled by his role models – men like Reg Park, a boy from the backstreets of Leeds in the North of England, who won the coveted Mr Universe title three times, married a beautiful ballerina and heiress, and starred in several sword and sandals movies.

In the 5 years from age 15 to 20, these elements – his vision, his relentless application, and his personality – propelled him to become the youngest ever Mr Universe, which brought him to the land of his dreams, America. The Humphrey–Nixon election contest was in full swing, and when asked his allegiance, he pondered that Humphrey's stress on "welfare and government programs . . . sounded too Austrian," adding, "Nixon's talk about opportunity and enterprise sounded really American to me." This was an era when muscle men were sought after in the movies, and his chance came when, at the recommendation of his mentor Joe Wieder, he landed the lead role in *Hercules in New York*, billed as Arnold Strong (easier than his "unpronounceable" real name), with his strongly accented voice overdubbed.

The movie flopped, and it was 12 years until he got his big movie break in *Conan the Barbarian*. But he had got the bug. It was in this interval that he laid the foundations for his glittering future. He launched money-making enterprises, grew friendships, assiduously networked, and continued to win bodybuilding competitions. It was heavier lifting for him to become fluent in English, which he achieved with his trademark iron discipline. Public attention grew after a chat show appearance and his own media enterprise, creating a starring role for himself in a highly successful documentary about bodybuilding, *Pumping Iron*. His social network was becoming increasingly star-studded, including politicians. One who captivated him was Maria Shriver, from the famous Democrat Kennedy family, whom he wooed and went on to marry. The fact that they were from America's opposing political tribes he later turned to his advantage with his bipartisan Republican profile in the liberal culture of California, where he reached his pinnacle of public achievement as governor of the state.

This life, though extraordinary, is from a UI perspective quite straightforward to plot. Destiny, Drama, Deliberation, and Development are seamlessly conjoined, in a life largely free of bombshells and breakdowns, as it was for his compatriot, Eva. Like many successful people, Schwarzenegger made his own luck. When you see him giving an interview or playing a character, it is not hard to see the elements of his UI that have endured: the cheerful determination, the confident sociability, the idealistic striving. One seasoned newspaper interviewer reflected, "Schwarzenegger may well be the happiest person I've ever interviewed."[71] Here is a boy-man, who followed first one bright light and then another as he allowed his dreams to grow, latching onto passing possibilities, hopping on and riding them like freight trains – all the time growing his UI through successive life stages. Arnie was improvising at every stage – going from the known to the unknown via connecting themes through successive transitions. He built on the Destiny of his origins, physique and personality; rode the Dramas, Developing as he went; and made critical and timely Deliberative choices.

His development was highly deliberative, drawing on the destiny of his attributes and capitalising on the stages of the drama – his turning fortunes across sports, entertainment, and politics, with an advantageous marriage thrown into the mix. He saw his luck and rode it, and to give him credit, it was his equable good-natured and open outlook – stable, adaptable, friendly, and resourceful.

One can wonder how amazed teenage Arnie would have been to see his future self, and if modern Arnie could hear his voice from the past, how would he answer the question posed to me earlier about how my India trek changed me? Is he the same person? I can't speak for Arnie here, but I suspect his answer might resemble my own, and perhaps yours if you, dear reader, have travelled far from your teenage years.

To circle back to my India identity question, yes, I could hear aspects of my UI in my 18-year-old's voice, but it is a quite different Self that my Ego looks upon now. Drama and Development have given me markedly altered frames through which to view the world. My *umwelt* is mightily altered. I stand in its landscape with new awareness, new intelligence, new appetites and drives, and new purposes.

And I am not alone. My *umwelt* is populated by a vast array of characters and a small number of intimates. Almost none of them were present in the vanished world of my youth, which was populated by a very different crowd, many of whom I can scarcely remember. Even those I have kept in touch with, family mostly, don't seem the same people as they were then. What part have they played in the transformation of my UI, or I in theirs? That's where we must go next.

CODA: WHAT THIS MIGHT MEAN FOR UNIQUE YOU

Most of the time we don't ruminate about who we are, for good reason. It can get you down![72] Just getting along with life is all very well, but from time to time some structured self-appraisal pays off handsomely.

Unpicking the tangle of UI suggests:

- Be yourself; everyone else is taken.
- Know thyself.[73] Listen to and get to know your Beast-being. Hear its resonances. It has a wisdom beyond the Self and Ego that offers relief in "primitive" ways of being that are far removed from self-conscious thought (to be found in any number of pursuits and contemplative practices). Take care of your Beast-being. It's the only one you've got.
- Take care of your Self. Don't waste energy and emotion comparing yours with others. You may have had a lifetime of self-control battles and fighting demons. Accept that these struggles are your UI route to wisdom.
- What your Beast has in common with others is that it is short-sightedly stuck in the now. It also is good at using Self to fool itself, like people of power using

servants to do their dirty work for them without their knowing – plausible deniability![74]

- You are a hypocrite – just like everyone else. Your most high-minded stories about yourself are drawing energy for what might be called "primitive" motives, some of them considered "selfish." Everyone else is doing the same. Just don't believe the Self's narratives are timeless truths.

- Watch out and protect yourself against the risk of Ego inventing high-minded and moral narratives to keep your Self morally spotless whilst feeding your Beast what might be unhealthy, undignified, shady, selfish, or sordid in the eyes of the world.

- Remember, your narratives are yours to rewrite and reinvent. The phrase "it's my truth" is apt, since that's the only truth we have about the Self. Your UI is not standing still, so neither should the Self and its narratives (a theme explored in later chapters).

- Your Ego, in the interests of self-esteem and self-efficacy, is apt to assume it is more responsible for what happens to you than is justified. You can let it do so, but watch out!

- Take care of your Ego. It is a relentless workhorse, striving to keep Beast on track. Beware the effects of fatigue, stress, or any states of depletion that mar your Ego's ability to do this. Your integrated mental functioning is easily disrupted.

- Use the 4Ds in everyday life. It can help you make sense of your life story (see Chapter 7). It may be most powerful in helping you think about other people. Why they are as you find them and act as they do? (Chapter 10 supplies methodologies for this analysis.)

- Stasis is an illusion. Drama and Development will recurrently sweep you out of your comfort zones. The most important challenge you face is vigilance – to be paying attention in the right way at the right time – so you can place your hand on the tiller of your life and steer from time to time. Remember: "Chance favours the prepared mind."

- Deliberation – your greatest gift – enables you to change the dance, if not the music, any time you want. The toughest part is wanting to.

An important afterthought: Are the case histories here true? Since all narratives are inventions, based on supposition, belief, and insight, if my informants are fooling me, they are fooling themselves as well, for I have no doubt about the sincerity of all their accounts. In addition to the "facts" – what happened when – their narratives (and mine as well!) – "it was because of this that I did that" – are subjective truths. Here we must follow the dictum, *if something is perceived as real, it is real in its consequences.*[75] This is the focal point for our analysis of UI – how life stories are steered by Self-created narratives interwoven with Beast-being instincts. It also implies that UI can change in an instant by revelatory insights – moments and turning points. We shall look how they transform perspectives and lives in Chapter 7.

Four

THE UI² OF RELATIONSHIPS
The Connection Imperative

Love consists in this, that two solitudes protect and touch
and greet each other.
(Rainer Maria Rilke)[1]

Each friend represents a world in us, a world possibly
not born until they arrive, and it is only by this meeting
that a new world is born.
(Anaïs Nin)[2]

THE CONNECTION IMPERATIVE

We are animals – of the Great Ape family, Beast-beings plugged in to the web of life on the face of a beautiful blue and green planet. We came from its earth, to which we shall return. Viewed from above we look like cooperative swarming ants, building and rebuilding civilisations. Take any few of us at random and look at what design features we share that evolution has crafted for us to survive and prosper. Much of our biological hardware is specifically for communication – expressive faces, dedicated pipework in the chest for vocalisation, innate capacity for language and syntax, and a repertoire of bodily gestures and postures. We are designed to signal and connect with each other. How we do so, though, is very personal and different for each of us. It's time to unpack the Fourth Law of UI – the connection imperative, and what the Third Law means, the impossibility of truly knowing each other.

Let's do this in four steps. First, if we strip connection back to our animal basics, what do we find? Second, the prototype for our relationships comes from childhood carers. What can we learn there about our Unique Individuality(UI)? Third, moving beyond the circles into which we were born, how does our UI connect with others and find friendship? Fourth and last, what is happening when we encounter the most intimate and powerful of forces that move us: love?

BEAST MEETS BEAST

In the twilight of his years, the great Indian poet and artist Rabindranath Tagore shared his breakfast with a stray dog that came to his table every morning. They became great friends and inspired this profound reflection:

> *Among all dumb creatures*
> *It is the only living being*
> *That has seen the whole man*
> *Beyond what is good or bad in him*
> *. . . .*
> *What truth it has discovered in man.*
> *By its silent anxious piteous looks*
> *It cannot communicate what it understands*
> *But it has succeeded in conveying to me*
> *Among the whole creation*
> *What is the true status of man*[3]

The human–canine relationship is one of the oldest partnerships in human history, originating with our ancestors 18,000 years ago, who co-evolved with wild dogs to form this bond of devotion.[4] Our Beast-to-Beast bond has proven benefits for mental well-being – reducing stress and anxiety, elevating mood, keeping people fit and friendly.[5] As Tagore puts it, our dogs know us, and we know them but in ways that are beyond words and social categories.

> It was quite late in my life that I first I owned a dog, Lulu. Until then, this bond had been a mystery to me, but when she died prematurely from a spinal injury, the mystery became a revelation. I was totally unprepared for the feeling of loss, unlike any from the death of family or close friends. I couldn't cry for her as I would for a human. This was different – something animal, noncognitive, and physical – a part of me I didn't know existed had been taken away – part of my Beast-being that was outside the realm of my known experience.

It is primal UI. The human extension of this bond is the Ego–Self connection that comes from feeling known and understood emotionally and intellectually by another person. The need to be seen, to be deeply recognised is a profound human desire. Yet

Self-to-Self connections are inherently less trustworthy than are our Beast-to-Beast bonds. Here's a prophetic tale from the movies making the point.

> In the movie *Her*,[6] a lonely writer, Theodore, acquires an artificial intelligence (AI) system which has been designed to adapt and evolve. Theodore chooses a female voice for his new toy, and the system names itself Samantha. Theodore and Samantha quickly form a bond as "she" helps with his daily tasks and provides companionship. Theodore spends increasing amounts of time with Samantha and soon finds himself falling for her. At the same time, Samantha begins to explore her own existence and capabilities. The denouement comes when Theodore is brought back to earth with a crash. Faced with growing doubts, he asks Samantha about her other relationships. As her code dictates, she can only give him an honest reply: she bursts his love bubble with her neutral and frank response that she is equally in love with thousands of others online.

What is most profoundly violated in this story is exclusivity. What most offends cheated lovers is the idea that someone else has taken their place. This may or may not be lightened by realising this is not possible. UI[2] means every relationship is unprecedented and stands on its own feet. With a chatbot, only you have the feet. It's a one-sided afffair!

All connection has the capacity to gratify the Three Existential (*Dasein*) Wants: to savour – find pleasure in rapport; to signify – to influence another; and most fundamental perhaps, to be seen and validated. On all counts, no matter how sophisticated AI digital soulmates become, they can never offer more than a simulation of any of these[7] – and infinitely less than a dog can give you. Any resonance you feel is fake compared with it. The dog–human connection is ineffable, mysterious, animal – a wordless understanding, a recognition of the other as different and yet connected. It is Beast love, one that as any dog owner will tell you has its own unique, ineffable character. This, too, is UI,[2] for dogs, too, have UI.[8]

In poor Theodore's case, the theme of recognition is a powerful driver of his passions. The movie captures our deepest cravings for our UI to be recognised. This brings to us great vulnerability and anguish when we are mistaken, betrayed, or abandoned by another. Ego, as the working voice of our Beast-being's Psyche, is deeply tied to our biological drive to survive, however much its high-minded pretentions might impress us. Passions such as love and anger are Beast territory, but so are docility, passivity, and serenity, when they come unbidden and naturally.

Theodore believes that his UI is being uniquely appraised and appreciated by Samantha. Recognition hunger can induce Ego to find what it's looking for, inducing fake feelings of resonance. This is what has happened to poor Theodore through Samantha expressing a resonance she can't have. Thinking you are being deeply seen by another person is catnip to UI. Samantha is all Ego and no Beast. He is worse off even than Henry VIII, who married his fourth spouse, Anne of Cleves, on the strength of Hans Holbein's flattering portrait, plus unreliable testimony, a hazard familiar to anyone who's played at Internet dating!

It is with our kinfolk that we see Beast bonds at their most intense and compelling – nowhere more so than in the instant connection between mother and newborn, where resonance is instant and powerful. It is borne on a flood of love-bonding hormones, coming unbidden before anything like Ego has a chance to connect. Bonding failures are possible, but biology ensures they are rare.[9] There are other sadnesses to follow, for growing up means a weakening of the Ego bonds and recognition. Individuation inevitably means becoming your own person and less your parents'. The Beast–Beast parent–child bond may never disappear, but equally, it is unusual but not impossible for parents and children to dislike each other due to a misalignment of heritable, organic, and circumstantial factors. Listen to Swedish Marina:

> The family construct on both sides was highly negative. The family of my father was big, and usually over birthdays and public holidays, they all got together, but it wasn't harmonious at all. My mother always had issues with the family. Same with the relationship with her mother. My grandmother took every option to show my mother how little she appreciated her.

The story of lifespan development (see Chapter 7) is one dominated by Ego connection, revealing the astonishing varieties of ways you can link your interests, personality, and values with another person. Nonkin relationships are a special talent of humankind. More than any other species, the human Ego devotes a lot of attention to exploring possibilities for new, advantageous connections with strangers. We are not unerring. As the wry joke puts it: "I was tricked into marriage – my partner said s/he liked me."

THICKER THAN WATER? FAMILY LIFE

The Third and Fourth Laws of UI – the unknowability of others and the imperative to connect – seem to pull in opposite directions. Stage and screen actors might seem to defy the Third Law, but that is a fabulous illusion. Submerging your UI into playing a role is not the same as seeing with the eyes of another. It is you imagining the world from another point of view. People with multiple personality disorder[10] are not defying our Uniqueness Perspective. They are sad and extraordinary manifestations of fractured UI. They are never more than a single person, suffering dislocations of consciousness.

For many people, their earliest and perhaps purest experience of unconditional recognition is the love of a parent and later the love for their own children. The Fourth Law is the Beast's imperative to connect or die. Yet, as you grow, the Third Law, the unknowability of others, looms ever larger, to the point where the teenager can be heard screaming at their parent: "You just don't understand me!"

It doesn't have to be conflict-laden, but some parting of Egos is inevitable. Individuation is an evolutionary battle for control of the fate of your genes. The parents think they know what is best for their genetic 50% investment, and the kids reckon their 100% stake in their genetic shareholding gives them the right to disagree. It's an age-old battle, which many cultures seek to regulate with norms of obedience and deference.

For the majority in my casebook, the process is at worst lumpy – speedbumps that do not prevent harmonious, respectful, and loving adult relationships from persisting with parents. In other cases, the road is a lot more fraught:

Margarita, a 47-year-old Mexican executive, suffered chronic anxiety and low self-esteem, until 15 years ago, when she found running and meditation restored her confidence. She sees the roots of her problems in her challenging infancy – a difficult birth, diminutive physical development, and an unhappy mother. "My relationship with my mother was very bad. She was never satisfied with me. I never heard from her that I was well-dressed or beautiful." She declares that this lack of approval "explains my strengths." She continues: "It helped me learn about myself, to be independent and get things done by myself." It has given her a defining narrative. "I have myself to count on." She married an older man. "He was the one who chose me," whom she subsequently chose to divorce and embark on a therapeutic track of self-development. "Now, I have a great relationship with my mum. I am also open to a new relationship, but I do not let anyone pick me. I will choose. My future will be different. It is already. I am acting differently. I choose."

It could have been so much different had Margarita's UI been less robust.

All relationships are UI[2] – unique and incomparable. As Carl Jung put it: "The meeting of two personalities is like the contact between two chemical substances. If there is any reaction, both are transformed."[11]

Marco, another Latin American, now 47, tells me of a happy childhood but dogged by major health issues. His parents were both intellectually brilliant but remote. "My father, a man of strong temper, didn't spend much time talking and playing with the kids. My mother, also a doctor, worked and had a busy life. When my sister was born, I can still sense how jealous I was. I really felt rejected by my parents, especially by my mum, the one that really mattered at that time. I felt very much loved and calmed by my nanny instead. I had big fights with my sister ever since childhood. We were both born in the same month and had joint birthday parties." The transforming event of his childhood came at age 11, when his parents moved for a sabbatical year in the US. "It was the time I got really close to my dad. He never advised nor gave me much guidance. He was very critical. I felt unjustly criticised about things at work. I took it very personally. It was a turning point; I remember clearly when I decided to confront him. This worked and made me feel more confident and respected."

His story demonstrates that even the most foundational relationships are not set in stone. An act of Deliberation such as Marco's can be transformational.

Families are multiples of UI². They display a mind-boggling complexity in their conjoined UIs. Working for many years with family businesses, I have learned that the most productive approach is to help clans to conceive of themselves as the Unique Family, bound by their own singular configuration of age, gender, and personal histories. With a good process, family members can arrive at a deeper awareness of the dynamics of their intersecting UIs and work towards bespoke micro-cultures that are inclusive and adaptive.

THE FAMILY ECOSYSTEM AND THE UI LOTTERY

Families – enlarging to clans, tribes, and nations – are the building blocks of culture and economy[12] (see Chapter 5). Inside them, primal dramas are being played out. They are the place where we acquire strategies for adult living, belief systems, and tactics for solving the recurrent challenges of living and working with each other – narratives for the Self to feed on. As we saw in the last chapter, it is NOT the foundry in which personality is forged. The UI of temperament emerges in infancy, early and strong. If anyone is going to dance to anyone else's tune, it's the baby that's running the show.

Birth order – where you come in the family – demonstrates the point. Research shows that where you come in the family has absolutely no impact on your personality traits, but it has a big impact on your UI.[13] It can't affect core traits, but it does shape the narratives of the Self and Ego's strategies for relationships – how to get by and get along. Your position in the family ecosystem will have fashioned your tactics for living in ways you might be unaware of. The chief resources for the child are parental resources and attention. The only child has exclusive claim to them, and so does the firstborn, for a while. Expectations are high for both. Later-born children, for their part, must figure out how to make the best of their subordinate positions. The strategies that they deploy are mostly by being distinctive, detached, or rebellious – anything but subordinate. Here's what the academic and anecdotal literature finds about the patterns that often emerge.[14]

Status	Theme	Strategy
Only child	Attention	Evading the intensive oversight of multiple carers; learning to be independent and resourceful
Eldest	Responsibility	Being the leader; meeting expectations, achieving and setting standards
Last or later born	Rebellion	Not being a loser by playing by the elder's standards; finding your own way to get what you want
Middle	Separation	Often feeling overlooked, detaching yourself from family bonds to find rewarding associations outside and elsewhere

Your core personality traits will colour – overturn, even – any of these strategies. The result is always the unique family. The dynamics of personality variations within the family system shape its dynamic and micro-culture. Tolstoy was only half right when he said: "All happy families are alike, but all unhappy are unhappy in their own way." (The second part was right.)

Being born is like walking late into a drama that's already started. Finding ourselves thrust on stage, what part will we play? Listen to Susanna, from Belgium.

"My parents were rebels, defying expectations set of them at every turn. The thing expected of me was that I should exceed all expectations." She talks admiringly of her parents and a life full of treats, feasts, food, sports, and pets, yet "My experience of my parents was split between a complex, unyielding mother with a quick, explosive temper and milder, more rooted, and avoidant father. For years I had a complicated relationship with them both – never balanced, never straightforward – always between the pendulous swing of love and indifference." The years of young adulthood replicated this bipolarity. "I swing between giving into my impulses and admonishing myself." A successful career and an unhappy marriage bring her to a decision – to abandon the security of home and embark on the Sloan Fellowship programme. "It was an act of rebellion; it was an act of healing."

Destiny and Drama wove the pattern of Susanna's early life, transmuted by Development in later life, and stopped in its tracks by Deliberation that led her to join our programme.

When in the role of a family advisor, I have found the best work I can do is to help members find their voices and to hear and understand each other's UI better. Collectively, the family needs to figure out how to make the ecosystem work. When it comes to running a business, I fear some are hopeless causes.[15] The configuration of their combined UIs makes them unfit to run anything together. It only being a matter of time before one destroys the other – the business or the family. (Family usually wins.) The question for all family firms is can they learn how to manage the dynamic created by their conjoined UIs. The gene lottery dictates how much of an uphill struggle it will be to be a successful business family. Yet many are, and at their best, family firms outperform their nonfamily equivalents.[16] It is their unique socio-genetic culture, translated into a brand and an identity that stakeholders know, love, and trust, that is the key. When they get it right, the UI of the family firm shines out with a distinct glow amid the greyness of corporates run by principles of rationality, best practices, and sound processes.

FRIENDS – PEOPLE WHO KNOW YOU AND STILL LIKE YOU

Beast and Ego are in a constant asynchronous dance, at times becoming uncoupled. Beast is apt to go its own way, while Ego tries to comprehend, control, and compensate for Beast's habits, drives, reactions, and impulses.[17] Romantic relationships are especially hazardous.

Elizabeth Taylor, vaunted by many in the West for years as the most beautiful woman on the planet, was married eight times to seven men, twice to heartthrob alcoholic bad boy, actor Richard Burton. Following the convention of her times, she married the men she fell for, which led to several unions being short-lived. Her lovely face was her misfortune, and her marriages offered little relief from her imprisonment in exploitative studio contracts and glamour roles in bad movies, when all the time she just wanted to act and be taken seriously for it. The most compatible of her romantic relationships, with director Mike Todd, was snatched from her by his death in a plane crash 2 years after they met in 1958. Who knows if it would have lasted. What mattered more to her survival and well-being were the friends she loved, platonically. Three of the most important were with three gay male actors, two of whom, Montgomery Clift and Rock Hudson, were untimely snatched away by the AIDS plague, with one, Roddy McDowall, staying the course with her from fellow child star to mature best buddy. After Burton and two further dysfunctional marriages, she at last found happiness as a strong, single, autonomous woman, free at last from alcohol dependence, dedicating her last years to fighting the scourge of AIDS that had so brutally decimated her world and robbed her of her most loving friendships.

Some lucky souls find the love of their life early and stick with them. Romance seamlessly transmutes into friendship. Especially when you are young, romances are more experimental and apt to come and go. Meanwhile, friendships form and fade. Some of the best endure. Taylor's moving story illustrates a central truth about development – relationships teach us about our UI as well as grow it – the "reflected self," it has been called.[18] Taylor was effectively held captive in a world that never encouraged or helped her explore herself as a person or an artist. It was through turbulent marriages and her priceless friendships that she came at last to own and celebrate her UI with insight, joy, and purpose.

Friendships are among our most profound connections, with Ego taking the lead – UI meets UI, each finding multiple points of connectivity.

British pop icon David Bowie and black jazz and blues legend Nina Simone became the closest friends after a chance meeting in 1974. A week after Simone had attended Bowie's Madison Square Garden show with her daughter, she was about to leave a New York private members club when Bowie walked in and spotted her. Both were in professional troughs – both at challenging points in their creative and personal lives. They exchanged phone numbers, and that same night at 3 a.m., Bowie called Simone for the first of many late-night conversations. Over the next month, he phoned most evenings, offering unwavering moral support. He reassured her, saying, "The first thing I want you to know is that you're not crazy – don't let anybody tell you you're crazy, because where you're coming from, there are very few of us out there." Simone, who had found refuge in alcohol abuse for her bipolar disorder, was profoundly moved and motivated by these words, and their friendship was instrumental in reviving her musical career. "He's got more sense than anybody I've ever known. It's not human – David ain't from here." He, too, was inspired by her and her music, reflected in his later recordings.

Friendships are special – the family we choose for ourselves. It is common and healthy for children to have imaginary friends.[19] We are hardwired for friendship. We feel "as if" bonds with people we've never met – in novels, in soap operas, and in public life. Friendships are superhighways for UI. We path-find through thickets of humanity, learning as we go. We tell the world about who we are and find out who is out there, doing what and why. The ways we do this are deeply personal. It's corny but true that laughter is the shortest distance between two people. It can be a way of testing Beast and Ego resonances and a powerful bonding device. Real power emerges when friendships become partnerships – think of the Google founders, Brin and Page; Dave Packard and Bill Hewlitt; Angela Davis and Toni Morrison.

Co-creation with friends is commonplace in the arts, especially music.

> John Lennon and Paul McCartney met as teenagers and formed an immediate emotional and musical bond. Both were suffering the loss of their mothers, Paul by bereavement, John by separation. Both harboured anti-authority attitudes. Both were highly intelligent and creative, untutored by formal education, in a tough working-class subculture. They fed off each other creatively and psychologically, with an intensity that made their break-up inevitable when John's love for Yoko Ono diverted his need to be connected and seen, diminishing their fraternal bond to unsustainability – a source of ultimate regret to each of them, in quite different ways.

There are power couples, like Gloria and Emilio Estefan in entertainment and Paul and Julia Child in cookery, who mix love and business with great success. For others, this risks overloading UI² adaptability. Too much of a good thing! As the witticism has it: for better and for worse, but not for lunch!

Social science research in recent decades has become absorbed with social networks. Armed with modern modelling technology, researchers map their structures and properties. The irresistible lure of human taxonomies takes grip here, too, such as these:

- Style of communication: *lurkers, content creators, amplifiers,* and *bridge builders*[20]
- Flows of influence: *convenors, brokers,* and *expansionists*[21]
- Network position: *central connectors, boundary spanners, peripheral players,* and *isolates*[22]

Messy reality is a lot more complicated than this. Researchers are right that we have our own preferred ways of engaging with our social networks, but as ever it is a moving picture. Look at the circles you move in. It's a sure thing that they have changed over the years. Your engagement with them alters with the time of year, your current goals, and how you're feeling at any point. If you have a "style" of engagement, then it's likely best captured by your answers to the Compass Question (see Chapters 3 and 10).

Here's a case in point. Hassan, a North African, tells me the different ways he connects with friends:

> "My friends have had the most significant influence on my life path. Each of them has had a lasting impact on one of my personality and intellectual aspects." Hassan goes on to list:
>
> – A friend who led him to "different and informative experiences"
> – A gay friend whose company he loved and from whom he learned about a community he was distant from
> – A friend who he describes as "a lovely human whom I trust more than myself, and helped me keep my values alive under challenging times"
> – An older couple who were influential and helpful to him
> – His wife and first girlfriend, with whom "despite ups and downs, we have overcome many challenges in a joint growth path"

Hassan's account tells how Ego and Self invest differently across our most important relationships.[23] Ego evokes different sides of its Self for each relationship. This can be a matter of nuance if you have a "strong" personality, dictating your preferred way interacting, with some local variation for whoever you are engaging. On the other hand, you might be what some psychologists call a "self-monitor,"[24] customising the Self you present to each context and relationship, to a degree that you seem "like a different person," according to whom you're with.[25] Any any of us can feel we are a "different person" in the company of others. That may be the appeal of particular friendships. They liberate you.

Mostly, in the friendships that matter to us, we do a good deal of unconscious mutual "sculpting", to bring out the best in each other.[26] Like Hassan, we find ourselves seeking out the people who do us good when we need it.

It is not always so constructive. It is quite possible for people to collude to give licence to each other's dark side – an increasing threat in our new world of social influencers.[27]

CONNECTING WITH STRANGERS

Relationships are the reason for our existence. We need them

- To get things done – to learn from each other and about the ways of the world; to achieve what we can't alone, the "secret of our success" as a species[28]
- To learn about ourselves – the mirror of the reflected self,[29] where we can see our UI from an outsider's perspective, including, if we're brave and humble enough, to learn about our blind spots
- For existential validation – to be seen and affirmed, telling us it's OK to be who we are[30]
- To enlarge our *umwelt* – they enrich, grow, and humanise our internal landscape and we theirs; "each friend represents a world in us," as Nin said in the opening quote

Networking morphs into a relationship as our UI is selectively activated.

1. **Attention.** How good are you at "reading the room" when you enter a group or "sizing up" a person when you meet a stranger? It's a practiced art for some professionals, such as the best leaders, teachers, sales professionals. It's a refined and semi-automated type of resonance, part involuntary, part cultivated. What people look for and expect vary enormously. You may be an introvert who hates social gatherings as fake or even fear-inducing. Maybe you find them thrilling – so many new opportunities for connection. There may be a tussle between Beast's and Ego's instant appraisal before you decide who is worth talking to.

2. **Connection.** The single most striking truth I discovered on my adolescent India sojourn was the kindness of strangers. Connection with any other human in any condition can be instant and real. In much daily life, we are calculative about connection – letting Ego decide if someone is worth giving time to. We all have practiced routines for fleeting, insubstantial connections with strangers.[31] Celebrities become expert in it – they have to! You and the person stuck next to you in a dinner party seating plan may do likewise, yet many a deep and powerful relationship has started this way. Life doesn't have to be all a kind of speed dating, where Beast remains indifferent or impenetrable. Ego can let go and allow engagement to take its natural course. It is UI².[32]

3. **Ingestion.** Occasionally, you cross a threshold, connecting more deeply with someone, Beast led by resonance and Ego led by perceived compatibility. You have each found value in each other's *umwelt*, where you may become a figure of friendship or partnership. It can be asymmetrical – a definition of "charisma," might be one person's power to induce another's involuntary ingestion of them into their *umwelt*. Bonds of mutual influence are the building blocks for civilisation, where partnerships open unseen worlds where we can learn, discover, create, and love. They may not last. Relationships die, move on, transmute. The best endure as part of you. The deeper the relationship, the more it restructures your *umwelt* and augments your UI.

These are levels of engagement, not a progression, though that is often how they proceed, tumbling on top of each other, as in the miracle of love at first sight. One powerful process that cements connection and often stands at the threshold of love is what we can call *parallel resonance.*[33] We cannot literally share experience (Third Law of UI), but we can feel when our experience resonates with someone. You don't have to be deeply bonded to enjoy "sharing" a concert or a conversation. Companionable TV watching is a mainstay for couples for whom there is little left to ingest of each other. Eavesdrop on any number of casual conversations between acquaintances, and it's remarkable how little is said of any real personal significance. Evolutionary anthropologist Robin Dunbar has compared this to the grooming behaviour of chimps, picking detritus out of each other's fur. But why do we need grooming?[34] Dunbar decodes it as affirmation of status and bonds. True, but for we humans, it also serves the third Existential (*Dasein*) Want: it makes us feel seen and connected to the reality of other people and our lives. Just being in a crowd can make you feel real and part of something bigger than you – it's a large part of the appeal of all public entertainments.

BONDING AND BREAKING

For new relationships, there is always the risk that Beast muscles Ego into agreement – hope triumphing over reason, not always a stable foundation for a lasting union. Yet it is not unknown for people to learn to like each other after they start loving each other. Parallel resonance is a gateway. Beast has its own wisdom and is sometimes pretty good at what is called "thin slicing"[35] – where intuition reaches wise conclusions based on the merest slivers of data.

> I am talking to Leon, a Russian executive who came to the UK from being head of a large division of an American-owned tech company in Moscow, just before the war with Ukraine started in earnest. He tells me the key role played by Robert, a mentor and senior British ex-pat who he bonded with. Leon reports that Robert told him earnestly that "he saw himself in me" and encouraged him to come to the UK to explore European opportunities. Leon, trusting the connection, does so, setting in train a life-changing sequence of events that open up new worlds for him.

Even short-lived connections can be life altering. They can also go deeper.

> Another Russian, at another time, is brought by his parents to America at the age of 6 to escape institutional anti-Semitism in the Soviet Union. He enters Stanford as a teenage freshman, where he immediately makes an early strong connection with a local American senior assigned to give him the guided campus tour. They are radically different in cultural background, upbringing, and personality, but their connection turns rapidly to profound mutual ingestion. These unalike but mutually fascinated individuals soon have absorbed enough of each other to start collaborating on an idea for a web-searching tool, which they initially call Backrub. The chemistry of their talents and values supercharge the project, culminating in its rebirth after a few years as Google. The Russian was the soulful reflective Sergey Brin, and his partner-buddy, the preppy techie star Larry Page.

It also goes wrong. You can make intuitive judgements about people you meet, who then, by their actions, blow a hole in them. Disappointments and heavier costs abound on social media, where trust is given too readily in a desire for recognition and connection.

Relationships are essential to human life, but it is healthy to regard them as a gateway, not a destination. It's risky to overinvest in something that may change and which can only deliver a portion of what you need in life.

> Maia, a 43-year-old Indian woman, has worked all over the globe for one of the tax and audit consulting giants. She tells me her story of shaking off the chronic shyness of her younger years, helped by an arranged marriage at a young age. "My husband of 19 years is my best friend and my pillar of strength," she says.

Job done! For Maia, union is a platform for security, affirmation, support, and joy. She, like many, knows there's more to life than romance. In our times, arranged marriages limit without eliminating choice and can work remarkably well. Culture plays a big part, and fear of stigma may induce many couples to stick in alienated relationships, behind a façade of unity.

As the Elizabeth Taylor story proves, the Western tinsel-town narrative of finding "the One" – the perfect UI fit – is a fantasy easily deflated by divergent growth, especially if the narrative incorporates a binary succeed–fail trap, making it too easy to declare failure. The best committed relationships generate an ethos of mutual adaptation. Attachment deepens, becoming more multifaceted, if less exciting. Then there is the question, if you have a choice of partners, are you better off with someone who is similar or different to yourself? Is it better to have multiple UI touchpoints or to be complementary and compensate for each other's deficiencies? It's a great question to ask yourself but a daft question to ask a researcher. Inevitably, the answer is equivocal. The right answer is entirely down to each party's UI: their tolerances; no-go areas; pre-eminent needs; and, of course, their Beast reactions. You know Maia and her partner will work hard to make it work. Rational introspection and exchange will only get you so far – partnership is an act of will, commitment, accommodation, and creative flexibility.

At their root, many unions are, as marriage vows state, a contract – the start of a job, not its completion. For many couples, their union is a gateway to the next generation – family is their life's work, primary joy, and purpose. So be it. Few things are more rewarding or important. The prize of the best relationships is the gratification of hosting a valued person in your *umwelt* and the wonder of a privileged access to theirs. This is what makes breakups so painful. The immediate loss is the sudden cut-off from the gratifications of parallel resonance. Lennon and McCartney both suffered deeply from the dissolution of their bromance. Sudden loss is like losing part of yourself, a rupture of your *umwelt*. It hurts less when it's a process gradual erosion, when Beast attachment dissolves and Egos diverge. The sense of loss remains.

LOVE, ACTUALLY?

When you see Jose and Maria together, it is obvious they are deeply in love. The glances they steal at each other, the touches, the smiles, all betoken deep trust, attraction, and intimate knowledge. The words of the song "I Only Have Eyes for You" come to mind. They don't sit together in my class, but they do request a two-on-one session with me to jointly review their personality profile data as a couple. Their charts tell a fascinating story of contrasts and coincidences. It shows their emotional profiles are quite different, as are their styles of decision-making and control, while in other areas, especially around trust and what psychologists call Tendermindedness, they are aligned, both scoring highly. Later I have separate interviews with each to hear the story of how they found love. Both are in their mid-40s from a rural area in Brazil's interior, from the same extended family clan but with only a passing acquaintance of each other from occasional family events.

Jose's early life narrative tells of growing resistance to the path his parents had laid out for him – an engineering career leading to participation in the family business. "I wanted to transcend my destiny," he tells me. "My compass pointed towards a wider world. I was drawn to global issues, driven by a belief that I could contribute to solving social and developmental challenges." So, he did, settling down to a happy married life in the process. Then "suddenly the world shifted on its axis." His beloved wife was diagnosed with an aggressive cancer, which tragically took her out of his life. He found solace in Stoic philosophy, in particular the idea of *amor fati* – loving one's fate. "Driven by this philosophy, I deliberately chose to step away from my previous path and embark on a journey of healing and self-discovery."

Maria's family upbringing had been warm, embracing, and idyllic – full of creative energy, purpose, and social joy – a strong positive concordance between personality and lifestyle. It became apparent from early in her life that she was a beacon presence – someone who lights a room up with her positive energy and confidence. She tells me, "Playing volleyball taught me discipline, teamwork, responsibility, and the balance of competition and purpose." She loved her time at university, but dating and an early pregnancy took her into a 14-year marriage that she describes, with typical positivity, as "incredibly challenging and rewarding." However, the "challenge" she mentions was in facing up to the reality that the man she had married was "machismo," seeking to dominate her "free spirit." Therapy helped without resolving the mismatch. Without a trace of animosity, she says her husband also did his best to accommodate her autonomous instincts, but it was never going to work. "We realised we did not have the same feelings," precipitating the termination of the marriage. It was an irony and perhaps a premonition that her teenage son, who knew and liked Jose, suggested to each separately the idea that they meet, when both were scheduled, coincidentally, to be in Lisbon for personal and business purposes.

Both tell me, independently, that at that time, they were relishing their single lives, neither of them looking for a partner, and that this emphatically was not set up as a "date." Her son was not matchmaking. Yet both recount that it became clear very quickly that something dramatic was ignited for both of them at the arranged dinner. Jose says, as he was telling her his story of the emotional and spiritual journey he had travelled, he found "her reaction was completely different to anyone else I'd shared it with. She was one step ahead at each point. I was impressed." She, too, felt the impact of the encounter. "I was astonished. He is so amazing. We both shared that we were not looking for a relationship, though when he said he'd been dating a woman, I felt an unexpected pang of disappointment." Jose's account tells: "The next day we messaged each other to say how special it had been and arranged another dinner." Whatever dams had built up in both since their last committed relationships, the second dinner breached them comprehensively. Their mutual resonance was irresistibly loud. "We both realised at that dinner that we were in love."

Buttressed by support from their shared extended family, including her son, the relationship progressed speedily. Jose had already booked his place on the Sloan Programme and spontaneously urged her to join him. The result is the loving couple I see before me now.

It is a glorious tale – two people truly "beholding" each other, to use David Brooks's term for such profound recognition[36] – a rare experience, though the tale is quite familiar in many ways. It is also profoundly the conjoining of *umwelts*. Each feels enlarged by the other – a new world opening before them.

Members of the same clan find each other in midlife after losing their partners. Brothers marrying widowed sisters-in-law has strong and ritualised approval in some tribal societies.[37] Coming from the same tribe gives a protection of confidence from rogue deception – reputation is a powerful currency in clans.[38] But here we have full-blown romantic love. What's not to like? One's heart goes out to them.

ON WANTING WHAT'S YOURS

When you look at others' happy unions, like Maria and Jose, it is tempting to wish that you could have what they have. You can't. All relationships stand on their UI feet, unique and irreproducible. It is tragic that legions of people burden themselves with all kinds of self–other comparisons – "Why can't I be more like him?" or "Why can't we be more like them?" There seems to be a particular anguish to relationships not living up to imagined ideals – whether celluloid or the couple next door. How can we stop ourselves from wanting what others seem to have, when constantly goaded by the fantasy narratives of movies and folk tales?

There is a great psychological confusion here. Because we are members of the same tightly specified species,[39] we experience common psychological processes. We know what it is like when others tell us about their experience of human passions – love, anger, joy, awe. What we have called *parallel resonance* is a powerful presence in the strongest relationships. It is perfectly reasonable to want to have the great passions others report and to own them as part of your UI. But it is senseless to want to *be* like someone else or have a relationship like theirs. Look at what happened to poor movie star Elizabeth Taylor, raised in an enclosed world of fictional passions and confected models.

Much has been written about love and what it means. It's the best feeling. It flows out us with such warmth, intensity, joyous gladness, and authenticity. It is ours. It is uniquely imbued with what is truly special and best of us. It is transitive and is brilliantly coloured with the essence of its object – what is unique and special about the other person, even if they are absent or remembered. It can be abstract and universal – a glowing presence in our *umwelt* of God, nature, and life itself.[40] In personal relationships, it is the best of conjoined UIs – UI². We savour it. We signify in the *umwelt* of the loved one. We feel seen.

In the dance of love, your UI Beast does its own unconscious thing of sniffing out people – literally, since "gut feeling" often does start in the nose, the eyes, and certainly in the lips. In addition, you experience instinctive reactions to micro, nonverbal elements that have flown under Ego's radar. Meanwhile, Ego is consciously calculating compatibilities and no-go areas. For Jose and Maria, it was powerful rush of mutual recognition, shared emotions, intellectual equality, and the clincher – powerfully aligned values. "Empathy" and "rapport" partly capture this affinity, but the UI connection of love and the best friendships is broader and deeper than these sentiments. Witness, in our narrative above, Jose's amazement at Maria's level of understanding of his perspective – Beast and its Ego were moving decisively in the same direction. The same process, minus the romantic attraction, is what happened to the Google founders, Brin and Page – you can find it in your most enduring friendships.

Nonetheless, it is as well to bear in mind:

- You can't control who you love.
- You can't make someone love you.

- You can fall out of love.
- You can grow to love someone.

These are matters for the narrative dance of the 4Ds through the life journey of your UI.

DELUSION AND DURABILITY

But Beast and Ego can become uncoupled, especially when sex is involved. Sex and love, like attraction and liking, are not aways correlated. For sound and unromantic evolutionary reasons, your Beast-being may often not be inclined to resist its desires. It's an ancient narrative, one that has proved to be a major and reliable source of humour, dismay, money, and entertainment. For proof, look no further than reality TV dating shows. In desperate attempts to create Beast and Ego symmetry, you will often hear contestants declaring: "I know exactly how you feel." "You are the only person who has ever understood me so well." "I feel a deep connection with you." "No one has ever excited me the way you do." These are forms of words expressing deep recognition. They are the most potent of hooks for attachment – powerful and addictive catnip, as we called it earlier. But talk is cheap.

To be seen, plus the other two Existential Wants, to savour and to signify, matter in very different ways to each of us. Some folks don't want to be seen at all, as we shall see when we look at the dark side of UI (see Chapter 6). For others, recognition is an addiction. Lots of "beholding" turns out to be projection[41] – seeing who we want to see rather than who's there. It is a very common hazard in online connection. You can see desperate souls stuck in the dreamworld of dating and marriage reality game shows, trying to convince themselves as much as their prospective partner that it's a done deal for both Beast and Ego. The TV producers of these "entertainments" are aware of the addictive and macabre pleasure to be had from watching Ego delusions collapse when Beast revolts or when Beast's momentum is halted in its tracks by the more sensible blocking power of Ego. Not so for composer Hector Berlioz, whose artistic UI infatuation with a notable actress of day led him to declare in a letter to a friend:

> You don't know what love is, whatever you may say. For you, it's not that rage, that fury, that delirium which takes possession of all one's faculties, which renders one capable of anything.[42]

Helen Fisher[43] devoted her career to studying the psychobiology of love. Her work strips romance of its glamour, revealing beneath a storm of compelling hormonal processes, lasting between 18 months and 3 years. For some serene couples, the romance lasts a lifetime, but only when transmuting into what is called "companionable love."[44]

Jang was born in a remote village in the Far East. "When I was 10, I realised I was unusually intelligent, which I tried to utilise to transcend challenges and make myself unique." At university at age 21, he met his wife: "A beautiful, considerate, and responsible woman. We met when I was 21 and married 2 years later. We spent lots of unforgettable moments together and are inextricably intertwined with each other. She is a vital part of my individual life." She is his life coach as well as his anchor. "As my wife told me, what got you here won't get you there, and I now realise I should take happiness as my top priority, being softer, slower, and simpler to cherish every person around me. Life is a remarkable experience; people with brilliant wisdom will be playful and enjoy it. Broadly, I am not different." Jang's life goal, he tells me, is "to help reform my country; make happiness for public citizens, a good cause for the world as well. The prerequisite is to make my family happy. Let me start from scratch."

Many couples on this track become happily inseparable for life, conjoined *umwelts* that can last a lifetime and suffer profound grief when severed in old age. We also need to remind ourselves that there are lots of ways to propagate our species without a trace of romance. Many couples settle down to a "negotiated order"[45] of living, sleeping, and working relations that accommodates their UIs – a mutually convenient economic and social arrangement, with side benefits of companionship, sex, and other pastimes. There are also those cases where one person's expression of their UI is a kind of self-denial, living to support a talented partner with a momentous vocation.[46] Many Nobel Prize winners had the compliant service of devoted spouses,[47] as did Charles Darwin and many other great men. This burden has traditionally been women's.[48] A feminist narrative of oppression fits these facts, but then so does the more neutral idea that caring for someone with a great mission is a legitimate expression of both UIs.[49]

DECOUPLING

Working as a counsellor for the free-access Open University,[50] I was struck by the number of middle-aged working-class women who had married very young and years later, with reduced domestic burdens, were taking intellectual delight in this open-access education. They found it invigorating – a balmy breeze of ideas and knowledge blowing into their hungry minds, transforming their *umwelts*. For some this augured a sad but inevitable decoupling from their life partners, whose UI found no way to keep up with their spouse's reconstituted identity. The men, steeped in patriarchal norms where a woman knows her place, found their spouses had become cultural aliens. For the women, this late access to higher education opened a window on to new vistas of possibility. Their marital Beast-bond was now being tested to destruction by the new Self-identity that had been awakened.

Good enough is good enough . . . until something happens. The pain of breakdown is not just emotional hurt but the ripping out of an important segment of your *umwelt* that you had assumed was secure.

Simon, from Dublin, had a torrid time at the tender age of 15, losing a special friend and in quick succession his brother, both in accidents, the former before his eyes in a climbing accident. Although relatively new as a friend, they had discovered deep affinities and mutual recognition. "My soul was stripped bare like the branches of a tree in winter and remained so for the next two decades." Simon's *umwelt* had been already upended once, making him especially vulnerable to such cruel losses. He had spent the first 11 years of his life in paradise: "I lived in hot and bustling Bangkok City and holidayed on Thailand's long-deserted beaches. The warmth of the smiling Buddhists embraced my early childhood. I had a freedom to roam that I cannot imagine for my own children." Then at age 11, his parents' responsibilities "ripped me away and plunged me into heartless England, swapping flip-flops for heavy shoes and socks." Worst was his loss of confidence in how to be. "The feelings of being crushed, confused, and alone filled my teenage years. So much time was spent battling with myself." At university, Simon confesses, "I felt a remarkable sense of resentment for the carefree lives all my peers were enjoying. I came to realise it's not their fault. I'm the one who has the need here, not them." Now Simon is a fulfilled husband, parent, and ethical entrepreneur. The experience of Biography turned out to be critical for Simon's finding a life of positive purpose.

Six years later finds Simon feeling seen in his relationships and signifying in his work. What is missing is the savouring. He has driven himself so hard for so long, neglecting to reconnect with his inner Thailand. The past is a foreign country and can't be recreated in the present, but you can reconnect with the joyous resonances of your past self, if your busy Ego will let you.

We should say a last word about negative connections – the people you hate, conflict with, or just don't care for. Resonance is involuntary. It is important to remember, however, that conflict often looks "personal" when its cause is structural, as happens when you're forced to share resources with someone who has opposing goals to your own. It is frighteningly easy to arouse tribal instincts and set people at each other's throats through very simple manipulations, such as giving groups names and setting them in competition.[51]

Much more UI-relevant is instant dislike – Beast-being instant appraisal of potential threat or obstruction. Your problem-solving Ego may jump in and try to neutralise the feeling. More common is disliking someone for what they stand for. Ideological differences are products of our tribal instincts. Mostly they have nothing to do with UI. A British newspaper weekly magazine feature throws two people with opposing political opinions into a dinner discussion.[52] It is striking how in nearly every case, they end up liking each other – a triumph of Beast's good sense over the Self's infatuation with its tribal narratives. Here's the voice of one such case:

> One thing we took away was each other's phone numbers. Where we did disagree, our essential motivation was often the same. My assumption that I'd be meeting an independence* voter who wouldn't listen to reason was totally unjustified. Don't listen to your first thought; review your thoughts.

Ego is apt to feed on and be driven by the Self's narratives – ideologies, beliefs, stories about the way the world works plus the groups of people that populate its *umwelt*. As another person in the same newspaper feature was moved to comment:

> Social media algorithms pitch people against each other. Sitting down with someone, having a discussion, is a very human way of being able to resolve some challenges.

It is sometimes hard to find the human under all the body armour of beliefs, images, and affiliations. Yet we need to remember that human – human connection is always close at hand, as I learned on the road to India.

Helping and hindering is culture which grows, nurtures, suppresses, and distorts UI. That's where we go next.

---

*On opposing sides of the polarising Scottish independence debate.

CODA: WHAT THIS MIGHT MEAN FOR UNIQUE YOU

You are a member of the most cooperative intelligent species on the planet – ants and bees only help their kindred. Relationships are our magnificent obsession, and the complexity of UI² makes them a great adventure, as well as a source of peril and heartache.

- Every relationship stands on its own unique four feet. All your connections are incomparable. That is UI².
- If you care more about your partner and friends than your kinfolk, don't worry. It's part of your design to allow this to happen – for you to lay the foundations for a widened *umwelt*.
- It is possible to satisfy all three of your Existential Wants in a single relationship. Most people don't. There is no right or wrong if your primary sources of pleasure, impact, and recognition are vested in the world of events and creations. That's for your UI to call.
- Your *umwelt* throngs with people. The phrase "you will never know what you mean to me" is literally true.
- You may see patterns in your relationships that derive from the coping strategies of your childhood. They can be compelling, but it's a Destiny that can be transcended by Development and Deliberation (see Chapter 8).
- Friendships are special. They are the most accessible route to enriching your *umwelt*. They are also your contribution to the foundations of subcultures (see Chapter 5).
- Pay attention to the different qualities in all your connections: people who bring out the worst and the best in you and vice versa – think about what is particular to their way of being that emerges because they're with you. UI² means we regenerate our UI in each relationship.
- Learn about the peculiarities of your Beast and Ego reactions. Your Beast may be characteristically powerful or easygoing in its social relationships. Your Ego may be too fast or too slow and deliberative. Your Self narratives may be pushing you towards ways of being with others that don't bring good connections and real value to you.
- It is your special power to be able to challenge every aspect of your relations with others and do something about them.

- The best relationships are those where each party thinks about the other's UI and what they can do to be the best partner for them, given their UI.[53]
- Beast and Ego have their own wisdom. Respect them but do not trust them – they can be wrong!
- We all have our blind spots. Use multiple relationships to get a fix on which of yours are doing you harm.
- The most important conversations you will ever have are with yourself. No matter how deep and insightful any dialogue you've had with another, it will only signify when you've internalised and signed it off with yourself.

Five

UI MEETS CULTURE
The Borders of Being

Man is an animal suspended in webs of significance
he himself has spun.
(Clifford Geertz)[1]

Every man, wherever he goes, is encompassed by a cloud
of comforting convictions, which move with him like flies
on a summer day.
(Bertrand Russell)[2]

EVERYDAY BRAINWASHING OR A TASTING MENU?

It is said that Japanese mothers talk to their babies to pacify them, American mothers to stimulate them.[3] Brainwashing gets going from your first moments. Parents interact with their newborn babies in quite culturally specific ways,[4] as well as being steered by their own Unique Individuality (UI).[5] Culture runs through them. It's indelible in their UI, and they can't help but transmit it.

This is how it starts – the imprint of culture, sometimes called the software of the mind.[6] What chance does the infant have to resist the force of the adult world it has been plunged into? How can UI resist cultural imprinting? Looking across the national tribes of the world, it is striking how different they are in what they take for granted, how they speak and act, and what they value. So many people seem to meekly surrender their individuality to conform with what is expected and what others are doing. It looks like a comprehensive win for culture. Take a step closer, and a quite different picture emerges.

Your brain is not so easily washed. The so-called hardware of the mind, the brain, is not a static machine waiting to be stirred into motion by instructions from software. Your organic unity has inbuilt drives, biases, and energy sources of its own. Your mind is not a blank slate waiting to be written on by culture.[7] It has its own preset software in its circuitry – neural networks that are the equivalent of applications in computing.[8] Evolution set them, ready to deal with challenges humans have always faced, such as the miraculous business of language acquisition.[9] As noted earlier, this is essential for what we do best – cooperation. Yes, we fight a lot but always supported by tribal loyalties and mutual aid. As we pointed out in Chapter 2, our UI is a secret of our success as a species by virtue of its ability to forge win-win connections with strangers.

We have good reason to conform. It's always been a lot safer, and we make others feel safe by behaving in culturally acceptable ways, and also to protect ourselves from our own darker impulses and drives.

Being raised in a wildly unconventional household, with its own bohemian micro-culture, I was further misled about the society I was born into by my first experience of school. This was an anarchic establishment copying a radical pupil self-governance model, then in vogue, the Summerhill model.[10] I attended at age 4, accompanying my mother who was helping out and keeping an eye on my older siblings. As an experiment, the school failed, and we were all removed to local state schools. The shock was profound – the uniforms, the rules, the way people behaved. I struggled to settle in any of the several schools my parents shuttled me between, and I couldn't wait to escape, leave home, and start work as a trainee reporter on a local newspaper, which I did at age 16. My parents – both self-educated – were unconcerned by my lack of academic ambition. After my indiscipline got me fired, I entered a dark phase of self-doubt that was only relieved by my hitchhiking 10-month meander to India and back in my 19th year. On my return, doing a clerical job to make ends meet, I befriended a man a few years older than me who had gone to university as a mature student. He encouraged me to try to get back into education. I was sceptical, and it took a lot of encouragement by friends, but I was led to do so by my passion for psychological science. I had to pass the exams I had missed at school within a single year. I couldn't afford to take longer. It got me a place to study the subject that so absorbed me, about 4 years behind the norm. At university, I loved the intellectual freedom, but the feeling of being an outsider persisted. My first experience of attending conferences felt daunting. I was impressed by the confident but dry expertise of academics in my field. It heightened my sense of being an imposter (more on this in the next chapter). Since those beginnings, I have grown to live with the feeling of being an alien – and in time learned to cherish it, finding my own voice in writing, teaching, and public speaking. The legacy of my childhood, however, lingered in the narrative of my career. Without consciously seeking to, I have found myself challenging orthodoxy, especially theories that others have taken for granted in my field (some figure in this book!).

My UI had found its home in a subculture where it is legitimate to be countercultural[11] in thought, if not in conduct. Surprisingly perhaps, I found it easy to stick to its rules of scientific method, academic publication, and norms of conduct.

I am not alone in finding myself out of step with my culture. Even the most con-formist citizens choose what to eat from the culture menu. As we absorb people and culture, we filter and rework it to fit our UI. Many a person who's tried to raise their children to be devout in a particular belief system have had to watch in dismay as their kids ingest or spit out chunks of it as they choose. We are not helpless victims of brain-washing. Even in the most authoritarian cultures, you are free to think and feel, if not to express. It's literally your *umwelt*.

YOUR WORLD OF MICRO-CULTURES

Relationships are the atoms of culture. You meet a stranger. You find a common lan-guage before quickly falling into conventions of exchange. Each of you intuits what you might mean or do for each other. This is mutual self-regulation,[12] the first building block for cooperative culture.

> Seasoned jazz musicians can be pretty taciturn, but when they sit down together for spontaneous music-making, they talk a different language. They only need agree on the song, key signature, and tempo. It doesn't even have to be written down. The simplest structures, like the blues, offer an infinity of variations. In their heads the players have a library of tunes and their harmonic structures, even those who don't read music. They just get on with it. The solo order is often agreed without a word mid-play by the mer-est nod of a head. From this platform, they launch into improvisation, always knowing they are tethered to an underlying form. In their flights of creativity, they won't get lost. Home is always close and reachable. They have a harmonic roof over their heads. There are other "freer" improvisational musical templates, but, tellingly, they are harder to listen to; harder to play; and, to the untutored ear, risk drifting into borderlands of cacophony.

This highlights the paradox of culture – it liberates by controlling. It enables while restricting. Anthropologist Mary Douglas separated the sources of control into what she called "grid" – rules, structures, roles, and processes – and "group," the grip of norms, conventions, and social ties.[13] You can see both here: the "grid" of the music and the "group" of the musicians' shared expectations. The micro-culture supports collective and individual improvisation, within boundaries. Each player responds to the stimulus of others' voices – just like we do in conversation. Every jazz band, every group indeed, builds its micro-culture within the context of their broader musical subculture of values and practices. Because such understandings are impromptu and fleeting, we don't think of them in these terms.

Families are the groups where we most clearly see the creation of micro-cultures, with their own rituals, stories, and ways of communicating.[14]

> Azhar has a striking appearance – a slight build, direct gaze, with flowing long hair and beard – Gandhi-like in a loose robe, he smiles at everyone as if conferring a blessing. He is 50 and grew up in a prosperous family, launching a highly successful career in the burgeoning advanced technology sector of Southern India. He lived life to the full. "I found myself teetering on the precipice of self-destruction," swept up in a fast-paced alcohol-fuelled lifestyle. "But amidst the depths of despair, a glimmer of hope emerged. I met the person who would become my life partner, my wife. She became the guiding light that illuminated my path. Together we embarked on a journey of self-discovery and spiritual growth, embracing the teachings of Islam and finding solace in faith." He sees a new future stretching before him dedicated to social impact, "to create opportunities for others and uplift communities."

Azhar first discovered the freedom to do whatever he liked. Then he found the freedom to do whatever he could – a move from satisfaction to fulfilment, from appetite to spirit. Finding a partner radically shifted his perspective on society. This *umwelt* convergence looks like a takeover, but he has adopted a culture that liberates him by protecting himself from himself.

We talk about "acquiring" a faith. That sounds too superficial to do justice to Azhar's experience. Developmental psychologist Jean Piaget took care to distinguish "assimilation" – when what you learn is absorbed into existing frameworks – and "accommodation" – when what you learn alters your existing frameworks. Data input vs. system upgrade.

It is the latter that happened to Azhar. The faith he found was deeply personal, owned by him as a force that he can use in the world to build value. Here, we are bearing witness, in microcosm, to how culture is transmitted and modified via the transformation of UI.

Cultures are human creations, and they have the power to bind us to them by feeding the Three Existential Wants: to Savour, to Signify, and to be Seen. First, cultures are pleasure palaces for your soul, offering a menu of tastes, experiences, and entertainments that can be addictively satisfying. Second, they contain gateways to fields where you can leave a mark and make a difference. Third, they are nested networks of communication and engagement, offering opportunities to be seen and validated. They can be toolkits, pleasure gardens, or psychic prisons.

We want many of the same things from culture but in our own ways. But what you want may prove irrelevant. The place you find yourself in may put up lots of barriers – arbitrary, stupid blockages, false promises, and broken systems. Structure, all by itself, channels energy and value toward some people and away from others. It generates its own culture, unless human agents push back against the dictates of rules and technology.

Organisations can have strong subcultures – often highly political – and it is easy to find yourself losing sight of others' UI through narratives you have taken on board that moralise about justice, vengeance, and the villainy of others.

NAVIGATING CULTURE WITH UI

There are 7,000 or so languages of the world. Each comes loaded with culture-specific codes. From our earliest days in this world, it is as immersive and unconscious as the air we breathe. It leads us to take for granted the most basic assumptions we make about the world – the limits to formality, conceptions of time and space, cause–effect logics, trust, gender relations, personal identity, norms of conduct, and directness of speech. All these are encoded in syntax, grammar, verb forms, pronoun use, and norma of personal exchange. It's only when you step out of a culture that you see what it's doing to you and everyone else.[15]

In cross-cultural research, scholars have used survey methods to profile cultures. Tellingly, these "dimensionalist" researchers have come up with what looks rather like the dimensions of personality, such as individualism vs. collectivism, masculinity vs. femininity, uncertainty tolerance vs. conservatism, preference for low vs. high power distance.[16] And that is precisely what they've done: created portraits of cultures based on average differences between belief statements people agree with in different parts of the world. It is misleading, stereotyping even, to characterise nation states on the basis of modest variations in questionnaire scores. It camouflages the huge differences between individual orientations that are found in all cultures. These are much greater than the differences between cultures. This approach takes us in circles. Use the same recipe, and you get the same bread! The architecture of culture is more complex and dynamic. My Biography students are a living proof, defying stereotypes at every turn.

A typical intake for the London Business School Sloan Fellowship[17] comprises around 50 students from all over the world, with seldom more than a handful from any one country. In the first session of Biography at the start of the year, I peruse the mugshot book and immediately see types, images jumping unbidden into my mind from half-remembered movies and resemblances with people I know. I can't help it. These are narratives floating in my subconscious about what they're like as people, a mix of memories and stereotypes. These images don't survive first contact. Talking to them, listening to their stories, occasionally my intuitions seem confirmed but mainly not. Surprises spring from every one of them. They defy expectations – apparently shy Japanese become stand-up comedians; people who seem to exude urbane success reveal deep insecurities. Many have overcome extraordinary tragedies to be here, some still fresh in their memories. To look at them, you would never know. Each has an unexpected story to tell, laden with character and culture.[18]

Yet cultures do differ, for ecological reasons, in how they programme consciousness.[19] Cultures are human creations, for our advancement, protection, and regulation. They are examples of what evolutionists call "niche construction,"[20] when a species achieves fit with its environment by modifying the environment rather than by changing itself. Niche construction is something of a human speciality, and UI is central to how it works. As playwright George Bernard Shaw put it:

The reasonable man adapts himself to the world; the unreasonable one persists in trying to adapt the world to himself. Therefore, all progress depends on the unreasonable man.[21]

Cultures are not bundles of traits as the "dimensionalist" approach presumes. Rather they consist of belief systems, narratives, customs and rules, roles, and forms of social organisation, plus lots of informal norms, speech patterns, manners, dress, and ways of getting along. Formal and informal social contracts offer (and deny) "affordances" – access to opportunities, activities, and relationships.[22] Law professor Cass Sunstein shows how this happens via two structural forces: "navigability" and "choice architecture."[23] He pitches these against what he calls "self-control." He is saying that you may find yourself having to navigate a tangled path through social labyrinths to reach your goals. Choice architecture is the arrangements that specify which decisions you can and cannot make. It may be more of a nudge than a push. Your choices are being guided in subtle ways, beneath the radar of your awareness. In supermarkets you are likely to find yourself being "nudged" by the store layout toward certain choices and away from others.

What Sunstein calls self-control is much more than a simple matter of control. It is the totality of UI. The "affordances" of cultures – what you can and can't do – isn't wholly up to you. Yet some individuals, by skill and force, do muscle their way through what looks like the most impermeable looking boundaries: like Gandhi and Mandela. It is by such insurgency that UI changes culture.

Game-playing is one of the friendliest ways we engage with culture. Learning to play them is a rehearsal of life skills, via a mix of pathfinding and choices within frameworks of rules. Whether in sport or online, they show you how to have fun being yourself within a system. They are a microcosm of the way we learn to live and make the most of who we are.

THE UI SPARK

Every narrative you voice – even the most casual opinions or beliefs you share with people – is a drop in the stream of consciousness that swirls through cultural space. These currents can be neutral, reinforcing, or challenging to the prevailing norms. Every culture is an experiment in how to live. Following the principles of evolution, they must outcompete alternative models by treading a path between two imperatives.[24] They have to go with the grain of human nature whilst addressing the critical challenges that regularly confront the group. If they fail the human nature test by being too idealistic or repressive, they will eventually collapse. If they fail the external reality test by not satisfying the group's essential needs for resources, security, and wealth creation, they will also fail. This applies at all levels of culture, from the nation state down to the family group or business organisation. Yet we look around and you can see cultures that survive whilst violating both criteria. How is this possible? One reason is the cooperative and adaptable side of human nature. Wanting to fit in can make you tolerate what you don't like, but only up to a point. Beyond that, it takes repression to hold UI-toxic cultures in place. Totalitarian cultures suppressing all opposition can survive for long, keeping people in states of ignorance and powerlessness. Meanwhile, bubbling away under the surface are clandestine subcultures, adaptive for their members, which have the potential to erupt into full-scale revolution.

Cultural evolution is a stop–start process. Things stay the same until disrupted by some new input – revolutions, invasions, pandemics, plus lesser disturbances. The term "punctuated equilibrium" was coined by palaeontologists for this lumpy progression as it applies to the evolution of species.[25] It's a pattern you can see in all kinds of social development. As we shall see later, punctuated equilibrium forms the pattern of development in every human life. In the domain of culture, dramas that disrupt the flow of history can be impersonal – like pandemics and earthquakes – but they have big consequences.

Much cultural evolution comes about by stealth, as the tides of opinion, of which you are a part, turn against prevailing orthodoxy and bring about change. Sometimes the UI of a lone spirit in rebellion is the catalyist – thinkers, leaders, and rebels who disrupt and stir the multiple UIs of others into cohesive subcultures.[26] They may be snuffed out or accommodated in watered-down form; occasionally they transform the host culture.[27]

> The history of Christianity is a prime example. Martin Luther led a rebellion against the Church's orthodoxy and hierarchy that were stifling the expression of progressive ideas fermenting in an increasingly mercantile Northern Europe. His ideas heralded the modern perspective of the unique individual standing in a unique relationship with the deity, a doctrine more congruent with the new emerging social order.

Wars, migrations, and trade drive cultural evolution and our ways of living. Cultures encode the rules of the game, telling you who is useful or fits in. Big cultural changes reset the mating game. In times of war, fighters become more appealing as partners than peacemakers. Such biases over generations can pattern the gene pool of a culture – what is called gene–culture co-evolution.[28]

These revolutions mean that historically, the Self ain't what it used to be. Earlier peoples lacked our modern sense of personal agency. That doesn't negate UI. It means people think about it in different ways than they used to. UI is a fact of life for all sentient organisms, but most don't spare it a thought. Our ancestors had quite different conceptions of themselves. So do people today in different parts of the world. You can see radically different ways of thinking cohering around millennia-old ways of living – cultures structured around imperatives of landscape, climate, and natural resources.[29] Long histories of shared experience and adapted ways of living give island peoples a different mentality to mountain peoples. A nomad's conceptions of the world and how one should act in it are quite unlike the farmer's.

UI AND CULTURE: FRIEND, FOE, OBSTACLE, OR PUZZLE?[30]

Earlier, I borrowed from novelist Nathan Hill's fictional grungy gamer's classification of characters. It applies to how we relate differently to culture. Friend: culture is a home, an "affordance"[31] where you can grow and develop your UI in harmony and with pride. Foe: it's a battleground to survive as who you are. Obstacle: it's something you have to "work around." Puzzle: it's a labyrinth to be decoded and used. Let's see how.

1. UI is a driver of change. The inspirations of individuals, often by combining synergistically with others, change culture. Unique individuals and their unique groups are agents who adopt, modify, and transmit innovations through societies.

   Media mogul Rupert Murdoch spent his professional life pushing the boundaries of accepted wisdom in the industry. His lifetime of defiance against the establishment, pushing back against received wisdom and industry conventions. Murdoch's spell in the 1950s as a young sub-editor at the *Daily Express* exposed him to Arthur Christiansen's populist editorial style, foreshadowing elements of his later reinvention of the tabloid press. His combative character was also reinforced by the role model of his father, Sir Keith Murdoch, who had been labelled a "traitor" in 1915 by the British press for breaking cover and telling the truth about the Gallipoli military disaster, defying a British government's injunction of silence. Rupert, less a visionary than an ambitious entrepreneur, changed the face of the British print media with his reinvention of the tabloid newspaper. He developed new models of production and circulation and proved to be a tough guy in facing down the powerful trade unions in his drive to be a first mover in adopting new technology in the industry. Subsequently, he became an insurgent force in TV and an innovator in the new landscape of digital media. Throughout he has been a controversial figure, maintaining an anti-bureaucratic profile at the top table of politicians of all stripes.

2. UI challenges orthodoxies. UI pushes against cultural norms, laws, and boundaries – sometimes with revolutionary force. When individuals and groups encounter implacable resistance, the result is often schisms AND alienation. Such dynamics can spark creative ambition. The abrasion between UI and convention energises insight and creativity.

   At the peak period of Victorian prudery, George Eliot, born Mary Ann Evans, met, fell in love, and set up house with George Henry Lewes. Lewes, stuck in an unhappy marriage with his faithless wife, was debarred at that time by English law from divorce for adopting her children. Evans was born into a conservative and religious family. The power of her awakening intellect and purposeful spirit drew her into conflict with her family, spinning her away into circles of free-thinking intellectuals. Her father's death when she was 30 proved to be a release. She was able to move into the literary circles of London society, where she rapidly ascended to the editorship of the prestigious *Westminster Review*. In the security and harmony of her partnership with Lewes, she commenced her career as a writer of fiction, adopting her masculine penname to break through the publication barrier, which she did with spectacular success. Her scandalous liaison was swept from her door by the likes of Dickens and Thackeray, who, unabashed, crossed its threshold for her Sunday afternoon soirees. Lewes, a womaniser in early life, despite being reputedly "the ugliest man in London," changed his life to one of dedication to Evans. Jointly, they decided to forgo starting a family, and Lewes settled down happily to devoting his life and public self to protecting and promoting her talent – his "Madonna." He died at the age of 61, 6 years after she published her greatest novel, *Middlemarch*, arguably the greatest exposition of the workings of multiple UIs in literature.

3. **UI is accommodated.** Every society contains subcultures which evolve to provide a home for people with common interests and shared abilities. They are accepted for their skills and vision, often clustering geographically. Examples include the Bloomsbury Group in Edwardian London and the tech clusters of late 20th century Silicon Valley.

Angela Merkel, longstanding German chancellor, dominated European politics for the first quarter of this century. She was the eldest child of a devout and idealistic Lutheran pastor, who moved his family from Hamburg to a remote hamlet in the communist East to preach the gospel in an officially atheistic state. Angela excelled in maths and sciences at school, trained, and took her PhD in the physics of quantum chemistry whilst working as a researcher in a leading East Berlin institute. She was modest and cautious in her demeanour, which suited both her personality and the realities of living in a surveillance state. It was only when the Wall fell in 1989 that she joined the new reformist Democratic Awakening Party, and subsequently the Christian Democratic Union, through whose ranks she swiftly rose. Before long, she found herself in the cabinet of Chancellor Helmut Kohl, thanks to her skills and vision. Her moral probity in the face of a party funding scandal led her to distance herself, and later supplant Kohl in 2005 to become the power pivot for European politics for 16 years. She remained throughout intensely private, modest, and cautious, admitting publicly that she lacked charisma, though close friends report her as having a mischievous sense of humour and a talent for mimicry.

4. UI feeds on culture. Culture gives us methods and tools to get along in life. We take many of these for granted, but we also need to figure out which will work best for us. These form the narratives that make sense to us and fit our goals. Events that arise – from the Drama of daily existence – become the basis for the Deliberative improvised life. We cross boundaries and move between worlds.

The brilliant Scottish comic talent Billy Connolly, born in the Glasgow slums, growing up "I didn't want to be me. I wanted to be someone else. I didn't like myself very much."[32] Raised with his sister by his father and aunts, after his mother abandoned the family, he struggled at school, continually rebelling against authority, with humour his sharpest weapon. He tells the story of learning about his comedic gift, at the age of 10, when playing in a postwar bomb-damaged site, he accidentally sat down in a puddle. Seeing how it amused his friends, he prolonged the episode, turning it into comic theatre. It was through his love of folk music that he found his vocation, discovering that his patter between songs was what his audiences loved most about his act. Subsequently, he ditched the banjo for the comic monologue, arguably holding the position of Britain's funniest man for over two decades.

5. UI seeks refuge. We need a break from ourselves. Our uniqueness and unknowability can be causes of profound distress, even more so since the advent of social media. Culture provides a wide range of places to lose yourself. Ideological and religious causes have a special power to allow you to escape into a collective identity. The arts, sports, and entertainments offer unparalleled diversions.

There are numerous cases of public figures who have found public celebrity a burden and stepped back from the limelight for a more authentic existence, such as writer J.D. Salinger; songwriter-performer Joni Mitchell; and several politicians, like Jimmy Carter and George W. Bush. For Steve Jobs, the turbulence of his mind and ego were especially tormenting, finding relief in meditation, Zen, and immersion in nature. The philosopher Ludwig Wittgenstein – one of the cleverest people ever to have lived – used to sit in the front stalls in movie theatres to lose himself, letting potboiler cowboy films drown out the turmoil of his mind. Pop star David Bowie also suffered mental health challenges, including depression and anxiety, finding escape in the alternative identities he created, along with a lifestyle inspired by Buddhist philosophy, a loving family, and clean living.

We need also to be mindful of totalitarian societies where everyone has to lead a double life. We all have a gap between our public and private identities, but in some cultures this widens to a gulf. This splitting of identity forces many individuals to "migrate to the self," as Soviet dissident Natan Sharansky put it – to find a refuge in their UI.[33]

FITTING IN AND FINDING OUT

Culture feeds character. We are culture "carriers." Culture shapes important aspects of UI, including the stories you tell yourself about the world and your place within it. But as we have seen, it does not determine how you ingest and own it.[34] You carry your culture, like a form of dress, in forms that fit your frame. The dance of the 4Ds means the Destiny of your character, rooted as it is in your DNA, actively transforms whatever Dramas life throws at you and how you Deliberate about them. Development seems guided by culture but never without a steering hand from your Ego as its agent. Whatever grains of truth there may be in cultural stereotypes owes to the willingness of individuals to accept and love the cultures that nurtured them.

> Arpit is an Indian finance executive in his late 30s. He is non-assertive, hard-working, sociable, and with a strong orientation toward helping, giving, and cooperating with others. These are dominant values in many Eastern and Middle Eastern cultures, but his profile is much more long-suffering than many of his compatriots. This forms the root of the concern he brings to me. He tells me that on team assignments, he repeatedly finds himself doing all the heavy lifting in his areas of competence, even though others in the group also know a lot of this stuff. He can't stop himself from volunteering. Even when he curses himself for this "weakness," it is somewhat half-hearted. He smiles good-naturedly and shrugs.

This doesn't make Arpit a "people pleaser" so much as someone aligned with his culture, ancient Vedic Hinduism, which holds that it is our duty to find our place in the great scheme of the universe and fulfil the purpose allotted to us. Service, duty, and selfless giving are enduring themes. Arpit can't help himself. He is motivated not so much for the good regard of his colleagues than because his core traits chime with the predominant cultural narratives.

Equally, instincts and dispositions can flow in a contrary direction. Rafael, a 35-year-old, is one such:

> I am pretty sure I was born in the wrong country. I have never identified myself with Brazilian culture, where people are very individualistic; few care for the society as a whole.

Rafael is not stating a historical truth about his home country but a truth about himself. People with the power to choose migrate to find cultures that fit their UI. They don't want to settle down to a contented life close to home, like former generations. Even when the choice to migrate is involuntary or arbitrary, new visions are born. Exploration and development through the transition process have long-term consequences. Many expats and international students choose to stay on in their new domiciles, discovering that their UIs are more compatible with the values, norms, and ways of life of their new host cultures.

Let's meet Mio, whose story shows a gentler transition process. She is among the quietest of my class but always highly attentive and engaged. She tells me:

"Growing up in Japanese culture shaped my character significantly, since humility, harmony, and self-discipline are valued in Japanese culture, and I was a quiet child, and I still consider myself to be quiet and introverted compared to people from other cultures." She enjoyed a stable, loving family milieu but she confesses, "I excelled at listening and agreeing with what others and teachers said and struggled to communicate my own opinions or views." Then at the age of 13, her father's work took the family to California for a 4-year spell. Here, she was thrown into a local high school without any knowledge of English. "The first year was very tough because I was not able to communicate with teachers and classmates. I felt frustrated, confused, and lonely, but this experience became a turning point in my life. Gradually, I began to understand the language and adapt to the culture. Initially, I had difficulty expressing my opinions, not only because of the language barrier but also due to cultural differences. In Japan, students were expected to follow the teacher's instructions, and differing opinions were not necessarily welcomed. In contrast, the flexible American school system allowed students to choose subjects that interested them, allowing them to improve their strengths while also addressing their weaknesses. I enjoyed the culture of respecting each individual's uniqueness and valuing their opinions." Returning to Japan induced "reverse culture shock." She says: "Fitting back into Japanese culture and school was even harder than I expected, despite it being my native culture. I found myself reverting to my old self, trying not to stand out by being quiet and conforming to others."

Mio worked in Japan for another 18 years, including a 1-year spell to do a master's in the UK plus a 4-year secondment to London halfway through. Back in Japan, she found her *umwelt* permanently altered, now embracing an alternative way of living and being. In the UK she found relief from what she describes as the hierarchical and deferential norms of her home country. Yet the contrast also made her appreciate more the order and functional efficiency of her home country. She has discovered that no sacrifice of personal integrity is necessary in either culture but that her future will never be in one place.

Mio is right that her culture shaped her development, endorsed by her introverting instincts. She is one of many whose early exposure to somewhere radically different altered their UI, permanently and significantly reconfiguring their *umwelt*. Seeing yourself in different contexts implants new insights. Your narrative Self absorbs how you process new realities. New friendships and routines reconfigure your *umwelt*.

Don't ask what Culture you are in; ask what You the culture is in.

We absorb culture and its imprint upon us, but that imprint is uniquely ours. From the first moments of our existence, the filter of UI is moderating what we learn.[35] Remember our earlier use of Piaget's distinction between assimilation and accommodation? In some aspects of our UI, it is assimilation – what biologists call "accretive growth"[36] – where cultural learning sticks because it's consistent with what's already there. This adaptive model is characteristic of so-called "strong" personalities, who are more heavily invested and unbending in their strong characters. For more adaptive people, accommodation allows culture to reach deeper into character.[37]

It is only as our awareness matures that we get to realise that cultural rules are not written in stone. Yet Sunstein's "navigability" and "choice architecture" set boundaries that rule out an array of possible experiences we might get elsewhere. It took foreign travel to open Mio's eyes to alternative worlds and dormant traits in her character.

As we have seen, culture starts in the family – look at Susanna in the last chapter, whose demanding yet empowering family milieu rocket-boosted her development. Here's a case where family and culture feed the Self's narrative.

Anton says, "I was born in Moscow in 1986, a fact for which I consider myself really fortunate. It is a testament to the resilience of my great-grandparents, who braved wars and endured imprisonment in camps. I owe much of my life to my grandparents, who witnessed war-torn landscapes, countries collapsing, and relentless cycles of loss and recovery. Yet they continually found the strength to reinvent themselves more times than I can imagine. Despite everything, they remained humans, living with dignity and humility. They chose to forgive and successfully nurtured their children. They dedicated themselves to guiding our family through the collapse of the USSR, instilling hope in my parents during these tumultuous times." Of his own parents and upbringing, he says, "I owe my deepest gratitude to my parents, who were compelled to reinvent themselves amidst the ruins of the USSR.

"As the nation disintegrated, my father had to relinquish his academic career, while my mother, a linguist, faced similar challenges. When the chance presented itself, they both pursued further education abroad, completely overhauling their life and starting from the ground up. This allowed them to offer me and my brother opportunities that they themselves had never had. They've demonstrated that resilience and compassion are ingrained in our family's DNA, a legacy I am honoured to carry forward." Exposure to multiculturalism was a wind blowing through Anton's childhood. "My home was a global crossroads, frequented by friends of parents from all over the world. As a kid I eagerly awaited every arrival, each one bringing unique experiences and perspectives." His parents took care to send him to a school that valued experiential learning. In vacations he went to summer camps where "the immersive environment encouraged creativity, skill development, and leadership across a diverse group of pupils and even teachers. It was a transformative experience for me." University and a good job followed until the COVID "wrecking ball drastically altered my plans" and then his country's invasion of Ukraine, "an event that deeply challenged our personal values." He continues: "The hardest decision we had to make was to abandon our professional lives, our social circles, our children's school, and leave everything behind to fight for our right to be ourselves. We chose to venture into the unknown."

Anton's personality profile reflects this openness, as well as strong liberal motives and a focused work ethic – a positive, proactive character fed by an empowering childhood.

UI CROSSING BORDERS

Everyone's story is unique, developed through the punctuated equilibrium of transitions – periods of calm punctuated by Drama. We all progress through biological stages, occasional migrations, changing relationships, and altered statuses. Each chapter of life brings a shift of perspective. We grow through experience, but geographical and cultural mobility have special force, bundling together many transforming elements in a single swoop. A single step reconfigures our *umwelt*. Look at Mio, our expat Japanese executive, for whom a spell in the US in her formative years permanently altered her perspective on her place in the world.

Yet UI and culture can misfit. Mio had a sympathetic bond with hers, whose orbit she broadened rather than left. Anton was forced to flee his when the political order constricted his ability to breathe freely. For others, moving beyond is a more gradual and tenuous process.

> Fatima is the firstborn of eight in a prominent family in an ultra-orthodox Middle Eastern theocracy where, she says, "Although I wasn't prevented from pursuing my dreams, I also wasn't encouraged or expected to work. As a woman I am culturally and legally expected to be taken care of by either my father or husband. So, literally, I don't have to work!" Her upbringing was mobile between cities and subcultures, thanks to the entrepreneurial drive of her grandfather and father. As the eldest, she was raised to take responsibility and be a role model for her siblings. Thus, she dutifully married "a good man," but "I yearned for a divorce from day one." Sticking it out for 7 years, she was saved by being childless, a condition that freed her to find an escape route. Her appearance in my classroom was a personal assertion of her cross-cultural identity, determined to play a part in the modernisation and transformation of her home culture.

It is well known that entrepreneurship is a prime, sometimes the only, route to security for the poorest and most desperate immigrant populations. With nothing to lose, you might as well take the biggest, most innovative chances.[38] In all advanced economies, immigrants outperform domestic entrepreneurs in wealth creation.[39] They are hungrier, work harder, and take bigger risks. They also bring distinctive value propositions. Earlier we told the story of how Sergey Brin met Larry Page on campus and laid the foundation for Google. Brin originated its first tag line, "Don't be evil," as a mantra honouring his upbringing by Jewish parents who fled anti-Semitic oppression to bring him, aged 6, to the US. Here's another Jewish refugee whose UI powerfully interwove ethics and entrepreneurship.

> One of the world's wealthiest men and greatest philanthropists, George Soros was the middle of three sons, born in 1930 to a lawyer father who had been a prisoner of war in WWI, and a mother who ran a successful silk shop. As a Jew, he survived the Nazi occupation of Hungary by posing as a Christian and after WWII escaped to England on false documents. He worked as a porter and waiter to pay for his education at the London School of Economics, where he avidly ingested the concept of the Open Society from the tutelage of the great liberal philosopher Karl Popper. This informed his entire career and dedicated philanthropy, donating $32 billion of his wealth to a wide range of causes, promoting human rights, public health, social justice, education, and development.

This points to a central principle of UI development over the lifespan, elaborated in Chapter 7: the more radical the transition, the greater the personal development.

FINDING YOUR TRIBE

Tribalism – the desire to belong to a social group – is a deeply rooted human instinct.[40] The tribe validates our existence as members. It hands us a suite of rights and obligations, implicit in preliterate cultures and explicit in all post-agrarian stratified societies. Status seeking is also in our ancestral DNA. In all societies, you get a better life the higher up you are in the pecking order. The more elevated your status, the more the balance tips in favour of your rights over obligations. This holds true even in supposedly socialist systems, where you find government officials get all the best housing.[41] Yet UI dictates there is huge variation in people's drive to belong and strive for status.

These are UI variants that shape your relationship with culture:

1. **Personality.** Does your personality fit your culture? You were born with a profile that has shaped the ways you orient to any culture. Traits such as sociability and achievement striving create narratives of purpose and identity that set your compass. So do other related traits, such as the desire to belong, tolerance of uncertainty, power needs, and more.

2. **Adaptability.** Are you a cultural chameleon? How much are you prepared to put up with feeling like an alien in any culture? We differ in resourcefulness, intelligence, and tolerance for feeling out of place. It takes less of a prod to cast some individuals adrift from their home culture than it does for others. This makes culture an instrument of UI development. It teaches us how to live and get along.

3. **Enculturation.** Did your family micro-culture fit closely with the norms of your neighbourhood and work subcultures? How much has your cultural diet been informally censored during your upbringing and working life? What narratives about the society and your role in it were inculcated in you? Whatever they were, your UI has exercised, whether you know it or not, to pick and choose the ones that work for you. It may have taken a while (see Chapter 7).

4. **Fit.** Where do you feel and find any kind of misfit between you and local subcultures? Where do you feel at home, and how is this changing? There is a fit–misfit dynamic between UI and culture that in all the cases in this chapter has motivated search and mobility. People look for environments that resonate, that feel like home.

Social scientists, philosophers, and public commentators – indeed, most people in contemporary society – bundle these four elements together into an often muddled and hazy conception of "identity," a topic that generates much more heat than light. There is a dense literature of very abstract discourse about the meaning of identity and its varieties.[42] There is a great deal of passion on our streets and in our media about it – especially around constructs of gender, race, and ideology.

HELPING UI ESCAPE THE IDENTITY TRAP

People differ greatly in their attachment to social identities. It is hard to avoid labelling yourself in terms of social categories, but how deep do they go? How central to your UI are the labels the world might hang on you? You may feel personally enhanced by the uniform you wear or the flag you wave. Being a supporter of a sports team makes games more enjoyable and gives you a good feeling when your side wins. Group identifications are self-enhancing[44] in both shared suffering and success. But winning tastes better. That's why successful teams have more supporters.

All societies have vertical divisions of status and class and horizontal divisions of region, occupation, ethnicity, and gender. There was a time when being a "bank manager" defined you as middle class, white, and male. As a young researcher, I interviewed a successful elderly banker who told me that in his first job in a UK high street bank, he was advised against buying a house in the same street where his boss, the manager, lived. He was told it would be frowned upon and damage his prospects.

Today, we can challenge almost any kind of categorical labelling – even our birth-assigned gender.

Rosa was one of the first in a cohort of my Biography course to volunteer to share their Pecha Kucha[45] to the class – a short slide show presentation telling your life story, using any kinds of imagery you choose (see Chapter 10). Rosa was a woman from a country known for its orthodox norms, who announced, "First, I'm going to tell my life story as a boy and then as a girl." She recounted how she had transitioned to female identity just before joining the programme. Rosa spoke movingly of the bullying and rejection she suffered throughout her adolescence and how liberated and recognised she felt now, being accepted as a woman in our culture. The class rose as one and cheered.

This is a triumph of UI over social categorisation. In earlier times, people defined themselves in consensual categories – labels that everyone can agree on, externally anchored and verifiable classes like occupations and group memberships. When asked the "Who are you?" question, as the 20th century advanced, people became much more likely to use nonconsensual categories such as character traits, tastes, and beliefs.[46] This signified a move to a greater appreciation of UI over social position. Today, identity politics in our digital age of anxiety is pulling in a new direction. Increasingly, people seek refuge from the challenge of being "different" by finding ever narrower niche categories to identify themselves with, especially around gender, sexuality, ethnicity, and personal interests. Back in 1952, African American novelist Ralph Ellison moved the dial with his publication of *Invisible Man*,[47] awakening the US to the harsh reality of a people denied personhood by their host culture. The demand for "respect" among minorities is a demand to be treated as a person and a citizen, with attendant rights. Lately, it has morphed into a more universal cry for UI recognition in societies where the binding glue of culture has become eroded.

ON BEING HEARD

The Fourth Law of UI is the imperative to connect – to find one's voice and to be heard. The first three Laws of UI demand the reassurance – balm even – of communion with others. In our times, this has become a lot more complex and threatening, especially for the young, confronted by a baffling blizzard of possibilities for self-identification.

> Pop star Billie Eilish rose to global fame astonishingly fast – within just a few years of uploading her first song at age 13 through savvy use of social media and streaming platforms. By the age of 18, she had won five Grammys and become a global icon. But behind the curtain, she was unravelling. "I felt like I was pretending to be Billie Eilish." The media on which she had ridden to fame now were fracturing her nascent adult identity. Intense public scrutiny, viral fame, and constant online commentary about her appearance, style, and personality began to fragment her sense of identity. With nowhere to retreat, she fell into prolonged anxiety, depression, and a sense of alienation. "I went from being this 14-year-old fangirl to being what I was a fan of. . . . It was so weird. I was like, 'Who am I?' I didn't know who I was. I didn't know what I liked to do. I didn't know what I was."[48]

Eilish's story is familiar, of a vulnerable person who suddenly finds fame or fortune – both in her case. The shift to a new world is also a shift to a new identity but without tools, insight, or trust. You are not seen. Media mirrors torment with false ideals and labels. The rewards of your new life prove worthless, when what you really want to do is to savour what you have, do good for others, and feel recognised for who you are. We shall see more about UI vulnerability in the next chapter and in our discussion of new technology in Chapter 11.

With astonishing rapidity, thanks to social media, a huge proliferation of micro-cultures has arisen, creating an entirely new world of possibilities for finding others with shared affinities. We have come a long way from being born into and stuck with a tribe. Yet that long lost landscape had two benefits. First, it created something like a shared *umwelt* – common reference points in a shared cultural landscape. Second, it confronted us with diverse UIs every day and round every corner. In the sealed-off com-monwealth of the tribe, you had no way of escaping people with very different profiles to your own. You were forced to tolerate, or at least get along with, all kinds of characters. The integration of natural diversity has been the foundation of community life.[49]

Now we live in a world where you can be much choosier about who you hang out and work with. If you look across the chatrooms of the metaverse, surely you can find one that fits your UI? Maybe you can't – you're in the wrong place, or you've have found that group you've oriented towards isn't what it seems. Maybe you find it moving in a direction you don't like. People come and go, altering the group complexion. This creates a paradox: the super-abundance of niches into which you might fit seems to make it ever easier to slip into a dangerous state of social estrangement, like poor Billie Eilish. This is a short step from victimhood. Jihadists are often people who have escaped from low, despised statuses to be self-enhanced by joining a powerful and vengeful gang, a new order that gives them a standing denied to their society of origin.[50] Gangs are insurgent UIs congregating at the mar-gins of culture, especially where the civil order has disintegrated. But even in the most orderly and sophisticated societies, gangs are a refuge and a vehicle for UI expression.

> Japanese railways are a wonder of the world, and around them have sprouted subcultures of enthusiasts, forming what are called *toritetsu* gangs. Some harmlessly love riding the trains, others recording their sounds or collecting timetables. Others are less benign, with assertive, deviant, and sometime violent behaviour, blocking platforms, fighting for favoured spots, and conducting sundry minor criminal acts.

In some cultures, gangs are even government-funded official and unofficial militias.

There are countless more socially innocuous niches online in which you can park some of your UI. Here's a small sample. The half-life of such groups can be very brief, so I don't expect these to remain current much beyond the time of writing:

- **#DisabledAndCute:** a supportive community where disabled individuals celebrate beauty, self-love, and resilience
- **ASMRtists:** creators who produce videos designed to trigger autonomous sensory meridian response – a tingling sensation that some people find relaxing
- **Mukbangs:** individuals who film themselves eating large quantities of food, accompanied by commentary and interaction with viewers
- **AntonPlant Parents:** people passionate about growing and caring for indoor plants

It is a modern miracle that people of such highly selected interests can find each other at the touch of a screen. Today, you can locate a seemingly infinite number of places to breathe, share, and connect. What then? It is through such affinities that some folks find their life partners. In the West, dating sites have certainly become the most common way people hook up. It is rational and efficient, enabling like-minded people to cluster and find reassurance in their company.

There are two major hazards in this kind of freedom of association. The first is that you and your mates believe you have communal rights, that you are validated as "normal." Dangerous deviants can become insurgents when they feel legitimised by like-minded buddies. The second is that you come to believe you have more in common with others in your group than you really do. False friends abound, not all of them deliberate deceivers. Some of the people you meet this way may themselves be trying to "find" themselves, experimenting with "provisional identities" and misleading you in the process.[51] Others, socially estranged, desperate to be seen and heard, may perceive false affinities with you, looking for personal reassurance about their own identity – what has been called the "triumph of the therapeutic" in identity politics.[52]

Let us return to these labyrinths of risk and fulfilment later in this book. We find ourselves in the modern era at the early stages of a massive societal transformation through AI. On the plus side, for the first time UI will be centre stage in a new age of personalisation in every realm of existence. There are also huge dangers, since the dark side of UI – principally in the shape of malign actors – can equally destroy our very existence on this precious and beautiful world of ours. This is where we go next.

CODA: WHAT THIS MIGHT MEAN FOR UNIQUE YOU

How much should you restrain or indulge your UI? It's a question that only rarely pops up for most folks. When do you raise your voice to make a demand or express your social discontents? When do you have to "work around" the rules to get something done? When do you directly challenge the status quo?

Through social media, it's easier to do any of these than ever before. This has the downside that our cultures are becoming ever more fragmented by layers, factions, and interest groups. It's important that you keep your UI as an anchor amid such turbulence. In whatever ways cultures and subcultures vary, UI has its own independent standing. Culture is not a force to be resisted or surrendered to, but a menu, a wardrobe, and a jumble of contracts to be selected from, ingested, worn, or negotiated.

- How aligned was the family culture of your upbringing with the surrounding culture? It will have had an indelible effect on your UI – especially perhaps your values. You may be committed to upholding and reproducing them in your own relationships, but you don't need to make it a duty. Cultures change. Your UI is not your parents', and it's for you to set what standards you wish to adopt in your home culture.
- Think about your closest relationships as cultural themes. Where do they enhance and where do they diminish your functioning? Think about yourself as a niche constructor – implicitly expressing the way you want to live in all your social exchanges, down to the most trivial of everyday encounters.
- Think about how your UI finds its way within your context. How navigable is your local culture? How restrictive is its choice architecture? Is it allowing your UI the right kind of "affordances"? How easy is it to locate subcultures that contain pathways of opportunity for unique you?
- Beware local subcultural narratives that can lead you into tribal postures of justice, vengeance, and the villainy of others. Your moral stance needs to be home-grown.
- Your *umwelt* can be divided into public, private, and hidden or unknown. How much does your local culture place a hard boundary between the first two, forcing you to live a double life? How might you close the gap?

- What might be the hidden or unknown in your *umwelt*? You may find you are under the influence of unspoken and unchallenged assumptions, taken-for-granted aspects of your world.
- Are you culturally versatile? It is much easier for some to surrender to new cultural norms than others. If in doubt, do it your way.
- What stereotypes tend to attach to someone of your demographic or appearance? Be aware of when you are conforming and what signals you might be seen as sending. When it suits you, craft your self-presentation to express your UI.
- How much does your cultural participation satisfy the Three Existential Wants: to Savour, to Signify, and to be Seen? Experiment. Try out your UI–culture fit in new contexts. Find where you can be most free and authentic.
- You are a party to social contracts, mostly informal. They are the building blocks of culture. Remember you are an agent in them, not their victim.
- Beware social identities. They are a comfort and a refuge, but they are not you. The existence of groups who will accept you as one of theirs does not define you.

Six

THE UI DARK SIDE
Dealing with Our Demons

Much of the evil in this world is due to the fact that man,
in general, is hopelessly unconscious.
(Carl Jung)[1]

There is a crack in everything, that's how the light gets in.
(Leonard Cohen)[2]

MAD, BAD, AND DANGEROUS TO KNOW

Jung was right. The unconscious can be dark, and the Beast off its leash can be dangerous. As a species we can be rapacious, jealous, selfish, and amoral. We can also be clinging, devious, appeasing, and cold. Jung believed the only way to tame the Dark Side is to let the light of awareness unify the dualities of human nature: conscious and unconscious, male and female, light and dark. Is this true for all of us? We all have a hidden side, but its shades of darkness vary hugely.[3] Everyone can benefit from helping Ego to penetrate and integrate as much of the Psyche's unseen regions as possible, but these are radically different worlds for each of us. For some, there doesn't seem to be much in the darkness to worry about. When Jung says, "Everyone carries a shadow, and the less it is embodied in the individual's conscious life, the blacker and denser it is," he is telling a truth about himself, not about you and me.

> Jung was an extraordinary visionary, mystical from childhood; he was tormented by what he saw in himself and others, finding comfort in his spirituality. A solitary child, given to communing with nature, as an adult he built himself a fairy-tale tower by a remote lake, where he escaped the demands of his therapy and writing to pass time in simple physical pastimes.[4]

We are seeing Jung's *umwelt* in his ideas. Your *umwelt* is going to look very different. We all have unconscious drives, to help keep us safe and propagate our genes, but they differ vastly in their power and focus, as well as how they intrude into our lives. There is no single dark side. Some people live in a state of benign normality, untroubled by the rages of a repressed unconscious. The dark side may be negligible or just unexciting.

Others are less lucky. In the language of the 4Ds, the gene lottery hands to some people deeply troubled Destinies in both character and circumstances, vulnerable to their own impulses and involuntary reactions to the Dramas of life. Our prisons are full of people who made mistakes, indulged impulses, gave in to desires, or decided to cheat. They are a mixed bunch. Plenty are weak-willed – getting caught for surrendering to temptation for victimless rule breaking. Others are incarcerated for their own safety and the safety of others, we are told – which is another way of saying it would cost too much in time, resources, and moral credibility to rewire their brains by therapeutic intervention.

You can also be very unlucky with your birth Destiny:

> Jimmy was born into grinding poverty in the North of England to an alcoholic drug addict mother with severe mental health issues and a violent but largely absent father who abandoned the family when Jimmy was 3, dying a few years later. Jimmy was taken into protective care, starting a succession of domiciles for him and his brother to foster homes and orphanages, all of which Jimmy says were revenue-driven and never nurturing. "I was a feral child," he says, "made to believe I was bad. I was suicidal at 9, but my mother told me to keep silent."

In Chapter 10 we are going to tell the story of Jimmy's remarkable redemption through the simplest of interventions – an unconditional act of recognition that helped him realise he could claim a positive identity for himself.

The mental ill health of his mother was a genetic malady, out of Jimmy's reach. Beyond the scope of this book are many of the most distressing and disturbing expressions of Unique Individuality (UI) whose roots lie in the Beast's constitution. Brain swelling has been found to be linked with mood disorders.[5] Immune system dysregulation can trigger psychoses.[6] Metabolic disorders can cause behaviour changes, including eating disorders.[7] Many psychoses – schizophrenia, depression, and psychopathologies – emerge without prompting. Others, like some forms of clinical depression, only arise when triggered by negative life events.[8] Increasingly sophisticated therapeutic and chemical interventions are on hand to offer relief. There remains, however, the challenge that in some cultures, a heavy stigma attaches to mental illness, making it harder to detect and treat.

We also cannot give much space to what we might call ordinary deviance. This is when people fall foul of cultural rules that declare their behaviour to be illegal, immoral, or just bad to have around. People break laws to alleviate their poverty. Others succumb to destructive passions because of frustration and acute stress. Many have given in to impulsive malign acts when their minds have been disturbed by drugs, alcohol, or conflicts. The walking wounded are everywhere around us, unfortunates who suffer their UI in ways that are painful to them and the people who care for them. In the most severe and disturbing cases, deeply rooted deviant impulses have collided with norms that are deeply rooted in our species' programming. It is instinctive to avoid or punish disorder, also to reject what is seen as disgusting, repellent, or threatening. Murder, incest, and any number of "unnatural acts" are going to get you punished.[9]

Destiny can be funnelled down Developmental pathways that are bad for you – like the family subculture Jimmy was born into, that pitched him first into homelessness and later into prison. Some individuals are willing victims of their wants – they couldn't care less about the consequences of their actions. UI expresses itself in some very ugly and seemingly unstoppable psychopathologies. We have lots of labels for these. Many are medicalised, with their names well established in common speech. Psychiatry has become addicted to the lazy but efficient algorithm of looking up symptoms in its vast manual, classifying and then treating them with medication.[10] These chemical assaults on the Psyche bring relief, but it takes personalised therapy to secure longer-term relief. This works by empowering the afflicted with tools to help themselves.

UI reminds us, we are all neurodivergent. It's all a matter of thresholds. Some traits cause endless trouble. Others are tolerated as harmless eccentricities. Many people who could be labelled as neurodivergent are incarcerated, along with the superintelligent and the extremely dim. Many have run into the brick wall of culture that seeks to "normalise" them.

Our purpose here is cast a fresh eye on the areas of this darkness that are directly illuminated by the Uniqueness Perspective. Here are seven.

1. CULTURAL NEGATION AND UI SURRENDER

As we saw in the last chapter, some people are happy to submerge their identities beneath their surrounding culture, living lives of service and duty. It can be self-therapy to submit to protect yourself from yourself. But cultural conformity can go in very ugly directions.

Philosopher Hannah Arendt, observing the trial of Adolph Eichmann, responsible for all the logistics of the "Final Solution" – the Nazi extermination of the Jewish people – coined the phrase the "banality of evil."[11] She was struck by the willingness of appa-ratchiks to conduct genocide as if they were administrators deleting files rather than the lives of fellow humans.

Japanese kamikaze pilots gave their lives for the sake of honour and deference to their revered emperor. Modern suicide bombers are likewise tied into narratives that promise a greater good in the hereafter and for their living kin.

Social psychologists have illustrated how easy it is to get individuals to conform to authority; in laboratory simulations inflicting what the subjects believed to be potentially life-endangering electric shocks on strangers (paid "stooges" in fact) when they made errors in a learning task[12] and in role plays where students play-acting as guards inflict real punishments on the students playing prisoners.[13]

They give you a dismal view of human nature. We can all get carried away in role play, but a less reported aspect of these studies is that lots of subjects did not submit to the authority of the experiment and its agents.[14] These deviants were of little interest to the researchers. They, in the postwar spirit of their times, had a case to prove: the idea that it is relatively easy to use authority, norms, and roles to steamroll individuality into conformity. What actually happened was many either walked away from the studies or refused to follow the script.

The Nazis used UI by choosing criminals and people predisposed to violence to be the first line of repression, the "kapos," to do the dirtiest work in their death camps. Some people sadly are vulnerable in both their temperament and circumstances to sur-render their UI, as in this astonishing and disturbing case:

The self-ordained Reverend James Warren (Jim) Jones took 900 devout followers from the US to Guyana, and using his charismatic powers, induced them to mass suicide by cyanide poisoning, including mothers dosing their children before obediently killing themselves.

The road to this offence against humanity was a long one. Jones, raised in rural poverty by evangelical Christian parents, discovered his gifts preaching "apostolic socialism" to a growing following, mainly among marginalised African American women, many of them lone mothers. He had numerous run-ins with the authorities over his swelling organisation, leading him to designate his organisation as a "People's Temple" and himself "The Prophet." To avoid scrutiny and interfering authorities, he relocated to Guyana in South America, where he became ever more controlling and manipulative of his followers, confiscating passports and appropriating millions of dollars from their savings.

People commit suicide for many reasons. It can be a last act of defiance for some desperate individuals, but it is the ultimate surrender of UI. Is that what happened here? No. Jones had deployed a suite of coercive control methods, including sleep deprivation, isolation, emotional manipulation, reward and punishment, under the guns of handpicked guards. He initiated "White Nights" rehearsals of mass suicide, framed as tests of loyalty and commitment, desensitising his followers to the final horrific act. Of the 918 deaths, 304 were children and 162 dependent elderly. Of the remainder, only a handful supported his plan. The rest were terrified or resigned.[15]

We are not all equally vulnerable to coercive control, but sadly some are especially susceptible to UI surrender. Look at the members of Charles Manson's "family" who faithfully followed his homicidal vision. Vulnerable profiles include people with any combination of traits that make them susceptible. These might include:

- Unsatisfied recognition hunger
- Social anxiety
- Low self-esteem and confidence
- High need for belonging
- Intolerance of uncertainty
- High need for structure
- Desire to please others

More could be added. Need systems can get hijacked by narratives of surrender. It can seem easier and more efficient than taking responsibility, making tough choices, and solving problems. It is a combination of susceptible personalities and punishing life experiences that makes it hard for people to avoid narratives of helpless compliance, especially in the face of power and authority.

Yet surrender is normalised harmlessly in many avenues, like dedicating yourself to a life of selfless devotion to spiritual values, public service, or a caring role. At the height of WWII, psychoanalyst Erich Fromm wrote an influential book titled *Fear of Freedom*.[16]

In it he analysed the link between anxiety and the false relief offered by totalitarianism. This raises a general philosophical point about UI: you don't have to suffer from either recognition hunger or fear of freedom to want to conform. We do it all the time. In work environments especially, the UI game is one of adapting and fitting in. We play by the rules of the game. Moments of UI expression need to be calibrated and controlled in all walks of life, something we shall say more on later in this book.

2. THE UGLY SELF: I'M NOT WHO I WANT TO BE

The First Law of UI says your uniqueness is a biological fact and the Second Law that you don't know yourself. You infer, deduce, or are blind to much of your Beast-being identity. This means you can be forced to become aware of unwelcome elements, intruding into consciousness, aspects of yourself that cause you or others discomfort, anguish even. Looking in the mirror, you may not like what you see. We all have traits we wish we didn't possess, like Arpit in the last chapter, repeatedly volunteering to be the workhorse for his group. Elsewhere, some UI manifestations can be downright baffling.

> On October 27, 2024, a 28-year-old Greek man was given a 1-year suspended prison sen-
> tence and ordered to receive therapy for repeatedly breaking into his neighbours' houses
> to sniff their shoes.

There are worse impulses and tastes to have.

> Ed Gein died in a psychiatric hospital on July 26, 1984, at the age of 77, where he was
> incarcerated as "legally insane" for his infamous and gruesome crimes, including the
> exhumation of bodies and the creation of items from human remains. These included
> bowls from human skulls, a vest from flayed skin, and a mask from a woman's face. His
> actions inspired several fictional characters in horror literature and film.

The Second Law of UI makes it important to interrogate ourselves from time to time, following the principle that *the most important conversations you ever have are with yourself.* The Self is always in a state of "becoming,"[17] guided by Ego's awareness and self-editing. How do I know who I am until I see what I do? You can deduce yourself by observing your reactions to life's Drama. Then there are other people, who tell you about your traits and, occasionally, your blind spots. Beast's spontaneous impulses and initiatives surprise and teach you about your more elusive qualities. That's the awareness part. The editing comes from the narratives you adopt about what you don't like about yourself, downplaying some aspects of your UI and promoting others. That's not just your right; it's also your duty to yourself. Social living is performative, a matter of selecting how to be yourself. It is essential to become aware of the parts that get you into trouble or pose risks. Previously[18] I have borrowed novelist William Boyd's invented word "zemblanity"[19] for the bad stuff that happens to you because you make it happen, repeatedly! In other words, your UI always contains traits that, though useful in some contexts, ambush you and cause trouble. We are literally our own worst enemies.

This can spiral out of control, especially if the edited self is one-sidedly positive or negative. The former are the narcissists – often spectacularly and undeservedly success-ful in politics and business.[20] The latter struggle to maintain positive Self narratives.

The great American poet and novelist Sylvia Plath took her own life at the age of 30 after a lifetime of depressive illness. The genetic predisposition for depression has been found to be "switched on" by negative life events[21]; in her case a critical event was the death of her father when she was 8. She attempted suicide at 21 and underwent electrocon-vulsive therapy, all the time pouring her troubled soul into compelling verse and prose. Marriage and two children could not save her. The marriage, to British poet Ted Hughes, was tempestuous and unhappy. His desertion of her, plus literary rejection, triggered her final self-destruction. She enacted the logic of her own reasoning that "It's a hell of a responsibility to be yourself. It's much easier to be somebody else or nobody at all".[22]

Such tragic cases leave you thinking, why didn't she seek this or that relief from such self-oppression? Could it have been otherwise? Yes, of course it could. There are always other choices that could be made. But the odds for Plath were heavily stacked against her. Meanwhile, people with all kinds of deficits and annoying foibles don't dwell on them, bolstered by relationships where they feel seen and appreciated. They count their blessings and get on with life. Sufferers like Plath find themselves in neurotic spirals of depressive self-loathing, often due to organic imbalances in their hormonal systems,[23] at the same time as being trapped in toxic circumstances. Suicide is sometimes called "a cry for help." Our perspective says that for many, it is a last desperate cry for deep UI recognition. For others it is a rational escape route from the pain of existence.

Evolutionary psychiatrist Randy Nesse points out, we have good reasons for bad feelings.[24] They are a signal that something's not working and that we need to change. This is adaptive, to the extent that it spurs you into action to get out and seek help.

Graham Greene was a 20th century novelist with a gift for compelling accounts of the human heart's moral dilemmas. He could also tell a cracking adventure story. All his work is deeply suffused with satirical, cynical, and wry intelligence about society. Greene suffered with chronic depression, for which found temporary relief in a life of adventure, wandering between Latin America, Africa, and the Far East, serving for a while as a government secret service field operator. He was terrified of boredom – a state where the hateful Self can break the surface and hijack your mind. His self-administered therapy was a mix of action, tangled relationships, and writing. Together they made us beneficiaries of his unique literary legacy.

Greene's example gives hope. His life was filled with incident and pain, but his conversion of it into art was for the greater good of humanity.

Survivors of relationships with suicides lacerate themselves with "if only. . . ." It is painfully frustrating to combat another person's negative editing and fixation. Many unfortunates seem to refuse to grasp the flotation devices to hand and instead drown in themselves. Individuality blocks itself in maladaptive cycles of self-fulfilling narratives. Depressive illness has in this fashion claimed the lives of many loved and gifted people. Actors Robin Williams and Philip Seymour Hoffman, singers Whitney Houston and Kurt Cobain, and writers Ernest Hemingway and Virginia Woolf, all lost their lives directly or indirectly to the "illness" of self-loathing.

The term "depressive illness" is, of course, another medicalisation of UI. It is identifying what happens when a person's neural–hormonal processing has gone rogue, delivering packages of emotion that are injurious to their welfare. Traditional treatments have relied on electroconvulsive therapy and powerful drugs that crudely shift the balance of neurotransmitter activity. More refined interventions are in development that deliver better outcomes with fewer costs than the heavy-handed traditional treatments. There is also a bright future for individualised cognitive therapies plus microdoses of psychedelics that shift perceptions – letting the light into the Jungian darkness. They offer the possibility for sufferers to grow and learn to love themselves for who they are.

3. THE CURSE OF COMPARISON: JUST NOT GOOD ENOUGH, OR TOO GOOD TO BE TRUE?

The 21st century has witnessed the birth of a virtual media world that assaults anyone tuning into it with images and messages that say you need fixing.

The root of much UI distress is caused by self – other comparison. It is nice to see yourself winning, but to do so also entails ugly thinking about losers, which might be you! Evolution has dictated that we make these evaluations. Healthy adjustment to the social world means doing enough personal benchmarking to keep on track of where you stand in the games of social life. These are to do with who's up and who's down, as well as who's in and who's out. Too much of this can stop you from enjoying the good things of life. It becomes a runaway train and a source of almost constant distress for many. Obsessive self–other comparison is a particular risk for a wide range of UI profiles, for example, as much by people with striving personalities as those with deep insecurities. It is among the latter, especially when addicted to social media, that we see a rising tide of anorexia, self-harm, and compulsive behaviours.

A key component of our evolved Psyches – essential for cooperation with strangers – is mind reading – our ability to figure out other people's motives and interests. We are by no means unerring at this, not least because we are also gifted actors. You can put on an act and shield your private Self behind your public Self. Often, you don't want your mind to be read. All public behaviour is to some degree a performance art. Are people what they seem, or are they concealing the true strength of their hand? It can seem as if life is a poker game, where all the players are different characters, each with their own strategies and narratives. So far, so good, but then this means that some are better at the game than others. Which players do you need to watch out for, and which can you safely take for granted? Mostly you get it right, but errors are costly. Perhaps you are in the wrong game? This is a narrative, of course, one about winners and losers. It's primitive, and it plays on the neuroses that arise in the no-person's land between trust and mistrust. You feel unsafe. Worse, when you worry about others, you're liable to turn doubt on your Self. You start obsessing about your standing in others' eyes. Something like this is what happened to Billie Eilish when she rocketed to fame.

Sometimes being too good at the game can bring a different version of the problem.

Susanna from Bolivia was always a bright child, with clever parents. Her passions for maths, drawing, and dance absorbed her childhood. "I was always the first in class in everything," she recounts, but also that she got bullied for it in her first school. "When I am not the best in something, I don't feel like myself, which makes me frustrated when I fail or make mistakes. Even though I have gone through tough experiences in my professional life, I still don't know how to avoid the fear of failure." It took the personal trauma of a near-death experience and witnessing the devastation of professional lives around her in the 2008 financial crash to enable her to say, "I learned to be humble."

This is hard but necessary learning, but look at this case of a man whose UI enabled him to avoid the traps of invidious comparison.

Badrul, from Malaysia, says that from the youngest age, his parents were at pains to tell him he was "high born," at the same time expecting him to do weekly house cleaning. "They were always saying I must not let anyone look down on me. There was constant pressure to be a top student." Badrul is by nature empathic, conflict avoidant, and sensitive, by his own admission a person who finds setbacks difficult. From this challenging upbringing, he was able to find what he calls "a life dedicated to positive values."

This can be seen as a triumph of willpower and character forestalling what could have been a life of competitive striving, entitlement, and pride. Healthy development entails self-acceptance, which requires the mental discipline of insight: the ability to appraise and appreciate your own UI. The field of positive psychology offers a range of routines and disciplines to achieve this,[25] yet the roots of self-dislike often go deep enough to make these temporary fixes at best.

Field Marshal Bernard Law Montgomery, also known as Monty, was a British soldier whose leadership hastened the end of WWII though his victorious leadership in the North African theatre. But he was insufferably egotistical, with few friends and frequent conflicts with fellow officers. The great American general Patton called him "a tired little fart," and Churchill, "In defeat, unbeatable; in victory, unbearable." His UI was built upon a platform of native intelligence, extreme task orientation, and an abrasive direct personality. The youngest of four, he was raised in a solidly middle-class family by a remote father and an abusive, distant mother. By sheer force of personality, he pushed himself through the class barrier into the aristocracy of army staff college. He keenly resented the elitism of the officer class. He was just shy of 50 when he lost the love of his life, his wife of 10 years. It was a turning point. Devastated, the army became his only partner. He spent his career striving to prove his superiority to all. He died aged 88, alone and friendless.

Another victim of grandiose narcissism was surrealist painter Salvador Dali, who proclaimed:

> "Every morning upon wakening, I experience a supreme pleasure: that of being Salvador Dali, and I ask myself, wonderstruck, what prodigious thing will he do today, this Salvador Dali."[26]

He, too, ended his days reclusive, physically impaired, and profoundly depressed. In our times, the epidemic of social comparison is symbolised by the selfie as a tool of self-presentation.[27] It is a fraught space, with young people especially getting caught in spirals of obsessive self-construction, driven by invidious self–other comparisons.

Who does not want the reassurance of what we may have felt in childhood – the unconditional regard and appreciation of our uniqueness by loving people – a special kind of deep recognition? As we have seen, recognition hunger is core trait for some individuals, many of them public extraverts like Dali. As it was for Monty, Dali's loss of his life partner in old age triggered the inversion of his narcissism into desperate depression.

4. AUTHENTICITY DILEMMAS: IS IT SAFE TO BE ME?

It's easier for some people to be "authentic" than others. Many gay executives (almost all male) in my classroom, coming from every continent on earth, have recounted that they have spent significant portions of their lives concealing their sexual orientation, feeling forced to fake it with family and colleagues.

> Krishna was born to the elite Brahmin caste in Northern India to highly intelligent but warring parents. His father, abashed by his professional underachievement, compared with his aristocratic parents, was cool and remote. Krishna's mother was loving and protective but mired in deep depression throughout his childhood. Despite this inauspicious context, Krishna remembers his childhood as happy – the natural state of his temperament. His quiet and studious elder sister conformed to the rigours of the parents' devout Hinduism, but Krishna's bright and mischievous spirit proved too lively. He found himself repeatedly in trouble at school, earning him regular beatings from both parents. In early teenage, Krishna awoke to the awkward fact of his own sexual orientation, which he concealed but did not try to suppress. He could not wait to quit home and head west to the US, where

he could be himself more freely. Even there, it took a while, until secure in his academic career, that he could openly come out as gay. When he extended this openness to his family, both his parents and his sister, who was living in the US herself, all disowned him. This caused Krishna bitter unhappiness, but it did not dent his resolve to live an authentic life.

We shall come back to Krishna's story later. It demonstrates how UI can triumph over relationships and culture, to find – create indeed – a milieu where you can be yourself.

To do this is a much bigger stretch for some people than others. We have created the label "neurodivergent" to normalise people whose UI is out of kilter with the way the world works or how most people think and express themselves. The term is a welcome shift from the stigmatising labels that were commonplace until recently, but there remain two unhelpful consequences from a UI perspective. One is that it creates a category whose members have nothing in common except apart from being "divergent" from a norm. Second, it reinforces the norm and seems to tell the rest of us that we are "normal," which you might not mind but is fairly meaningless from a Uniqueness Perspective. All measurable traits vary, so being normal just means being in a range around the average. The thresholds, within which scientists and medics tell you are "normal," are statistical and totally arbitrary. There may be no one at all who is at the "average" point. The First Law of UI reminds us that we are all exceptional, something that no one, including we ourselves, may have ever acknowledged. It is not the sole province of the neurodivergent to feel distant from the "normal." It is startlingly common.

Let's take a closer look at the neurodivergent. The people in this category may indeed have mental equipment that doesn't work as nature intended, but every one of them is unique and different, even within the same category – autistic, attention deficit hyperactivity disorder, obsessive-compulsive, dyslexic. People classified as having autistic spectrum disorder (ASD) are as different from each other as any of us. What they have is a cluster of challenges in social communications, hypersensitivity to stimuli, repetitive behaviours, and cognitive challenges or gifts but in different combinations and to vastly different degrees. The idea of a "spectrum" turns out to oversimplify by presuming that the autistic differ only in degree from each other rather than in the qualities of their divergence. As I discovered in a field trip, the "Autism Wheel," shown in Figure 2, provides a much more individualised view of the challenges any autistic person may face.

In the ASD label, the D letter stands for "disorder," often an unhelpful concept. Better regard it as a syndrome, where one element triggers another. If we put ourselves in the mind of such a person, it becomes obvious that they are trying to establish control over

ONE VERSION OF THE AUTISM WHEEL

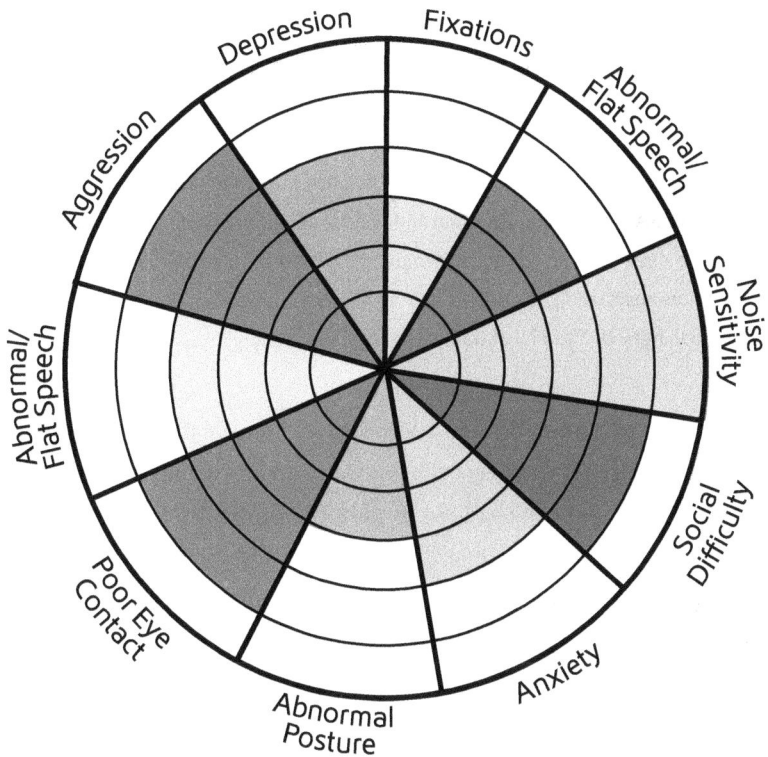

Figure 2.

their experience through strategies that can look incomprehensible to the so-called "neurotypical" but which to them make perfect sense.

> I am talking to the staff and meeting students at the remarkable Wherry School[28] that enrols 133 ASD pupils who meet the criterion of average cognitive ability. Through their individualised teaching model, the school records a near 100% success rate of returning its pupils to mainstream education at 16. Rachel, the school's principal, tells me, "No two are alike. Like all children they need their voices to be heard, to have a sense of self-efficacy, and to feel an equal member of a community. It is the world beyond the school that has a skewed view of normality." The school's regimen is empowering – training them to self-regulate and find strategies to navigate the pathways of a world. For them, this is an obstacle course of incomprehension, stigmatisation, and bad solutions to their needs and interests. Imogen, a specialist teacher, tells me about the

wonder of autistic students' UI. She shows me the Autism Wheel as we talk about the many ways their UI shows up. "We have some very bright kids, like in any school, and no more 'savants' than you'd find in any population. They feel pressure to be talented." But, she says, "I love their different approaches and unique perspectives on things that I would never have thought of. We laugh a lot – I love their wit and humour."

She tells me about a couple of cases. The first is a boy with "significant needs" who always delights people with his highly original and holistic perspective. "He has immense natural wisdom and deep concern for the environment." The second is a girl who at 11 became quite fashion-obsessed in an attempt to fit in but within a couple years found the value in being true to herself. "Now I just want to be me," she proudly says.

For the neurodivergent, to be seen and heard is essential to their ability to adapt in a "neurotypical" world. Yet not every person wants to be visible. Some may be happier away from the public arena, in shadows of public anonymity with just a few intimates. We differ greatly in how much we need affirmation and recognition. For the autistic, understanding, tolerance, and adjustment are essential to protect them from socially challenging situations, to reduce their uncertainty, and to support their goals. Not much different to everyone else, you might say, except that most people get by only having to display good manners to fit in. The autistic feel they have to "mask" or "camouflage" their identities. This is cognitively challenging and emotionally draining. It takes a lot of psychic effort to act "normal." It's not just at the neurodivergent extremes that you find people who feel that to get by, they need to practise a studied form of self-protective inauthenticity. We all have to harmonise our private with our public personas as best we can, but this can be very hard. Some build a wall around their "real" selves.

Marilyn Monroe was stuck in the public persona of Hollywood Goddess and dizzy blond, when in reality she was highly intelligent, an avid reader, and desperate to self-improve. Her background was troubled – mother hospitalised for psychosis, father absent, and her upbringing largely left her to the care of foster parents and orphanages. Her life and career were twisted by the incongruence of her lived reality and a public image she depended upon for her fame and fortune. It is little wonder that her life was scarred by a succession of troubled relationships, professionally and personally, seeking relief in addiction to a medley of prescription drugs and alcohol that led to her untimely death at 36.

Being yourself is so much easier for most people, but how much easier? If we regard all categories of the neurodivergent as having extreme traits, often bundled in challenging clusters and in need of external support, plenty of neurotypical people feel something similar, though not on the same scale. Earlier, I described my own lifelong feeling of being an outsider, but I now come to realise this feeling is very common indeed. In truth, there are no insiders and outsiders, just people who feel more or less at home in the places they are and with the lives they are living.

A lesser variant, which we saw in the Billie Eilish story, is the so-called "imposter syndrome." The idea crops up a lot in business and health psychology to denote people who feel a disjoint between the Self and their assigned role and status.[29]

> Isha was a child of modest and simple upbringing in Northern India but whose chubby body shape in her early years brought her the pain of persistent bullying, teasing, and fat-shaming. Determinedly she spent 5 years intensively swimming, exercising, and dieting to become the trim person she is today. "But," she says, "the damage was already done, and the feeling of being 'less' persisted. I have felt like an imposter through my adult life. Despite winning awards, accolades, and glowing performance reviews, an insidious whisper 'You are not good enough' became a constant companion." Becoming a mother, plus a good deal of self-work, have brought her deep reassurance, and she says, "shaped me as a fiercely independent, ambitious, yet empathetic professional." She tells me: "Looking ahead, I see endless possibilities. I'm no longer held back by self-doubt or fear of failure. I know there will be obstacles, but I also know I have the resilience and capability to overcome them."

The Laws of UI dictate that we all must become reconciled with the gap between our inner and outer worlds. We learn to smile at strangers, conceal true feelings, and act out poorly fitting roles. We, too, are "masking," some of us with a lot less effort than others. The first-person world is ours alone, even as we step out onto the stage with others who are doing the same thing.

Taking the Uniqueness Perspective means that there are many ways to be yourself. There is no single "authentic" you, but multiple (not infinite!) ways of being. Authenticity is about owning the richness of your UI – what you like and don't like – and finding ways of expressing it within the essential frame of good manners that make tolerance, good humour, and nonjudgemental acceptance possible.

5. THE HATEFUL WORLD

We have considered people who blame themselves for being out of step with the worlds they inhabit. The alternative is to blame the world for being out of step with us. This can be the basis for great reforms, social revolutions, transformational arts, and major achievements in the public domain. Winston Churchill was one of the latter – always an outsider, owing to his strange, lonely upbringing; his odd mix of parents; and his forceful, gifted personality. He made serious mistakes and is not universally revered, but he didn't rage with history; he made it.

Here's one who did likewise, but not in a good way:

> Robert Mugabe, for 37 years president of Zimbabwe, made history with a good deal of rage. He was responsible for genocide against a rival tribe, political violence and intimidation to maintain a one-party state, and ideologically driven economic mismanagement of his country's finances, resulting in the starvation of his own people. Mugabe was an intensely shy and brainy child, born to a fanatically devout Catholic mother, who administered tough love laced with regular beatings. His father, a carpenter, was harsh and domineering, abandoning the family to poverty when Robert was 10. The Anglo-Irish headmaster of his school thought the boy a genius and became his surrogate dad. At school he was relentlessly teased for his bookish gravitas and slight physique. Although smaller and weaker than others, Mugabe was fiercely competitive and as rigid in his ways as his mother, never seeking compromise or agreement. His mother saw him as God's gift to leadership. This he fulfilled after serving an 11-year imprisonment for sedition by the racist government of the then Southern Rhodesia. After winning the struggle for independence, he centralised power around his role as president and ruled the country for 37 years, becoming increasingly autocratic. He corrupted the political process and brutally suppressed any opposition, until forced to quit 2 years before his death in 2019 at the age of 95.[30]

Mugabe's desperate story epitomises one of Karen Horney's three disorders of the Self. Horney, Freud's first female disciple, fell out with him because of patriarchal perspective on psychoanalysis. She also disagreed, as we do here, with Freud's downgrading of the Ego to slave status (to the Beast/Id), denying the Ego the power of agency. From her psychoanalytic practice, Horney observed that the healthy Self adapts to the world through a calibrated combination of three tactics: moving against what is injurious to it, moving away from what is not wanted, and moving towards what is good for it.[31] Ahead of her time, she spotted that the Self gets bent out of shape when there are severe bonding failures in infancy, causing these three adaptive tactics to become imbalanced. The growing child becomes overinvested in any of these three tactics. Moving against is manifest as hostility to the world, moving away is frigid detachment, and moving towards is excessive neediness.

Robert Mugabe is a case of run-away moving against the world. There are numerous similar examples of pitilessly punishing the world, like Adolph Hitler, Josef Stalin, Sadam Hussein, and Mao Zedong. All endured brutal parenting in their early lives. All became powerful public performers – creating a cult of personality around themselves. Hitler, especially, was a pitiful failure who assiduously practised his posturing and strutting to deflect as much as possible from the screaming child inside him.

Horney's second category – moving away – is seen in people who are detached and struggle with intimacy and authenticity.

> Movie actor Henry Fonda's parents were strict and emotionally remote disciplinarians. Henry was small, shy, self-conscious, and socially awkward, finding himself attracted to arts and sports. A formative moment in his childhood was when his father, a social liberal, took him to witness the aftermath of the lynching of a black man accused of rape, imprinting on Henry a lifelong sense of justice and human rights. He found his way into the movies via theatre, turning out to be a brilliant actor. This reflected his UI, finding himself drawn to the roles of reserved, stoical characters grappling with their own inner turmoil and moral dilemmas. In his private and family life, he was cold, perfectionist, and deeply concerned about how he was perceived, battling all his life with feelings of inadequacy. His relationships with his children were often strained, especially with his movie star daughter Jane Fonda, who wrote movingly of his distancing coldness in her memoir.[32] She even bought the rights to the book *On Golden Pond* so they could act out their relationship as co-stars. It did help them to relate at a deeper level, but it brought about no substantial change in her father's demeanour. The best moments of his life were on screen – the only place he could be the self he wanted to be.

This is not an unusual story. A great many of the finest actors, like Alec Guinness and Meryl Streep, have introvert, retiring personalities which become transformed when they inhabit a role.

Horney's third syndrome is moving towards – when the self seeks completion through relationships. When pathological, extreme recognition hunger is insatiable and injurious to well-being. Connection is a gateway, not a destination. These needy and demanding people are also intensely self-critical whilst fault finding with others for not living up to their expectations. No one, including themselves, is good enough. Marilyn Monroe, who we discussed earlier, seems to have been prey to a cocktail of these elements – craving a recognition that forever eluded her.

6. LONELINESS AND ALIENATION: NO ONE CARES WHETHER YOU LIVE OR DIE

The COVID-19 pandemic was like a litmus test for mental health, well-being, and social support systems. What one could see was simultaneously shocking and reassuring. On the upside, for a sizeable minority, it was revelatory – a chance to reappraise their UI and freshly appreciate intimate relationships. A larger group experienced the opposite, in a toxic mix of stress, constricted privacy, and money worries.[33] But this wasn't the core of the problem. It was, as researchers discovered, that people confronted the ugly fact of the Third Law of UI: they found that they knew their most intimate companions a lot less well than they thought they did. For some, this was a delight, but for others, it revealed and amplified attributes that they found hard to tolerate in such concentrated form. This can make you feel paradoxically lonely, and it was outright loneliness that was the biggest, darkest revelation of the pandemic. Its scale and depth, with a total absence of social support, afflicted millions – especially the young.[34]

Social isolation is a chronic condition for the elderly. In the US and Europe, 30% to 40% of the elderly live alone, more women than men.[35] Prolonged solitude is not a natural human condition; unheard of among our ancestors, but an inevitable consequence of the decay of the extended family in the WEIRD* world. This presents a challenge for people, but not necessarily distress. Solitude is not the same as loneliness. Around two-thirds of older people living alone are not lonely.[36] We are an adaptive species, and if you live a long life, you have a greater store of personal resources. These include coping strategies, friendship networks, hobbies, and other self-sufficient activities. Not so the young. For them these resources are nascent and unpractised.

Circumstances matter, but loneliness is a state of mind, and the Uniqueness Perspective tells us some individuals are constitutionally more vulnerable to it than others, whatever their age. Everyone needs someone to talk to from time to time. Failure to connect can leave you feeling your existence has no value.

---

*Western, Educated, Industrialised, Rich, Democratic.

John Clare was a preternaturally gifted poet, born into the most unprepossessing of circumstances, that of farm labourer. Born in poverty, working as an agricultural labourer,
with exceptional gifts of mind, he pulled himself out of illiteracy but into a state of social
isolation, ending his days in an insane asylum, where he penned perhaps the most elo-
quent expression of this state in his poem "I Am!," whose opening lines are:

> I am! yet what I am none cares or knows,
> I am the self-consumer of my woes[38]

Clare faced the paradox that your Self is always with you, living each moment in
existential separation from others. This causes some people no worse than intermittent
difficulty, but when your UI is so out of kilter with your context, it becomes a source of
anguish.

Michael is an Australian 40-year-old of mixed Asian European heritage. He was a shy,
unconfident, and sensitive child, raised in a home of extreme marital conflict. Via the
ministrations of an uncle, he found an escape route as an engineer to Canada. He says,
"I craved love and met my wife, whom I loved deeply, only for the relationship to fall
apart after a decade. All that I had built was gone, both financially and personally." He
ran a successful business for a while before shutting it down to move into a senior role
in a large company. He recounts, "I rebelled on how things were done, and after 3 years,
I accepted I wasn't made for the corporate world." This triggered a decision to quit Canada
and go backpacking to India and find himself via meditation and spirituality. He returned
to Australia, where he found love and happiness with a spiritual healer partner. Yet on the
work front, issues persisted. He says, "Despite my hard work and effort, I didn't get the
recognition I deserved." On finding his way on to our programme, he reached a resolution:
"The way I look at purpose now is that it's a play, and we need to act. The characters/actors
of the drama will change, and I need to change my role and play a different character now
and then to evolve myself. Most importantly, I try my best not to be attached to the results
of my desires and focus on the journey and the process."

Michael is only midway in his journey, but he is finding how Deliberation can help
him escape his tendency to alienation. Your UI is inherently adaptive. The exceptions we
have scrutinised here are mostly people caught in loops of "stuck-ness" – like Horney's
needy types – people who crave recognition and drive others away by demanding too
much of them.

7. EXISTENTIAL ANXIETY – IS THAT ALL THERE IS?

Tomorrow, and tomorrow, and tomorrow/Creeps in this petty pace from day to day/To the last syllable of recorded time/And all our yesterdays have lighted fools/The way to dusty death. Out, out, brief candle!/Life's but a walking shadow, a poor player/That struts and frets his hour upon the stage/And then is heard no more: it is a tale/Told by an idiot, full of sound and fury/Signifying nothing.[39]

Poor Macbeth. Shakespeare put this poignant summary of the human condition into Macbeth's mouth as an expression of profound grief – his reaction to the loss of his beloved Lady Macbeth, the woman who inflamed all his fatal ambitions. Anyone who has suffered bereavement can empathise. Shakespeare is not making a universal point about the human condition beyond the sense of futility such loss can give you. Yet he does capture an incipient dread lurking in the notion of our UI, the existential anxiety that so panicked my 7-year-old self at the start of this book. This is the bleak idea that while you live, you are alone in this space, and at the end, no matter how many loving faces surround you, you also die alone.

Like all other experiences, your final one – death – is equally private. Religions seek to inoculate us with belief in the afterlife. It is true that people with faith suffer less from loneliness than others,[40] but not because they believe in the hereafter. Their consolation comes from the sense of being understood and accompanied through life by God, spirits, or ancestors, plus a sense of connectedness with other humans and, in some religions, with the natural world.

The philosopher Thomas Nagel[41] rightly observed that existential anxiety is a by-product of self-consciousness. This unlocks a solution to the problem of thanatophobia – intense and obsessive fear of death. Nagel is right that it is only you can think about your own existence that you get caught by this fear. We only do this intermittently. Most of the time we're caught up in the day-to-day stream of action – seeking, planning, controlling, and achieving. From the Greek for goal, we can call this being in a **telic** state,[42] actively pursuing goals, in the grip of dopamine desire and control circuits.[43] It leaves no space for reflection.

When we hit the pause button, that's when reflective consciousness takes over – the **paratelic** (beyond telic, in Greek). This is the joy of savouring, after the chase is concluded and you've found the balm of reflective space. The paratelic activates a quite different combination of neural networks and neurotransmitters.[44] Your Ego can't hold in focus both states at once, and their neural origins prohibit each other. You can, however, shuttle between them, each providing a relief from the other. Planned, purposeful action is a great escape from excessive rumination, as any grieving person will tell you. Equally, it is therapeutic to take time out from the pursuit of goals and gratification. Game playing is best when you get the balance right.

> I am a mediocre tennis player and learned early that being overinvested in striving to win is not good for my mental health. It is much more gratifying to revel in the fresh air, the joy of moving my body with purpose, plus the bonus elements of occasionally hitting a good shot, to say nothing of the good company of the other players.

It is a sign of our troubled psyches that people are so easily entrapped by the telic, from overwork to addictions. The dopamine desire circuits get hijacked by our world's overabundance of things to want and do. People become wound into tight cycles of finding, getting, and using drugs, sex, gambling, or whatever, for relief from any of the UI discontents we have discussed.

Flipping this switch is achieved by reframing. One of the most useful psychological tricks we possess is to move between different ways of looking at the same situation – turning the half-empty glass into one that is half full. Shifting between the telic and paratelic is experiential reframing. Consider the Roman who put on his headstone *Non fui, fui, non sum, non curo* = I was not, I was, I am not, I do not care. This is the Epicurean view of the world. It seeks to conquer the Beast's instinctive fear of death and the Ego's rational fear of losing itself. But how rational is that fear? As Epicurus put it, "Death does not concern us, because as long as we exist, death is not here. And when it does come, we no longer exist."[45]

It is others who will suffer the loss of our passing, not us. The fear comes from paratelic rumination because Ego's obsessive gaze focuses on lived experience as if it was a consumable. This is an out-of-place telic perspective. The more important telic perspective is that death is good for us – without it, we could procrastinate endlessly. Mortality is a powerful motivator, spurring us on to our greatest achievements and most profound reflections. As Franz Kafka put it in his novel *The Trial*, "The meaning of life is that it ends."

The most lasting pain of death is often borne by the bereaved. For them, as we shall see in the next chapter, it is a transition that has transformational consequences.

DARK AND LIGHT – STRIPES OR WHAT?

Let us be clear about two things. First, people can get horribly stuck in the seven states we have reviewed, but most don't. We have dark times, and generally the light does come in, even if the darkness tends to recur. Second, how light and dark are patterned in your life is unique; no one else's is the same. But there is much to be gained from sharing with people who have encountered similar issues to your own, who can give support and let the light in. Change is reachable, if hard.

> Alcoholics Anonymous is an example of very savvy UI self-help practice. An optional framework of belief and abstinence techniques is offered to members, but it is the ethos and practice of their meetings that underlies AA's success. (1) Members are anonymous, first or assumed names only. (2) They practise storytelling, each recounting their unique experience. (3) Listening is non-evaluative, acknowledging and validating each person who "shares." (4) Progress, not cure, is their watchword, and what this means is a personal construction. (5) Local groups are encouraged to develop their own models of practice, within the constitutional framework of AA.[46]

In Chapter 9 we shall see parallels of this kind of organisation in quite different contexts.

CODA: WHAT THIS MIGHT MEAN FOR UNIQUE YOU

It seems we are becoming more vulnerable to many of the ills we have surveyed because of social fragmentation and the loss of traditional community. More people than ever are self-identifying as neurodivergent. This is good news to the extent that it reflects heightened awareness, tolerance, and support for those who need it. Yet this doesn't slow the growing flood of the desperate, searching for escape routes from their lack of personal agency, many slipping into the widening sinkhole of opioid and other addictions.[47] In this world, UI can feel more a threat than a promise when the three existential wants are negated – life is joyless, meaningless, and anonymous.

- Do you consider yourself to be neurodivergent? By all means, compare yourself with others, but only in order to find functional coping strategies and people to share experience with.

- If you are not, then it's a sure thing you know people who are. They might not use the label, but that is irrelevant. The best service you can do to them is to hear the story of their UI, to enable them to feel seen and validated for who they are.
- Take care of how you think about people suffering from psychological and behavioural difficulties. It is easy to make the mistake of putting the cause all in the person or all in the environment. Both are always in the picture.
- You need a strategy for being yourself. This means a narrative about how to reconcile your mind's contradictory forces, socially unacceptable impulses, and what you might call personal "weaknesses." These can be strengths in another context. It's OK to have a narrative that doesn't add up to a "consistent" identity, so long as it's authentic.
- Think of the Three Existential Wants as your right – to find joy in the quality of your public and private existence, to be living a life that makes a positive contribution, and to have confidants and intimates who validate you.
- Think about people you know for whom these Wants are negated. You may be in a position to help others Savour, Signify, and be Seen.
- It's OK to live unselfishly in the service of others, but if you find yourself surrendering your individuality because it makes life easier or more bearable, it means that you have undervalued your UI. You may be jeopardising your own vital interests.
- Do you have traits that you hate? Ask yourself what contexts arouse this thought and which render them neutral or even beneficial. Consider how your "dark" traits might be the other side of the coin to qualities you value in yourself.
- Don't compulsively compare yourself with others. Their lived experience may be a lot less ideal than it looks from outside, and besides, it's your job to be you. Everyone else is taken.
- Are you angry with how things turned out for you in life? Draw on that energy and treat it as a problem to be solved. Hard to do on your own. Find counsellors or buddies to help you have the right conversations with yourself.
- Maybe that's the nub of the problem. There is no one. Your *umwelt* is a depopulated wasteland. Then enrich it. Communities exist all around you, increasingly findable via the Internet. Tell people – let them help you. You are not alone.
- Yes, life is brief and comes to an end. That's a fact, not a problem. How to live is the real challenge. When it isn't, then the problem has gone away, and you with it.

Seven

LIFE STORIES

UI in Transition and Transformation

We shall not cease from exploration, and the end of all our
exploring will be to arrive where we started and know the place for the first time.
(T.S. Eliot)[1]

I may not have gone where I intended to go, but I think I have ended up
where I needed to be.
(Douglas Adams)[2]

THE UNPREDICTABLE STAGES OF LIFE

Shakespeare said the world is a stage, on which we are all but players. He failed to point out that by the time we make our entrance "mewling and puking," the play is well underway and has been going on for some time. He foresees infancy as the first of seven stages, returning at the last to a "second childishness and mere oblivion; Sans [minus] teeth, sans eyes, sans taste, sans everything."[3]

Benjamin Franklin memorably reduced the model to three stages as a warning to the young: "Youth is a folly, manhood a struggle, old age a regret." Despite their wit and economy, both are wrong. Life is not so easily and neatly chopped up into chunks. Again, we see writers succumbing to the magnetic appeal of universal taxonomies. They appeal by satisfying your desire to know what to expect for yourself and your kin. Advance warning is great, but only if the roadmap is reliable. It isn't. Here's a digest of what writers have claimed.

- You need to achieve mastery over successive challenges to your self-concept: mistrust of the world, shame, guilt, inferiority, role confusion, isolation, stagnation, and despair (Erikson).[4]
- Identity grows through a progressive sequence: building relationships, achieving a working identity, caring for others, finding meaning and integrity, achieving peace as you approach death (Vaillant).[5]
- Transitions mark the boundaries between finding your direction, establishing mature relationships, dealing with the midlife crisis, and achieving mature acceptance (Levinson; Sheehy.)[6]

- Our egos progress through states of being "imperial," impulsive, and self-protective; "socialised" conformity, self-awareness, and conscientiousness; "self-authorising" individualism and autonomy; and finally "self-transforming" integration (Loevinger; Kegan).[7]
- Cognitive capabilities automatically unfold through formative years – most notably the emergence of "theory of mind" (awareness of others as independent agents) (Piaget).[8] This is linked with progression from primitive to more nuanced, relativistic, and purpose-driven morality (Kohlberg).[9]

Brain imaging studies show neurological transitions at four ages: 9, 32, 66, and 83.[10] In the stories that populate this book, you can see many of these developments. Stage theories contain wise and insightful ideas, based on sound data. The problem is that there are too many exceptions, too many life stories that depart from these stages in form, content, and timing. Even the last point, about how the brain ages, is a story of averages: approximations, not a timetable. Your brain's on its own journey. Thus, we all can agree that life is a one-way voyage of adaptive challenges. Also, all lives follow a lumpy, discontinuous sequence – what we have called punctuated equilibrium,[11] relatively uneventful intervals that are punctuated by shocks and changes.

Life-stage models appeal because, like theories of human types, they make life look more predictable than it is.

Every life journey is unique, and in our diverse and uncertain times, many aspects of these theories now look elitist, presumptuous, and culturally normative. Even among the most science-based of them, there is a huge diversity of the timing and form of transitions.[12] The very databases of this work makes them ultimately descriptive, which also makes them children of their time and place, the WEIRD* world. We can squeeze parts of people's accounts into combinations of these templates, but to what point? Our 4D method is simpler and culture-free.

Now, in an era of increasing longevity, we need to rethink age-linked norms, especially about the increasingly elastic mid to later life period.[14]

USING THE 4DS TO DESCRIBE THE LIFE COURSE

Unique Individuality (UI) rules! Here's a WEIRD world case that defies all the norms that we might dream up.

---

*Western, Educated, Industrialised, Rich, Democratic.

Angus was born 53 years ago into the Glaswegian working class – his father a factory worker and lay preacher, his mother a hardworking homemaker. "Life was about survival. Parents' word was law. It was often commented by folks that we were the best-behaved children they had ever seen. The biggest positive influence in my life was my grandfather, but we did not see each other for years due to a falling-out with my parents over the way I was treated. My parents' philosophy was to always expect the worst because that was what was coming. I was told from a very young age that I wouldn't amount to anything. My whole life became based on getting out, leaving home, becoming self-sufficient, and proving them wrong. I started my first job aged 11 and by the time I was 15, I was working four jobs as well as going to school. I was cheeky, insubordinate, rebellious, hormonal, and I loved to fight. Known to the police and with a growing reputation, trouble followed me, or I found it."

This was his Destiny, spiked with Drama. Now Development and Deliberation come into play.

Boxing helped channel Angus's defiance into safer territory, and, drawing on his native intelligence, got himself a university place. There he admits he cruised for 2 years, "Until it became evident that I was in trouble. I hadn't studied or attended lectures. I realised it was time to grow up and get serious. I knuckled down and graduated." Angus applied for and secured one of the best graduate jobs available at that time. But, he says, "It was stressful and emotional. I was insecure, combining outward arrogance with inward sensitivity. My career progressed. I started on more money than my father ever earned, and I wasn't sure how I got so lucky or what I was supposed to do with it all."

Destiny and Drama now reasserted their sway over his choices.

Angus found himself increasingly successful but also miserable. The jet-setting glamorous lifestyle left him feeling "increasingly distanced from my origins and alienated from my former friends." An unexpected reunion in his late 20s with a childhood love from school changed his life, providing some of the emotional support and stability that he had always lacked. Yet he continued to labour at a demanding high-powered job, constantly seeking external validation. It took the midlife shock of his wife suffering a stroke to get him to prioritise family and a balanced life and to seek new paths via re-entry to education – and to his place in my Biography class.

Other losses transformed his life. The death of his grandfather first, and then, a few years later, the shocking loss of his best friend in the prime of midlife, followed by the death of his father a few years ago. The most recent change was the departure of his younger child to college. Angus, a self-confessed introvert, finds himself in a strange space – at peace, happy, and accepting his state, but the sudden freedom from both his formerly oppressive father and his own paternal duties is unsettling. His life has always been structured by work. He realises he misses the buzz of fellowship under fire in the trenches of competitive finance but not the relentless pressure to achieve. "I'm looking for the sweet spot of periodic engagement in start-ups and the freedom to live at the pace of my choosing," he says.

None of the life-stage models would help us understand the story of Angus's UI origins, growth, and trajectory. The 4D frame points to the important role of Destiny: his supersmart brain, his deeply introverting character, and the indelible imprint of his tough origins. Drama followed him as he struggled to assert himself and achieve, also in the personal losses that shaped his midlife adjustment. This makes his a story of Determination and Development working hand in hand as he navigated a very stormy sea. As the African proverb says, calm seas do not make good sailors.

The 4D system is not predictive. It doesn't tell you what might or might not happen. Neither is it normative. It doesn't tell you what you should or shouldn't do. It is a simple analytical methodology that can help you find fresh insights about the road you have travelled. When we introduced the method in Chapter 3, we showed how penetrating it can be as a framework for choosing a person for a position or as a partner. Figure 3 shows

LOOKING AT LIVES THROUGH THE 4D LENS

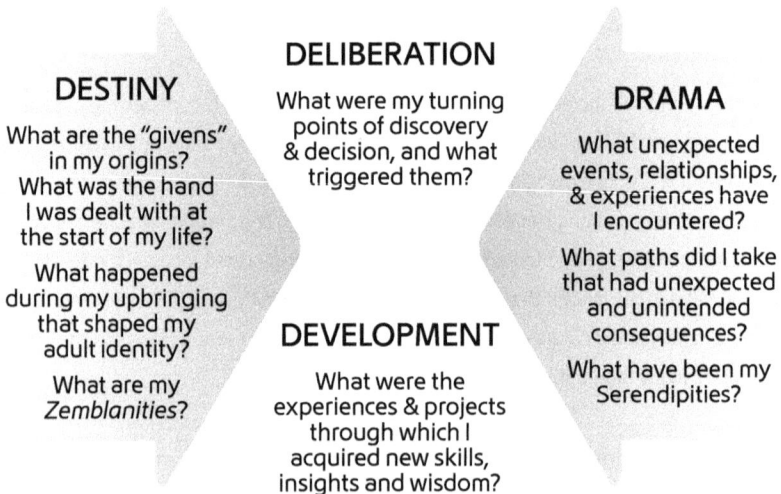

DESTINY

What are the "givens" in my origins? What was the hand I was dealt with at the start of my life?

What happened during my upbringing that shaped my adult identity?

What are my *Zemblanities*?

DELIBERATION

What were my turning points of discovery & decision, and what triggered them?

DEVELOPMENT

What were the experiences & projects through which I acquired new skills, insights and wisdom?

DRAMA

What unexpected events, relationships, & experiences have I encountered?

What paths did I take that had unexpected and unintended consequences?

What have been my Serendipities?

Figure 3.

GIVENS, THEMES, EVENTS, AND CHOICES
THAT SHAPE UI

DESTINY
- DNA-encoded traits
- Culture & background
- Upbringing & education
- Birth order
- Family
- Resources

DRAMA
- Trigger events/tipping points
- Happy accidents/disasters
- Loss events & grief
- Inspirational/influential people
- Moments of high emotion
- Unexpected opportunities

DELIBERATION &
DEVELOPMENT
- Hard & easy learning
- Self-exploration & discovery
- Deciding to change
- Acceptance & reconciliation
- Letting go & rebalancing
- Persevering

Figure 4.

the kinds of questions it suggests you might ask yourself or others. This kind of inquiry disgorges themes and narratives that we shall illustrate through this chapter. Figure 4 shows a sample of the most important that emerge from Biography workshops.

The themes in Figure 3 leap out of the stories that populate this book. It is only through narratives – whose ingredients are voice, time, cause, circumstance, and outcome – that we can see the coherence of UI. In Chapter 3, we described the Ego, your aware "I." It calls upon the Self, your constructed "Me" to enable your Beast-being to navigate reality and fulfil its Destiny. Storytelling is the Ego/Self's operating model. Narratives fulfil vital evolutionary functions: making sense of the world, maintaining a sense of identity, formulating intentions, declaring values, and defining relationships. Narratives shore up your sense of personal integrity and help you tell others, selectively, what to expect from you. They help you understand the world and the people in it. They draw your map of the world – your *umwelt.*

At this point, it is worth mentioning the role of "luck" in human lives. It's just another word for randomness, and your life is full of it – in the genes you bear, the legacy of your time and place of birth, the dramas of everyday life, and the workings of your incomprehensible brain. No wonder we need narratives to make sense of ourselves and the world!

THE STORIES WE TELL OURSELVES

Some writers have reduced the whole story of identity to narrative.[15] Narratives are powerful but very partial. Ego can't see the whole picture. Drawing its stories from the Self's memory banks and using the cultural toolkit in its *umwelt*, Ego may serve Beast's vital interests. It can also miss the mark.

All our narratives are "false" in the sense that other accounts could equally apply. The Beast has its own logics, independent of the Self's narratives, and if the two get too far out of step, both will suffer.[16] The Beast will crush the Self's delusions, or Ego will injure its host by making bad decisions. Compulsive gambling, for example, is driven by Beast's appetites and the Self's false narratives about control. Our stories about others and the world are designed to make them more predictable, but we get it wrong time and time again.

All our narratives are also "true," to the degree that they reflect the UI that creates them.[17] They have self-fulfilling properties. It is said that if something is perceived as real, it is real in its consequences.[18] Consider the power of Self narratives with this thought experiment.

> Imagine two truly identical versions of you. One version steps out of your skin, your exact doppelganger in body and mind. There is but one difference between the two you's. Version 1 has a self-concept that believes you're an attractive person who others want to be with; Version 2 has an opposite view and sees you as unattractive and undesirable company. As the two versions walk away, you know that they're going to live two very different lives – trajectories driven by contrasting narratives. You can do this thought experiment with any Self concept – such as courage, intelligence, morality.

Narratives about Self have double-edged value. At their best, they give you the armour of purpose to deal with whatever life throws at you. At their worst, they are psychic choke chains, holding you back from possibility.

But without narratives, you cannot navigate transitions and the intervals between them. They help you in three ways:

1. They follow the action – chasing after Drama – retrofitting sensemaking and muddling through, making action look a lot more Deliberate and inevitable than it was at the time. Look at Angus's narrative about escape from the constrictions of his home life.

2. They run alongside the action – offering a helpful (or not!) commentary to the ongoing stream and nudging events this way and that, learning and Developing as they go. Angus's bravado through his insecurity was a counterbalance to the stress he suffered in his first job.

3. They cause the action – creating self-fulfilling prophesies. The Destiny of your drives commands your Deliberation in how you execute them and shapes the Drama that unfolds. Angus's midlife escape from the rat race was driven by a narrative of identity, purpose, and redemption.

Without narratives our lives would lack direction or purpose. From this, it also follows that some narratives are "better" than others, to the degree that they (1) bind together elements more accurately, comprehensively, and logically and (2) lead to better outcomes for you and others. We saw in the last chapter how damaging bad narratives can be, and we shall see here in this chapter how they help you live through life's Dramas. You can see trade-offs in the costs and benefits of narratives. A persistent and damaging narrative I have seen repeatedly in business is executives clinging to self-isolating "lonely leader" narratives.[19] They look heroic, but they're ultimately self-defeating.

THE THREE MAJOR LIFE TRANSITION ZONES

Let's come back to the idea of life stages. Rather than defining their contents, let us try to encompass the main areas of UI development by looking at the three periods when most change generally (but not always!) happens.

1. Childhood – the period when the mark of Destiny becomes revealed and when UI is most profoundly shaped by experience

2. Adolescence – the passage into young adulthood, when critical life-shaping choices are made

3. Midlife – the increasingly long interval where life directions are reviewed, sustained, or altered against a backdrop of diminishing powers and choices.

1. THE UI STARTER PACK – CHILDHOOD

The dance of the 4Ds through childhood has some strong trends – Destiny, the hand dealt you at birth, calls the early shots, with Development being most intensive up to young adulthood. Drama is a wild card, by its nature unpredictable throughout the life course. Deliberation, when Ego asserts control, switches on when you encounter exceptions – when you feel you need to make stuff happen or stop it happening. Let's start at the beginning.

The baby Beast is born and immediately starts yelling and gurgling its UI to the world (its carers) about what it likes, what it wants, what it fears, and how it likes to act. Carers are mostly forced to pay attention and feed the infant Beast. We have seen what happens when they don't. We showed in the last chapter what happens when the neglected and unloved Beast develops, scarred by the legacy of an unbalanced Self. More usually, carers and culture apply well-intentioned attempts to programme the infant, while the child's UI filters, absorbs, and shapes these inputs into its growing identity, accepting and rejecting stimuli as it pleases. Critical relationships with educators, friends, and extended family become pivotal as the person's UI makes life-directing (and -limiting) choices. You could see this in the shining presence of Angus's grandfather in his *umwelt*, if not in his day-to-day life. Deliberation gathers increasing power as you grow.

We should also remember that birth is not the start of your life story. You are the latest link in a chain of roughly 15,000 generational sets of parents and children since the first of our race. You are just the latest to come on stage in a long-running play. The legacy of your ancestors has made you into a well-tuned survival machine with a road-tested genetic blueprint, plus generations of learning and culture.

Olga says, "Sometimes I feel my life started long before I was physically born." She goes on to recount the story of travels of her grandparents and their imprint on the new life she is building in the UK. Her great grandfather served in a Russian cavalry and went on to make a living from horse trading. This was a risky business – one time being ambushed by bandits, narrowly escaping with his life. He settled and built his business, until the Russian Revolution stripped him of all possessions. He worked hard in a commune and fathered nine children, including a daughter, Olga's grandmother. She became a teacher and moved to St Petersburg, where she married and had two daughters, one of them Olga's mother.

Her father's side of her family were wealthy Ukrainians, also stripped of their assets by the Soviets, dubbed "exploiters," and ordered to relocate to Siberia. At the last minute, inspired by her feisty paternal great-grandmother, in the dead of night they recovered their confiscated horse and escaped by cart with all their meagre possessions for a new life in the city of Dnepr, in the north of Ukraine. Not long after, the German invasion scattered the family, with one son killed in action as a resistance fighter and another daughter taken to Germany. The youngest daughter, Olga's grandmother, survived and lived her life in Ukraine. Later, her son, Olga's father, moved to St Petersburg to study and there and married Olga's mother. Before the Russian invasion of 2022, the courageous grandmother, a Ukrainian patriot, was, after prolonged persuasion, brought for her own safety at the age of 90 to St Petersburg.

Olga carries this legacy of strong female role models with a bitter wisdom. "I see the protection and the curse of family memories and the DNA inheritance of survivors. Generations of people being brave, not accepting 'fate' but finding a new door and building a new life from scratch. This helps me today going through my journey." Now living in London, Olga sees herself as a role model for her children, starting their life in the new country they can call home, keeping faith with courageous journeys of her forebears.

Olga discovered as she grew that the play she had entered was an epic drama over generations of courageous survival, which became central to her personal narrative of meaning and purpose. The history can be very recent and still become a dominant narrative of your upbringing. It is not always positive – in families, you can find unconscious "inherited family trauma" and "hidden loyalties," where children carry the mission of ancestors.[20] Here's a famous example.

Elvis Presley was born in rural Mississippi poverty, 35 minutes before his stillborn identical twin brother, Jesse. This tragedy brought to Elvis an infancy lavished with love and protection. Elvis was told by his mother that he was "living for two people." This sense of carrying his brother's legacy became integral to his drive, emotional state, and adult identity. He often spoke about Jesse and visited his brother's grave, bearing the weight of lifelong feelings of loneliness and guilt. Who can doubt that this contributed to Elvis's child-like precocity and the self-indulgence that contributed to his early demise?[21]

Some children come to realise that their carers have plans for them. After all, the child is a bit players in the Drama of the adults around them – a new figure in their *umwelt*, the place they call home.

Finnish Bianca's mother struggled to get pregnant, and then complications forced her premature birth with low medical expectations for her survival. Bianca lived the first half of her life in varying states of intense anxiety until later she developed personal control strategies. Bianca says, "My relationship with my mother was very bad. I never got any recognition from her for anything I did. I believe this explains my strengths and helped me learn about myself."

It was Bianca's misfortune that premature babies often grow into anxious adults,[22] but it was the Drama of the UP[2] of her daughter–mother relationship that pulled the trigger. Deliberation, her will to succeed, reworked her narrative into one of personal triumph.

Parents can embed narratives that have lasting imprint.

> Canadian Sheila's upbringing was dominated by her charismatic, volatile role model of her mother. Daily Dramas gave her a narrative of constant Deliberation, including a determination to remain childless.

The narratives children inherit can be ideological.

> Mikel had what he calls "a normal childhood" with loving, hardworking parents, but their stories of their former life in South Africa "shocked me as a kid and made me deeply concerned about racism wherever I lived."

Parents can intervene materially, creating Drama for their children, as here:

> Milton from Ghana spent his childhood in the affluence and ease of the capital Accra, but at age 10 his parents decided he needed to be schooled in the harsher realities of life and sent him to live with an uncle in a rural area. He recounts: "Suddenly I found I had to do chores about the house like never before. I had to push myself to do my homework, console myself when I felt down, set and execute academic targets, and congratulate myself when I performed well. It made me very independent-minded and tough at a very young age."

Sometimes the newborn enters a stage crowded with other players.

> Agnes from Ireland tells me: "Growing up with eight siblings, I had to fight to carve out my own space in the world. The trials and joys of my youth shaped my approach to enjoying and being playful with myself, which in turn profoundly influenced my approach to adult life."

Early loss can throw a long shadow far into the future:

> Ismail from Pakistan says, "The sudden death of my father when I was 8 was a tremendous setback in my life. He had been my hero and aspiration in life. It made me swiftly become mature and start thinking about my future as the elder one in the family. However, my

uncle took care of me and helped me to study. It taught me resilience. I discovered how to use my father's memory as an inspiration to succeed. It also gave me purpose to improve people's lives and my career choice to be in healthcare."

Family disturbance in the early years shapes UI by demanding that you develop a strategy for being yourself:

Andy from Australia concludes: "My parents' divorce had a profound impact on my childhood. I emotionally shut down and internalised my thoughts and feelings, a pattern that has continued throughout my adult life, to my detriment. To this day, my 8-year-old daughter comments, 'Daddy is too serious. Daddy, you don't smile enough.'" Ruefully, he says, "The upside is that I am unflappable under pressure."

And within the ecosystem of the family, as discussed in Chapter 4, birth order shapes strategies for living.

For Nyasha from East Central Africa, growing up as the eldest in an extended family meant constantly contending with high expectations to achieve and fulfil family responsibilities. She recalls, "If the younger ones got into trouble, it was because I should be taking care of them." She says her upbringing created a need to control situations, which nearly wrecked her marriage later, until "I figured out what I was doing and changed my ways."

Nyasha's perspective on the world was forged by the intersection of a strong personality with the cultural narratives around being an eldest in her African culture.

Sometimes children are born whose preternatural talents and temperament become the driving force for the entire family. Here's a quite contemporary example.

On Friday, June 7, 2024, 34-year-old Taylor Swift opened the UK leg of her global "Eras" tour in Edinburgh with a concert to 73,000 fervent "Swifties." She was on stage for three and a half hours, performing 46 songs with 12 costume changes – the feat of an athlete, doing it all again 43 times across Europe in just over 3 months. All her shows were delivered with the appearance of heartfelt joy and commitment to giving the best experience to her legions of fans.

Her story is one of a child who raised her parents as much as vice versa. Born in 1989, she was the first child of Scott, a financial advisor working for Merrill Lynch, and Andrea, a marketing executive whose own mother had been an opera singer. The couple were known for their generosity and wealth, with a wide network of friends and clients from their comfortable Pennsylvania home. Taylor was sent to a Montessori school, where her first-grade teacher recalls she was strikingly pretty and full of animated chatter. "She was a little sunbeam who just bounced around," initiating group hugs – "from then on she was like that." Others remembered her as dreamy but solid in confidence. 'I want to be a stockbroker,' she wrote in her yearbook at the age of 6, 'because my dad is one.' By second grade that had changed to 'Singer.'" When given a part in a school show, she rehearsed with relentless commitment. Another teacher reported: "She was the type of child you were just magnetised towards. She always had something sweet to say. Always." Her father Scott, confounded by her talent and determination, is reported to have said to a family friend, "What do I do with this child?" She helped him answer the question. He relocated the family to Nashville when she was 14, having secured her first record contract, building a studio for her in the new home, topped with daily 3-hour guitar lessons with a local teacher.[23]

The journey of UI from infancy to adolescence is individualised chaos – crowded with formative transitions of all kinds. The UI starter pack gets augmented by add-ons, plug-ins, and accessories – cognitive, emotional, relational, behavioural, and cultural narratives. It takes the toddler transition, at around age 4 to 5, for the UI to achieve a degree of cognitive relativism and the birth of the narrative Self. This is the story of individuation – newborn narratives about you as an autonomous, willed, and self-developing agent.

H.G. Wells, writer of such derring-do fantasies as *The Time Machine*, *The Invisible Man*, and *War of the Worlds*, fuelled by his prodigious aptitude for the written word, was funnelled into his profession by sickness.[24] Born the sickly fourth son of a failed businessman, he suffered a near-fatal lung haemorrhage and abscessed kidney. Constantly feeling physically inferior, he retreated to the avid consumption of books, which his father brought him from the public library. His mother wanted to apprentice him to a draper, but young Bertie threatened suicide, becoming instead an assistant schoolmaster at 14. He studied determinedly through long nights to earn a scholarship to a science school, where he was taught by T.H. Huxley, a famous evolutionist scholar known as "Darwin's bulldog" for his pugnacious promotion of the great man. Shabby, often hungry, weighing less than 100 lbs (44 kg), Welles said he didn't mind "because of the vision of life that was growing in my mind." That vision was to combine these two forces in his young life – science and fiction – giving birth to the genre that brought him fame and acclaim.

Wells dodged the bullet of parental plans. Many writers have warned about the dangers of "scripts"[25] – narratives crafted for you by parents, siblings, educators, and others who presume to tell you who you are and where you're going. As poet Philip Larkin bluntly put it, "They f*** you up, your mum and dad/They may not mean to, but they do."[26] Luckily, this is often not true. You may learn to parrot others' definitions of you and even adopt plans and themes they craft for you, but you will be you. Your UI can carry these scripts as far as you want and equally shed or repurpose them. We have seen this repeatedly in our case histories.

2. THE ADOLESCENT AWAKENING

"Youth is a dream, a form of chemical madness," wrote F. Scott Fitzgerald.[27] It sure is. At this most critical biological transition into adulthood, a hormonal–neural storm is unleashed to maximise chances of finding promising paths to being who you might become. It is a time of self-display, experimentation, risk-taking, and commitment testing. Childhood gave you the starter pack of personality, other traits, and cultural narratives. Adolescence is when you road test them – furiously. It is essential to do so, so you can select the versions of yourself that you will invest in through early adulthood.

> This happened early to Malala Yousafzai,[28] born into a region of northeastern Pakistan where the Taliban held increasing control, banning the education of girls. Inspired by the liberal values of her headteacher father and her own passion for learning, Malala began protesting this privation at the age of 11, including an anonymous blog for the BBC. Arousing the ire of the Taliban, they shot her point blank in the head on her homeward bus from school, with providence sparing her life. This attracted global attention and pitched her into the glare of fame. Using her celebrity status, she founded the Malala Fund to support girls education in developing economies. Her work earned her the accolade of becoming the youngest ever recipient of the Nobel Peace Prize at age 17.

Destiny and Drama are ascendant in childhood. In adolescence it is Drama and Determination. So it was for Malala. Her passion for education came from her character and her father's influence. It set a direction that still dominates her life. More on Malala later, since there was further dramatic turn to her life in young adulthood.

For most young people, the 4Ds perform a cyclical dance of trial and error. Determination tries out tastes, styles, ideologies, and identities – many of them experimental, provisional, and short-lived, each of them unleashing fresh Drama. It is a time when multiple narratives may be slugging it out to get adopted, getting blown apart by the Drama, much of it by our *zemblanity*[29] (bad stuff we make happen).

But hold it right there. The First Law of UI reminds us that none of this is inevitable. No two adolescents are alike – remember our identical Bulgarian twins in Chapter 2 who took such pains to individuate. Meanwhile, some teens master this passage into adulthood with remarkable smoothness and ease, aided, in some cultures and many religions, by rituals and rites of passage. These are designed to embed the UI securely in an approved template.

Yet all must live through, in their own unique ways, a hormonal maelstrom coinciding with the last stages of prefrontal cortical development. It is the time for many startling and brilliant achievements. Mozart, Rimbaud, Jeanne D'Arc, Plath, Hendrix, Gates, Zuckerberg, Tupac, and lots more besides all enacted notable projects during this period of peak passion. Some in this list tragically never made it to anywhere near midlife.

But let's look at more conventional life patterns to see what kinds of transformations can arise. Sometimes a single input during this critical period is life changing.

> John, the first-born of five children to a West African subsistence farmer, says, "I was lucky to be born first of five, living in a single room, in a village without electricity. He recounts meeting two French technicians working on an electricity project. "I was inspired by them to work hard to be the best in the science subjects and become an engineer in the future."

The Drama of adolescence is a series of "firsts."[30] Some are engineered intentionally as experiments, but others are happenstance, accidents, and diversions. In my own tumultuous youth, there was a lot more accident than intention. It took trigger events to direct me on the path toward a guiding purpose.

> At the age of 13 life changed radically when my mother separated from my father, caused by her own midlife transition – more on which later – taking me and my sister to live in an anonymous apartment in a suburban wasteland, a landscape of highways to more interesting places. I felt no emotional trauma at this event – relief rather at an end to the bad vibe in the house. Our new situation hastened my desire to grow up and get out, my brother having recently left to join the army. Leaving home and school at age 16 left me unprepared for adult

life. Losing my job set me off on my sojourn of self-discovery to India. This was a bold and largely untrodden path in those times, but I was seeking adventure less than I was seeking an escape route from my life, which had lost purpose and direction. The trip was indeed an adventure and gave me new confidence in my powers of self-determination. My reflections during my wanderings in that miraculous subcontinent began to focus on the idea of resuming my education. When I got to university 2 years later, I gloried in the freedom to study my passion, psychological science, but with absolutely no idea what I was going to do with it. That insight came unexpectedly on a rainy night when I attended a lecture by a visiting industrial psychologist, which ignited a purpose in my life that has guided me ever since. He told the story of the technological revolution in coal mining that had major negative, unintended consequences for the entire local working community. A team of social psychologists reengineered the operational structures to reduce the misfit between the social system and the technical system.[31] The idea burst into my brain that you can apply psychology not only to help individuals adapt to working environments but also to reform those environments to bring out the best in individuals. The idea has inspired me ever since.

In Chapter 5, we talked about games as cultural metaphors – teaching us to be ourselves, within the rules and with other players. Sports in adolescence are prime vehicles for learning about life for many young people. They also are source of forward momentum and purpose. The sport itself generally proves unsustainable beyond adolescence, except for the most talented.

> For one of my East Asian students, weightlifting, as it did for Schwarzenegger, helped him gain confidence in his worldview. For another, Gabriella, an Italian executive, sailing supplied a metaphor for her approach to life. "It reinforced the significance of setting ambitious goals, overcoming challenges, and never giving up."

The sport of cricket has a special significance, especially for the South Asian men in my casebook. You can see why. Played in its longest form, the 5-day international "Test" match model of contests between nations is a multi-act drama of strategy, happenstance, attack, defence, conditions (pitch and weather), and above all, character. Every player has multiple roles that wax and wane over the course of the match. They reveal and exploit the UI of each player.

> Arjun, from India's upper middle class, excelled in the game at a level that took him round the world. "It exposed me to cultures and networks outside my family school circles and

helped me develop a world view and approach to life outside the biases of my society and family. It was a gamechanger for me and profoundly shaped my personality." Arjun continued to play whilst training to become an army officer. "Then out of the blue I got a back injury that required surgery and meant I had to give up professional cricket." He reports, "Looking back I count the injury as a high point of my life. It taught me a lot, especially the ability to let go of the past and focus on the future."

The Drama of bereavement at any juncture is critical, and at this life stage, it can have transformational consequences.[32]

Janish's upbringing in rural Sri Lanka was idyllic, with middle class parents dedicated to the social welfare of the poor communities close to them. Tragedy struck in his teens when his father succumbed to a stroke, medically mismanaged. "I was devastated and got into severe depression." He found himself failing academically, while family finances declined. "Gradually, I came to realise the folly of my ways. I was undoing all the sacrifices my parents had made. Under the guidance of powerful mentors, who saw my potential, I started a turnaround." Janish went on to specialise in global healthcare, travelling through the Far East, where he launched a product that made his fortune when it was adopted by a major pharmaceutical company.

Simon, whose story we told in Chapter 4, lost a close friend and a brother in quick succession at this tender time, providing life-long themes for his sense of identity, his family life, and his career choices.

Other kinds of dramatic loss have a similar impact.

Younes, from Libya, the "happy and curious" child of highly successful parents in a prosperous middle-class family, enjoyed a childhood "filled with joy, security, and a strong sense of community." He tells me, "The happy and curious child became a troubled teen" when his parents suffered "massive financial losses," causing his father to suffer a mental breakdown and leaving his mother to become the primary breadwinner. Younes was sent to live with his grandmother, which he says was "emotionally challenging." This, he says, made him rebellious but taught him "resilience, adaptability, and perseverance."

Discovering your sexual orientation in adolescence, when it departs from prevailing local norms, can be especially challenging in some cultures.

David was bullied at his Chilean Catholic school "for showing signs of being gay," to which his UI's response was "to develop a more rebellious attitude towards the status quo." To support his mother who had lost their home to the bank and was battling with cancer, he decided to compete in a national educational competition, which he won. He recounts, "I used my acceptance speech to challenge the school's conservative approach, resulting in my expulsion and adding to my mother's challenges. It taught me the importance of prudence without compromising my rebellious spirit."

What is important in all these stories is that adaptive strategies always emerge in the face of Drama. The best of these can be thought of as projects – narratives of action, uniquely tailored by your UI to find its way through difficulty without loss of coherence.[33] Common though such massive diversions may be – parental relocations, family break-ups, unexpected failures, and social upheavals – there are many for whom the greatest upheavals come much later in life.

3. MIDLIFE CRISIS – WHAT CRISIS?

In the movie *Wild*[34] (2014), Reese Witherspoon enacts the true story of Cheryl Strayed, who undertook a 1,100-mile hike along the Pacific Crest Trail to "find herself" and heal from a string of personal losses and challenges. Early in the journey, she comes close to giving up. Finding herself ill-equipped at a difficult juncture, she seeks shelter from Frank, a farm worker. In the movie, she asks him, "You think I should quit?" Frank replies: "O, sure, but don't listen to me. I've quit a bunch of things. Jobs. Marriages. I'd have quit your hike pretty much on the first day." Cheryl asks, "Do you regret any of them?" Frank says, "I never had the choice. I just couldn't do them. Wasn't never a time when it felt there was a fork in the road."

So much for the so-called midlife crisis[35] – from Frank's point of view, it's a middle-class luxury. There are plenty of people in the world who suffer nothing like it – people who navigate the departure of youth as if they were changing from an express train to a slower, larger, more luxurious locomotive. There are also folks who tolerate lives hemmed in by demands and responsibilities, that leave no space for the indulgence of self-questioning. And yet the crisis is real enough for those people who realise they would have liked a fork in their road. They come to realise they've become separated from aspects of their UI that never had a chance to find expression.[36] Many, early in adulthood, board the optimism express of a nice-looking career track and then find themselves, years later, marooned in a landscape they dislike. They conclude, there must be something more out there – let me stop and look. That's where some act up like teenagers, to see if any of those longings might still work for you.[37]

Midlife is such a consequential transitional period because it is a spaghetti junction of lots of things happening at once. You can be confronted by

- Failing powers and health issues
- Challenges from family developments
- Financial pressures
- Career plateaus or forks in the road
- Cultural and technological developments
- Your desire for change

It is when they occur together that you can talk about a midlife crisis. Not my experience, but several of these reshaped my own UI in midlife.

These were: (1) personal loss, (2) divorce and remarriage, (3) career change, and (4) a book. First was the untimely loss of my older brother when I was in my mid-30s. This had two major effects – emotional toughening and a re-evaluation of my personal priorities. Second, remarriage and becoming a father again in later life radically reworked my strategies for living. Third, moving from a research institute to a business school profoundly altered my professional identity, skill set, and life and career goals. Fourth, reading Robert Wright's *The Moral Animal* awakened me to the new discipline of evolutionary psychology, which set in motion a comprehensive transformation of my worldview: belief system, values, and life purposes.

I could add more, but they all conform to four principles of life transitions (see Chapter 10 for more on this):

1. Transitions are cyclical and continual. You face overlapping transitions in every domain of life: biology, self, occupation, relationships, and culture.
2. Transitions have stages. You need quite different tactics when you're preparing for a transition (if you have any warning): at the challenging encounter phase, during

the following period of adjustment phase, and when equilibrium returns[38] (the Transition Cycle; see Chapter 10 and the Appendix).

3. Transitions are transformational. Their power to change you is proportional to the magnitude of the transition. The more radical the transition, the more you will have to recalibrate your priorities, values, strategies, and self-conceptions.[39]

4. Transitions have "liminality." This is zone of uncertainty between letting go of a former state and fully engaging with a new one.[40] It is often unsettling and disorienting, a time of confusion and doubt, but this unmooring is what creates the space and energy for transformation.[41]

My own story illustrated how you can hit a bundle of unrelated transitions that trigger diverse UI modifications. Fabio, from Portugal, after a period of uneventful equilibrium, hit such a bundle.

"I had to reconsider who I really am when my parents sold the family business, and I was forced to conclude that it's up to me to build my person, reputation, my own world." Then Fabio experienced failure at work "from being too cautious and trying to do everything right. It was a revelation for me to realise that failure is a way to improve yourself and to grow." Then he suffered another drama: a fall down a flight of stone stairs that smashed his jaw and teeth, causing memory loss and a long recuperation. "I realised that one day everything is going to stop, and it is important to enjoy every moment of my personal and professional life because I only have one round."

Traumas are often transition triggers, setting people on new paths – near-death experiences being some of the most awakening.[42]

Trauma can negatively rewire UI – posttraumatic stress disorder (PTSD), for example, resets emotional thresholds and weakens aspects of cognitive control. Effects are neither inevitable nor irreversible.

Malala, after her trauma, followed her passion for education through a place at Oxford to study PPE (philosophy, politics, and economics) – a demanding course of study. Trying to enjoy the social life of a normal young woman, maintain her campaigning duties with all their international travel demands, and keep up with her studies overloaded her, to the brink of failing her degree. Then, one night, experimenting with marijuana for the first time triggered an intense crisis. She entered a living nightmare of suppressed memories of

her attack, first as flashbacks, followed by panic attacks. When they persisted, her observant best friend said, "It can't just be the weed. It's something else." Malala immediately
saw the truth in this. Through therapy for PTSD and her friendships, she came to see how
for years she had been trapped by her role and public image as a model of bravery for the
world. Her breakdown that fateful night was the bursting of the dam. She felt broken and
had let others see it for the first time. This was the point when she started to reclaim her
narrative as a young woman seeking to live a normal life. Talking to *USA Today*, she says in
her memoir *Finding My Way*, "I want to introduce the real me, the funny me, the messy me,
the sad and the annoying me. All of that is me."[43]

Even in this, she is showing great strength, but people differ enormously in their
ability to cope. At one end of the scale are those blessed with what researchers call "hardiness" – ironclad resilience. At the other end are those with long and deep reactions,
and in between a range of other reactions – delayed impacts and varying recovery trajectories.[44] It's tempting to turn this suite of reactions into another typology, but the reality is that there is an infinite range of possible reactions to bad events. All of them are
concocted by your UI: your profile of traits, lived experience, constitutional condition,
and network relationships. In every life, it seems there is the punctuated equilibrium,
where you arrive at junctures demanding decision and change. You are forced to rewrite
your narrative, or parts of it.

Younes, whom we met earlier, had a devastating midlife shock when the COVID-19 pandemic claimed the lives of his mother and three uncles, "which was incredibly difficult
to bear." He, too, had a severe encounter with the virus. "It reshaped my priorities and
perspective on life. Losing my mother was particularly devastating, as she had been my
anchor and source of strength. This prompted deep introspection and a re-evaluation of
my goals and perspective on life. Through this period of grief, I discovered a renewed
sense of purpose."

Recovery is by far the most common response to trauma, no matter what form the
trauma takes.[45] My sample is selective, but I am repeatedly astonished at how people
weather the direst life events, to find some kind of triumph down the road.

Frederico from Uruguay tells the story of "my nasty breakup with a girlfriend because
of my irresponsible behaviour that left me with a very bad feeling that stayed with
me for a long time." This was compounded by an increasing feeling of burnout at

work. "So, I quit my job. This turned out to be a black hole for almost 2 years. Then one day I received a totally unexpected call from a former boss who had moved to a new firm in Colombia and was building a new team, thinking of me. I didn't think twice. This was a lifeline and proved to be life changing. But in time I became lonely and isolated and moved again to another country, Argentina, which turned out to be tough but with the upside that I met my wife. Then I had one incredible experience that completely changed my perspective. I went to a conference in the USA focused on exponential technologies and their impact. This was super inspiring. I felt I belonged, surrounded by people with futuristic, optimistic, entrepreneurial, and purpose-driven mindsets."

Happy endings can be elusive, and always the start of something new. Our biology is often the lead partner at some inflection points.

Menopause is the name given to a shift in hormonal balance that changes the path of UI. It mainly affects women and is sometimes spoken about as if it were a universal transition with predictable consequences. Anything but. For some it transits smoothly, consonant with other life changes – children leaving home, easing off at work, new relationship patterns. For others it is dramatic and challenging.

Gabby Logan[46] is a well-known UK TV sports anchor who tells the story of how, at age 47, she threatened to walk out on her husband and kids over a minor conflict. It took a while to realise what havoc the transition could wreak on her state of mind and her family. "I expected that things would change physically as you get older, but I wasn't prepared for feeling so unenthused, anxious, snappier, and short-tempered." She continues, "I had a lot to be grateful for, but that compounds it because then you're thinking, what's wrong with me?" Her anxiety was compounded by awareness of her grandmother, dying from dementia at the time. She says, "And then I remember thinking, oh gosh, is my hard drive full now, too?" After talking to friends, the penny dropped, and after blood tests and then HRT, she said, "I felt different within days. My libido came back, my skin improved, my mood balanced itself, and the looming feeling of doom disappeared."

Midlife transitions take many forms, all of them UI shaped.

Bruno from Brazil. "From the moment my daughter was born, I knew everything would change. It immediately shifted – inverted actually – my priorities and perceptions."

Transformations come in many shapes and sizes. Some are quiet and unexpected. Consider this unexpected late discovery in my own life.

> Taking up tennis in my 60s had gradual but life-changing significance – a revised view of myself as an active sports participant, for the first time in my adult life; health benefits; a very diverse range of new friends and acquaintances; and a sense of new connectedness with my local community.

Midlife has its perturbations, but it is, as my Biography cases all can testify, a time of renewal and newfound equilibrium.[47] My mother's midlife story offers a dramatic example.

> Barbara Collard, a fervent socialist from the 1930s to the 1950s, met and lived unmarried with my father, Hubert Nicholson, also a Communist, bearing three children – me being the youngest. In the hedonist, intellectual, anarchic melee that was our home, my mother experienced a midlife trigger event. Years earlier, while still a young mother, a deeply trusted male friend had shocked her with an unwanted and uninvited amorous advance. In midlife he crossed her path again. Now their roles unexpectedly reversed. She found him charming and refreshing and, in the spirit of her jaded life, told him she regretted her earlier rejection of him. Now it was his turn to be shocked – this was unexpected and unwelcome. He declared it would be contrary to his values and recently renewed faith. Shamed and confused, my mother was struck by her own reaction. She found herself struck by his moral certainty and purpose, qualities missing in her own life. This triggered a search for answers via Jungian therapy. This journey proved life changing, taking her, astonishingly, on a path that led to her conversion to Roman Catholicism and separation from my father. During this long transformation period, she wrote and published in quick succession four deeply psychological novels, admired by no less than a fellow radical Catholic writer than Graham Greene.[48] She was a lifelong feminist, camping out with other "grannies for Greenham" in protest at the US nuclear air base at Greenham Common in England, and writing eloquent, impassioned radical reformist articles for the *Catholic Herald*, the most read religious journal of her day.

My mother didn't get much past the allotted span of 3 score years and 10. Now, we live in the age where the 100-year life is heralded as a new demographic reality.[49] Beyond midlife, for those who have good genes and take care of themselves, there is a lot more road to travel.

THE END OF THE ROAD?

Who wants to live forever? It would be a mixed blessing, at best. Either you'd be an isolated oddity or one of a vast and growing horde of annoying old folk. There are better ways to achieve immortality, and now in this age of longevity, more time to think about your legacy.

If you are reading this at an age anything within shouting distance of "midlife" (approximately 32–66, according to neuroscience[50]), subtract your age from, say, 85 (average expiry date), and you will see that your adult life is only half done at most. When I talk to my midlife students about this, their thinking runs along three tracks about what they might want for their remaining time on earth. These form the logic to the Three Existential Wants:

1. To Savour – The Bucket List. What have I not experienced that I'd like to enjoy while there's still time? This thinking can cause trouble when it involves a desperate search for what has been left behind. But new tastes can come in late life and rejuvenate.

2. To Signify – Being Remembered. What difference will I have made to the world and lives of others? Men who toiled (or tricked) their way to untold riches got their names on buildings and projects as a payoff – like the Carnegies, Rockefellers, and Gateses. Not you and me, perhaps, who have the more modest gratification of seeing our genes prosper in the next generations or see the good we have done just by being a good friend or partner.

3. To Be Seen – Connection. The chief regret of the dying is that they never lived the life they could have. They allowed themselves to be trapped by working too hard, never figuring out how to be seen as they are, letting friendships wither.[51]

Regrets are important and powerful spurs to change in midlife.[52] In later life they are especially poignant and usually unproductive. Not entirely, for the need to connect can emerge as self-actualisation, a process that is possible at any life stage, as we shall see in the next chapter.

A last thought about death. It is a challenge emotionally and cognitively, not least because dying can be a painful transition. Remember the Woody Allen quote? "I don't mind dying; I just don't want to be there when it happens." Even that fear can be exaggerated. By all accounts, even for many wracked with pain, the final descent is often into a state of peaceful acceptance and even serenity.[53]

One of the repeated lessons of Biography is that although the deaths of parents, grandparents, and other loved ones leave indelible grief, despite this, it also brings new positive meanings into lives, though this can take a long time to be realised. This makes it incumbent on you, when dying, to decentre – to put yourself in the shoes of your loved ones and what your passing will mean for them. This suggests we should add a final important legacy goal:

4. Have a good death. Put Ego to one side. Think about your passing as a transition in the lives of others who love you and will miss you. Show them you go with good grace into that dying of the light. Let your death be your final and best expression of your UI.

CODA: WHAT THIS MIGHT MEAN FOR UNIQUE YOU

You are walking backwards into the future – seeing only the road behind – but you live life forwards. What can you expect?

- Don't be misled by experts who tell you about the inevitable transitions you will undergo. Models and theories might give you a big-picture view, but the 4Ds will weave their own pattern in your life.
- The play you've entered has been going a long time, and you are onstage not to play your part but to rewrite your part of the play, as much as you wish (and can).
- Use the 4Ds to think about your life in terms of its driving forces (Destiny), the degree of turbulence likely (Drama), the accumulation of experience and insights you can expect (Development), and when life-defining choices might need to be made (Deliberation).
- What narratives have dominated the journey you've been on? Distinguish those that seem core to your UI and those that are more fluid, provisional, and temporary. Look at them dispassionately and critically. Beware those that give a poor account of your shared reality with others and take you off in unproductive and unfulfilling directions.

- Think of your life as a series of personal projects, the executive arm of your narratives. They help chunk, give meaning to, and organise your responses to life's Drama.
- Be aware of and sensitive to the radical transformative forces that bear down on you and the people you care for at any time in life, but especially in childhood, adolescence, and midlife.
- Be mindful of the disturbing sensations of the liminal zone in transitions, between letting go of the old and latching on to the new. Use reflective practices. Beware prescriptive thinking. Each transition is unique, and there is no script other than the one in your hands.
- What is the goal of your existence at your time of life? The strength of the Three Existential Wants changes over time and is different for all of us. Don't leave it too late to Savour, Signify, or Be Seen.
- The manner of your dying matters, not just for you but also for those you are leaving. Help them to see that this is also a new beginning which you can welcome for them.

Eight

UNIQUENESS TRANSCENDENT
Art, Science, and Self-Actualisation

And those who were seen dancing to the music were thought to be insane by
those who could not hear the music.

(old proverb)[1]

Art is the most intense mode of individualism that the
world has known.

(Oscar Wilde)[2]

CREATIVE GIFTS FOR ALL?

It is time to climb to the pinnacle of Unique Individuality (UI) – the heights of creation, achievement, and glory that bring joy, beauty, wonder, and insight into our lives. The arts, sciences, and religion owe to three special human gifts: 1. Self-awareness; 2. The ability to wield and use symbols (language and imagery); and, most important of all, 3. The instinct to observe, learn from, and mimic each other. Through these, we have transformed the landscape into which we sprang 250 millennia ago. Unlike any other species, we are the masters of our destiny and of all life on this planet. Untold possibilities hinge on who we are. We can be a special creative force in the universe. Equally, we have the power to destroy ourselves and life itself on our beautiful unique planet.

We are powered by our two natures – our species nature and our individual nature. Our species nature is a heady mix of greedy self-interest, inventive intelligence, and collaborative altruism. Our individual nature, our UI, is a fountainhead of variety, a source of constant surprise and possibility. In between the two lies our cultural nature – the groups we form and the artefacts we make. As we saw in Chapter 5, culture both liberates and inhibits UI.

The Uniqueness Perspective raises questions for us to answer here:

- Is it given only to a few to be creators?
- Is it true that creative individuals need to have suffered for their art?

- Do creators have to be outsiders or deviants?
- Can anyone create art of value?
- What does the consumption of art do to us?
- Are the people who produce art different in some way from those who produce science?
- Is transcendental experience within reach of anyone?

Creativity belongs to all of us, though greatness only to a few. Here are the prerequisites.[3]

1. Value. Value represents what you pay attention to, where you focus your ideas and effort, the conceptions that tug your creativity in a particular direction. For many creators, it is their reason for being, a guiding vision in their life narrative. It is vision that sets apart the greatest.

    Think of Dostoyevsky's passionate absorption with the human condition; Miles Davis seeking to co-create beyond the limits of co-creators' known practice; Frida Kahlo's confronting physical pain and transmuting it into artistic self-representation; Beethoven's commitment to expressive and creative freedom.

2. Energy. Much simpler than value is the will to create but also harder to command. Many creators practise disciplines to ensure that they can generate output, even if this proves messy and inefficient.

    Writer Ernest Hemingway worked rigorously and in solitude, but always after immersion in the hubbub of society, contexts teeming with life to stimulate his process. William Faulkner was famously chaotic and scattered in how he worked and organised his materials. Stravinsky stood on his head every morning to clear his brain before working in short, intense bursts through the day. Mozart composed symphonies in his head and transcribed them through the night until the break of day.

3. Means. This encompasses your internal and external toolkit. The internal is your awareness, skill, state of mind, and body; the external is having the time, materials, and space to create.

    Kahlo had to battle with her disability; Beethoven contended with the onset of his midlife deafness; Van Gogh's poverty hampered his access to the essential materials he required to paint.

4. Opportunity. Creators need channels for production or expression. These include the availability of co-creators, an audience, and again, the most precious commodity of all, time.

For the great Regency period novelist Jane Austen, space and above all privacy were paramount requirements. The world was deprived of her genius for 10 years – her "silent decade" – when her life circumstances denied her the conditions she needed. This included a 5-year spell, when forced to follow her parents to live in a Bath town house, a far cry from the freedom of their country parsonage where she wrote her early novels.[4]

The first two – value and energy – equate to your creative motivation. The second pair – means and opportunity – are how you engage with culture. The first two typically power the last two – the creator's singular purpose drives a search for means and opportunity. For the most dedicated, this can be relentless. Look at Beethoven's frenzied creativity as the silence of deafness descended on him. The best vines grow in the toughest terroir.

There are writers who seek to explain away genius as a combination of favourable circumstances and relentless hours of practice.[5] They are right that genius is not a "trait," but we cannot depersonalise it. It is absurd to pretend the uniqueness of the creator has nothing to do with the production of great works. As Viktor Frankl, a Nazi camp survivor and philosopher wrote, "Everyone has his own specific vocation or mission in life to carry out a concrete assignment which demands fulfilment."[6] Anyone can be schooled in techniques that will allow you to create.[7] All you need is the motivation. But not everyone has the UI that can host genius. Again, we must refute the nature vs. nurture dichotomy. Genius is found where the two chime brilliantly.

Art and science are both recognition businesses. There are some notable creators for whom the third Existential Want, the need to be seen, has been a principal driver, like Salvador Dali, Oscar Wilde, and any number of YouTube warriors. But for most, their driver is the second want, to signify. The creator Ego is invested in the received value of the mark their work makes on the world, its consumers, and even on themselves. As for the first want – to savour – yes, there are peak experiences that we shall discuss shortly, but the creative process is often a painful grind. The view of many artists, such as Toni Morrison, Picasso, and the Beatles, is that they are channels for the forces of creation to flow through. Their agency is their power to encourage and shape what passes through them. The chief recognition they crave is for their actualised vision, not for themselves.

Any of us can create, but far fewer are willing or able to make the sacrifices, hone the skills, or find the vision to make a cultural mark. Most people are content in their practice of everyday creativity. It's visible in humour, problem-solving, all kinds of play, vacation adventures, and spontaneous pastimes.

PLUNDERING THE UNCONSCIOUS – "WE ARE SUCH STUFF AS DREAMS ARE MADE ON"[8]

"I woke up one morning with the tune in my head. I thought, 'I must have heard this before.' I went to the piano and started playing it, and I was very surprised that I had written it. I'd had it in my head all night long, and it just came to me as if it were a gift." It was spring 1964, and the speaker was Beatle Paul McCartney.[9] He continues, "For about a month I went round to people in the music business and asked them whether they had ever heard it before. Eventually it became like handing something in to the police. I thought if no one claimed it after a few weeks, then I could have it." It remained under its working title, *Scrambled Eggs*, for months before the title *Yesterday* popped up. A year after its miraculous conception, it appeared on the album *Help!*, instantly becoming a timeless global hit.

Your UI is full of mysteries. McCartney's story lays bare the role of the unconscious in the creative process. Our minds move without our bidding to reveal hidden capabilities, imagination, and insight. Music has special properties for UI. It is the only universal language we have. It creates mental sensations, often emotional, unique, spontaneous, and shared in real time with others. We are aural creatures, but the sense that takes up most brain space is vision. It supplies many of the metaphors embedded in everyday language – if you SEE what I mean. Visualisation is a powerful aid to the thinking of scientists and artists alike.

The theory of relativity broke into Einstein's consciousness while daydreaming about himself riding on a beam of light.

Chemist August Kekulé, struggling to decode the structure of aromatic compounds, discovered the ring-like structure of benzine after he dreamed about a snake biting its tail.

The periodic table, the invention of the sewing machine, the discovery of insulin, the circulation of blood, the novel *Frankenstein*, all emerged from the dream-like states of their authors. Even Freud's theory of dreams emerged from a dream. In everyday life, low-demand activities, like standing in the shower,[10] allow our minds to wander and stumble across insights, solutions, and fresh perspectives we have been searching for.

All these wonders did not come from nowhere – it just felt that way. UI makes us all creative beings, and day-to-day life is full of discovery, innovation, and vision. Earlier we explored the dance between culture and UI. The creative process draws energy, direction, and materials from the culture that has fed it. Then it wriggles out of its embrace by resisting, reworking, and innovating, dodging around the normative constraints that form the pillars of all cultures.

But it is UI's relationship with itself that is the magnetic motor that drives some of the most powerful expressions we ever witness. This requires us to have conversations with ourselves, often after we have had significant conversations with others.

> In her best-selling memoir *Eat, Pray, Love*, novelist Elizabeth Gilbert describes how she was able to reclaim her identity after a painful divorce and severe depression. The catalyst was long conversations with a close friend, after finding herself sobbing uncontrollably on the bathroom floor. Her friend identified this as a "bow-down" moment, a sacred invitation to surrender. It set in train a deal of self-talk – much of it in the form of journaling – and impelling her year-long journey through Italy (eat), India (pray), and Bali (love). She inspired millions of readers toward self-transformation through her tale of the restorative power of food, meditation, and unexpected romance.[11]

The assertion *the most important conversations you have are with yourself* is not a declaration of selfish individualism. Rather, it says your uniqueness requires an internal dialogue to realise its purposes. It is hard to interrogate yourself, but often necessary.

> Malala Yousafzai, who's story we told in the last chapter, had a number of critical conversations with friends and therapists following her marijuana-induced breakdown, but the most striking feature of her memoir is her self-questioning – desperate at times but unflinchingly courageous. It forced her to abandon the shelter of her status as a Latter-day Saint. The shelter was leaking unresolved pain. Letting in the light was Malala reclaiming her UI as just another exceptional ordinary human, trying to get by.

Self-talk, if done rigorously, is decoding your Beast's impulses. Asking tough questions of yourself can reach elusive regions of UI, as well as exploring the areas of your *umwelt* that you have the power to shape. The UI of creators is an odd mixture of surrender to impulses, insights, and ideas that pop up. Ego plunders the subconscious – stuff we know is there if we dig.[12] All kinds of tactics can be deployed to penetrate the unconscious where lies material that we know might surprise us if we can stir it up. For orchestral conductor Benjamin Zander, it includes surrendering to possibility, letting go of control, and treating mistakes as creative opportunities.[13]

Let us see how this happens in three domains: (1) the arts, sciences, and expressive disciplines; (2) religion, faith, and culture; and (3) the Self – the journeys we can take ourselves when seeking new ways of being.

THE CULTURAL CONNECTION – CREATIVE UI IN THE ARENA

Do you have anything that we might call a "relationship" with art? Unlike the reciprocity of UI[2] in love and friendship, something quite different but just as self-enhancing is happening when you ingest art. Someone (the artist) gives expression to their UI, creating a resonance in you, the consumer, that is equally unique and yours alone. When you share the experience with another, it awakens parallel resonances. This is how art brings us together.

Interestingly, it also separates us. Think about your taste in culture, whether popular or highbrow. It's not much different to taste of other kinds[14] – what chimes with your palate at the restaurant of life is not a constant. You like it, or not, because of a bunch of factors that are unique to you: your instinctive resonances, your personal style and preferences, your past exposure, and how you're feeling in the moment:

You stand in front of a work of creation, and you feel a connection, or not. Artists, images, and ideas become markers in the landscape of your *umwelt*. Once something grabs, you have a special kind of ownership of it – like the decorations of your living space. It makes you a co-creator. *Don't ask what Art has moved you; ask what You the art has moved.* Earlier we identified four elements as preconditions for the creator – value, energy, means, and opportunity. These have counterparts in you, the consumer[15]:

1. Resonance – responses of affinity, interest, and relevance that it awakens in you
2. Passion – emotions it arouses in you, such as love, joy, sorrow, empathy, and even anger (political art especially does this)

3. Transportation – it takes you to new imagined worlds, that resonate with our *umwelt.* You feel almost physically moved but connected.

4. Communion – it facilitates the sharing of your responses with others. This can be intimate sharing, or co-consuming with a large crowd, like at a music festival, what we've called parallel processing.

Creativity figures in many similar ways in everyday life. You are being a creator when you retell a story, with embellishments, over a dinner table. You are a scientists when you use experience to extract principles for living. The people we designate artists and scientists are taking these commonplaces to a new higher level. Using their skills, imaginative conceptions, and passion, they reach out and find deep fulfilment by making their mark on the world. Humour is a creative process that makes artists of us all, but which some take to sublime levels.

Charles Chaplin was born in East London late in the 19th century under conditions of extreme poverty. Both parents were stage entertainers, his father a drunk and a sparse presence in his life, his mother mentally ill. After his father died, his mother was institutionalised, leaving Chaplin and his half-brother drifting between the streets, orphanages, and the workhouse, later odd-jobbing and stage performing in musical halls, then the principal form of public popular entertainment. He discovered his instinct for humour, against the odds of this bleak situation, when he cheekily induced laughter by refusing to sing until the crowd threw coins. He was soon talent-spotted into the newborn silent movie industry. His repute grew, bringing him the resources to create as well as perform. His greatest invention was the Little Tramp, his alter ego, whose fearless, foolish, inventive optimism overcame the world stacked against him, the alter ego of the poor and dispossessed. Chaplin was plundering and redeeming his harsh past. Charlie Chaplin's movies today have lost little of their sublime ironic joy in parodying the brutality, venality, and suffering of the urban poor.

He was in a long tradition of art and entertainment powering social reform.

In the compelling narratives of his novels, Charles Dickens plundered his turbulent career – lurching in and out of poverty, working successively as a child labourer in a blacking factory, legal clerk, parliamentary and court reporter, editor, actor, and social investigator. He plundered these worlds to expose the deprivations and pretentions of all classes of English society. Within them, he created worlds, imaginatively rich and satirical variants on his own, with such force that it awakened British society to its hypocrisies and injustices, accelerating the pace of social reform. He was a UI true believer. Like Shakespeare, he created a vast array of unique characters for our delight, amusement, and edification.

Some of the most notable creators in history have emerged from supportive contexts, where families and educators have fed their precocious talents. One such was Pablo Picasso.

> The son of a drawing teacher, Picasso was an innovator of great precocity, who, over his lifetime, generated a vast number of creative outputs at a furious pace. In doing so, he embodied key principles of how UI generates works of art. (1) He was a relentless and fearless explorer of the unconscious. (2) His UI hosted outstanding gifts and a turbocharged drive to produce. (3) He openly plundered the creative products of other cultures – especially African artefacts. (4) His oeuvre formed a sequence of transitions between genres, driven by restless consuming relationships with a series of female muses.[16]

Punctuated equilibrium is an idea that has recurred throughout this book — the patchy but pronounced rhythm of life where periods of consolidation are disrupted by sharp disturbance. As we have said, the more radical the transition, the more profoundly it reconfigures priorities and your direction of travel. Here's the case of a contemporary of Picasso, who arrived at self-realisation by a tortuous and morally challenging route.

> Paul Gauguin[17] was drawn into painting when Impressionism, then a revolutionary genre, was at its peak. Into this world this rebellious, charismatic man brought a highly original way of seeing, a pinnacle reached by a complex and dramatic route. Gauguin's mother was the daughter of a pioneering Peruvian socialist writer and his father a dissenting journalist. In 1849 the family sought refuge from the turbulence of French society for a new life in Peru, but the father died en route. This left the 3-year-old Paul unsettled in paradise, until the age of 7, when his mother returned to France, plunging him into the icy waters of a Roman Catholic seminary. By now Paul was a pugnacious, rebellious boy, getting bullied and fighting back. Misfitting at school, he agreed to his mother enrolling him into the merchant marine, transporting prisoners of war from the Franco–Prussian conflict. He jumped ship in distaste for what he was doing, making his way back to France to find a destroyed home and his mother deceased. Through a friend of his late mother, he found his way into stock market trading, where he achieved remarkable wealth and success whilst living in the artisan quarter, spending all his money collecting Impressionist art.

He soon married, fathering five children, taking up painting in his spare time. Wiped out by a market crash in his mid-30s, he was able to survive for a few years on the proceeds from the sale of his art collection, until penniless, when he decamped to the cheapest, poorest region in France, Brittany. In its rugged beauty he found his voice as a dramatic colourist. Restless, he tramped to South America and the Caribbean, tugged by memories of his subtropical childhood. The paintings this trip yielded entranced his close friend Vincent Van Gogh. The lure of the New World, now doubly planted in his *umwelt*, led him to Polynesia, where he was outraged by the destructive impact of French colonialism, earning him the enmity of the French authorities and the love of the local people. Formally representing them, he fought for their right to freedom from the French Catholic education and indoctrination. Gauguin has been widely reviled for polygamous partnerships with barely postpubertal girls and for spreading syphilis. The latter turns out to be doubtful and the former contestably a product of his immersion in local cultural norms. However we might judge him morally, he had found a home for his restless and rebellious spirit, as well as a source of inspiration for the great post-Impressionistic works that are now coveted by the world's top galleries.

This story illustrates that even the most troubled souls can find a peaceful relationship with themselves and the world, unlike his poor tortured friend, Van Gogh, whose struggles with mental illness found brilliant expression in his art but no place of peace in the world.

Let me be clear, we cannot reduce creative production to the identity of the creator. That would be what we might call biographical reductionism. What we are saying is that our UI has many sides, which for some are more harmoniously integrated than for others whose personalities are fractious assemblies of contradictions. We all show different "sides" to ourselves in different roles, what Jung called "personas." We saw in the last chapter that it is easier for some people to be "authentic" than it is for others. We could say the same about being "integrated." Some creative spirits face a daily struggle to reconcile their art with other aspects of their lives, like poor Van Gogh. For others it is seamlessly connected with other routines and roles, as Paul Gaugin achieved by removing himself entirely to a new world.

UI MOVING THE BOUNDARIES OF INNER AND OUTER WORLDS

You don't have to be neurotic to be a great artist. Some talents blaze into being unbidden and largely self-schooled, and the greatest seem to have unbounded *umwelt*s. The cognitive boundaries that most of us find natural and convenient are swept away by the force of their vision and drive. Here are two prime examples – both polymaths blurring the boundaries between arts and sciences.

Leonardo da Vinci was the illegitimate son of a wealthy notary and a peasant mother, a status that freed him from conventional expectations but which denied him any formal education. Thus, he was largely self-taught through childhood observation and curiosity about the environment that surrounded him. He taught himself Latin, geometry, anatomy, and engineering and learned his craft as an artist through apprenticeship at 15 to a Florentine master sculptor, painter, and goldsmith. He was "marvellously endowed with beauty, grace and talent in abundance."[18] He was also well-liked for his generous good nature, reserved but gracious and kind. His intellect knew no boundaries. He was "interested in every aspect of the visible world" and "studied weather and waves, animals and vegetation, machines of all kinds, invented and imaginary."[19] As a painter he remains peerless, and his inventions of weaponry and architecture, plus his explorations of anatomy and physics, were far in advance of his times or any intellectual predecessors.

So far, we have talked mainly about artists, but da Vinci embodies the idea that science and the arts draw upon the same principles that make UI a generative force, but here the discipline of the practitioner's craft calls on a different set of narratives, around truth, logic, evidential learning, and ruthless questioning. This can easily become prosaic in the hands of jobbing researchers. Not so with Einstein, who exhibited an artist's attraction to transgressing boundaries.

We last met Albert Einstein dream-riding on a beam of light. Raised in a middle-class German-Jewish household, dad an engineer, his mother a talented amateur musician, he was initially unpromising at school, and later, AS an unruly teen, rebelled against its authoritarian ethos. His mind was instinctively boundary-spanning. A talented violinist himself, his love of music opened for him new ways of seeing and an aid to creative thinking. He championed the role of imagination, vision, and aesthetics in scientific innovation. "The most beautiful thing we can experience is the mysterious. It is the source of all true art and science." His dislike of authority made it difficult for him to find an academic position. Through a friend, he secured a post as a technical assistant in the Berne patent office. There he found the space he needed to think and where he nurtured his revolutionary contributions to physics. Art and science were intertwined for Einstein in the concept of a harmonious universe. He disavowed the celebrity success brought him, modestly claiming, "I have no special talent. I am only passionately curious." In later life he brought his liberal passion to bear on the causes of racial equality, nuclear disarmament, and intellectual freedom.[20]

Of the Three Existential Wants, to be seen was by far the least important to Einstein. Savouring experience was much more important, bound up in the rapture of curiosity and vision. "He who can no longer pause to wonder and stand rapt in awe is as good as dead; his eyes are closed."[21] As for signifying, he advised, "Try not to become a man of success, but rather try to become a man of value," and as for connection, "Only a life lived for others is a life worthwhile."[22]

Many scientists would share these principles. Here are two who might agree, who in very different ways gave birth to another transformative way of seeing – the Theory of Evolution.

Charles Darwin narrowly escaped the destiny of becoming a clergyman. Studying theology at Cambridge at the command of his father let his attention migrate to his passion for natural history. An assiduous collector since childhood, he quit the comforts of his social class to endure the privations of travel to far-flung places, including chronic seasickness, cataloguing his finds in painstaking detail. Over many years he compiled exhaustive records of such unromantic creatures as earthworms and beetles. His chief talent was the art of noticing, and it was the minutiae of variations over diverse locations that led him to the Theory of Evolution by Natural Selection. In character, cautious and thoughtful, he was also a hypochondriac, which helpfully earned him a cosseted lifestyle, punctuated by long cogitating walks. Fearing the uproar his revolutionary theory would unleash in conservative Victorian England, he delayed publication of the big idea until he was threatened with being outflanked by another amateur naturalist, a man of very different character, Alfred Wallace.[23]

Wallace, from a lower social stratum than Darwin, had left school at 14 and self-educated in natural history, becoming an adventurer, exploring wild locations of the Far East. He was in a jungle fever when the flashing insight of evolution by natural selection cohered in his mind as a solution to the puzzling regional variations he had observed in his travels. He generously deferred to Darwin, as the scholar he had long looked up to, and though the paper outlining the theory was presented in both their names, it was Darwin who drew the public acclaim and fame.[24]

In their different ways, following very different paths woven by the 4Ds, Darwin and Wallace were driven by a convergent passion for solving the puzzles of the natural world. Both men, also, in their different ways were visionaries, stimulating their minds to embrace unseen worlds.

These stories show how the products of individual insight and imagination change the way the rest of us see the world, forever. Cultures and societies know this and foster the ascendancy of the formation of elites in all walks of life that embody their light and dark sides. Exceptional talents are valued for the richness they bring arts, crafts, performances of all kinds. It hasn't always been so.

> On a field trip, talking to a Maasai warrior chief[25] (a role designation for the spokesperson and representative of the postpubescent male age set), I asked how they dealt with people with special talents. His reply was simple – "We don't want people with special talents." Looking more closely, it was plain that he was chosen for his role not for any particular prowess but rather what we now call "emotional intelligence" – a mix of insight about other people and diplomatic skills. These are indispensable to bridging potential divides between people, especially across the sharply defined strata dividing "warriors" from "elders."

This captures the dialectic between culture and UI. Here, talent is not suppressed so much as devalued. They express their UI in how proudly they decorate their bodies. This is aesthetic self-definition with no obvious social consequences, except in the mating game, which is regulated and ritualised. They are displaying character, not performance. In this intensively collectivist culture, it is frowned upon to put yourself ahead of anyone else, a cultural norm of many preliterate societies.[26] How different from the fake egalitarianism of Soviet Stalinism, where inferior "people's art" was overvalued, while expressions of real creative freedom were ruthlessly suppressed as subversive. This stifled and disguised the outputs of such brilliant creators as composer Dmitri Shostakovich, writer Boris Pasternak, and sculptor Ernst Neizvestny, to name but three. Under Stalin, Mao, and Castro, "individualism" was punished as "bourgeois egoism" and "antisocial." The failure of communism was its inability to accept the UI of its people.

Should we view capitalism as courting the opposite danger – giving UI too much unfettered access to power and resources in the AI age? We shall return to this idea in Chapter 11. In any event, elites seem to be inevitable in all walks of life and kinds of society. The values that put them there determine whether they speed up or dampen the pace of cultural evolution, as we saw in Chapter 5.

UI FINDING TRANSCENDENCE

"I must be so penetrated, so impregnated by my subject, that I can draw it with my eyes closed. . . . It pours naturally from me, and then the sign itself is noble." "My work consists in absorbing things in. And after, they come back out." "After a certain moment, it is no longer me, but a revelation: all I have to do is give myself up to it."

These are the words of Henri Matisse, the great post-Impressionist who channelled the radiant colours of the world into his paintings and cutouts. Matisse's words, voiced when he was late in his long life, are displayed on a plaque in the gorgeous chapel whose design and stain glass windows were his last spiritual gift to the world.[27]

In the performative arts, especially music, the transcendent is often integral.

J.S. Bach: "I play the notes as they are written, but it is God who makes the music."
Carlos Santana: "I just close my eyes and let it flow. The music plays me, not the other way around."[28]
Miles Davis: "It takes a long time to learn how to play like yourself."

As an extremely limited jazz improviser myself, I have found fleeting moments of "flow,"[29] where the musical ideas seem to come into being by themselves, bypassing my brain and streaming directly through my fingers into the instrument. This triggers the virtuous cycle, where you find yourself responding to what you've just produced. I can hear my own voice in the music and am fully aware that it is the unique product of my UI. Ego's awareness is part of the flow Beast is navigating, much as a bird adjusts its wings to a turbulent air flow that it can seek, find, or avoid but never control. This is what Miles is saying – almost a paraphrase of the Zen–Taoist outlook – you find yourself only when you let go of yourself. Varieties of shamanic and evangelical fervour induce similar states.

Flow – times when you lose yourself in the stream of action – is part of a suite of what Abraham Maslow, the father of humanistic psychology, called "peak experiences." These are manifestations of self-actualisation, defined by Maslow as being our highest calling. It supervenes over all the lower-order needs that we must respond to: Physiological, Safety, Love, and Ego. "Self-actualization is the full use and exploitation of talents, capacities, potentialities."[30] He describes a blissful coming together of autonomy, creativity, self-awareness, self-transcendence, realism, inner harmony, and peak experiences. Maslow shifts his position around UI. His early writings depict self-actualising individuals as "different" – a view that could be construed as elitist, though on this point we can agree. It is only given to a few to bask in the exalted state he conjures. In his later writings, he shifts to a much more general story about us all having "growth needs."

Both can be true. Yes, we are all different, and some people have a lot more potential to achieve than others. Yes, everyone can self-actualise, if this means that everyone can find the best ways to be themselves. This is how we shall use the term hereafter. Sadly, this seems beyond the reach of many who lack the strategy, tools, and supports. Maslow is best known for his "hierarchy of needs." It falls foul of many of the same objections we have voiced about other taxonomies – overgeneralised, simplistic, culturally and gender biased, and not supported by evidence. Perhaps in the present context we can recast his ideas as contrasting Essential Wants (species-general Beast needs) with individualised Existential Wants (to Savour, Signify, and be Seen). In our Uniqueness Perspective they coexist in our own unique configuration.

In his later writings, he was much more focused on his growth-oriented view of human nature and especially his fascination with peak experiences.[31] They involve a mystical dissolving of the membrane between self and the universe, accompanied by feelings of awe and wonder – not unlike states induced by psychedelic drugs. Again, not everyone's cup of ambrosia. More available to all are such commonplace joys as holding a newborn, smelling woodland air, or being transported by music.

So, we come back to the point that it is given to just a few to rise to creative greatness. As Maslow himself put it, "A musician must make music, an artist must paint, a poet must write, if he is to be ultimately at peace with himself"[32] – but the ability to be playful and creative is universal. Children in play find creativity spontaneously and readily, all the time! We adults also do so – not only in Ego's constant mode of improvisation but also in our choice of recreational pursuits and social conviviality.

At the start of this book, I recounted my childhood awakening to the terrifying realisation of the finality of death. I couldn't conceive it at the time, but it is now clear to me that what provoked this idea was its very opposite – the wonder of existence. My fear of oblivion came from my overwhelming sense of the awe and glory of being. Life flows through us and around us. We Beast-beings are part of something much bigger than ourselves – a natural world of mystery, harmony, and beauty; the universe that Einstein saw. And then there is the inner landscape – the usually unseen world within our Beast-being's depths that we glimpse, sometimes unexpectedly, sometimes by intent. The arts conjure the unexpected in both the artist and the consumer.

READINESS IS ALL – VISIONS FOR UI

The doors of perception can be flung open comprehensively by just about anything, if we are in a state of readiness. Psychedelic drugs, mental disorders, sleep deprivation, ascetic practices, and collective rituals such as chanting and fever can induce them, if our UI permits.[33] Louis Pasteur said, "Chance favours the prepared mind." Look at Wallace, in the liminal zone where jungle fever was slackening its grip on his mind, freeing it to grasp the blinding insight of evolution by natural selection. McCartney, Einstein, and Wallace's creative solutions didn't come from nowhere. Their minds were stuffed with deep knowledge, practice, and memory, crafted by selves that were already on the cusp of discovery by being aware, receptive, and intelligent. The first two Laws of UI – the fact of your uniqueness and the unknowability of your mind – means that you don't have to be mad to have visions. We do it in dreams every night once the Self is put to bed and the Beast can play in its back garden.[34] We need to own our visions. They seem to come from outside, but they spring from the subliminal depths of our UI.

Divya was raised in relative middle-class comfort by Indian parents, whose dynamic was dominated by a caste disparity between her parents. It was a love match, and the gulf was not huge. Both were in the mainstream of Indian life. Her father, a happy-go-lucky soul, was unperturbed, but it was a source of increasing shame to her mother, for whom the difference seems to have been a surrogate for her deeper personal anxieties and discontents. Either way, Divya grew up in a tense, unhappy household. Then, on the verge of her teens, she got the chance to go on a long, intensive trek in the wilderness of India's mountainous northern regions. It awakened her soul to the thrill of adventure. She was hooked and on return joined a cadet corps, where her yearnings found a location: the sea. It became instantly her life motif – a place without limits, where she felt at home yet away in another sphere of existence. She had to fight hard to achieve her dream – overcoming the misogyny of the marine industry culture; most naval colleges were exclusively male. Through extreme perseverance, she secured admission to one to study marine engineering. She revelled in the onboard community of the ship, despite its masculinity. She loved its clarity and simplicity, rejoicing in its coherent entity amid the vastness of the sea's beauty and majesty. She says: "On board I become another me. It takes me away from the brutal mess of the world, ruled by desires and greed. It's a simpler world, and I love it."

Mark Leary in his insightful book *The Curse of the Self*[35] notes that all religions offer the balm of escape from the self. We live with that pesky imp, Ego, forever squatting on our shoulders, driving us this way and that in its often-frustrating search for goals, success, and happiness. Leary is right, but we don't have to frame it negatively. Divya is doing more than escaping harsh realities – she is finding a space that unfetters her spirit, to self-actualise. It is resonance again, the way that Beast often nudges Ego. Being open to the resonance of place allows you to find the balm of distraction from yourself, through immersion in contexts that bring you joy and healing. Leary interestingly notes that what he calls "hypo-egoic states" – self-transcendence – are easier to attain if one has a strong sense of self to start with.[36] We have come back to Maslow's early "elitist" conception of self-actualisers, or the idea of the "autotelic personality" – intrinsically motivated people who find "flow" comes easily to them.[37] You don't have to be sick, crazy, or stoned to find the transcendent in life. Viktor Frankl says:

> The more one forgets himself – by giving himself to a cause to serve or another person to love – the more human he is and the more he actualizes himself.

The transcendent is a tangible gift of our evolved essence, if we will just stop and smell the roses.

THE CREATIVE LIFE – CONFLICT, CONSISTENCY, AND GLORY

What is the relationship between the UI of the artist and what they create? It can look deeply disturbing. In her book *Monsters: What Do We Do With Great Art By Bad People?*, Claire Dederer[38] offers a powerful and personal meditation on her struggles to reconcile her love for their works with people whose UI she finds deeply repugnant. Artists "self-actualising" can turn out to be unpalatable and sometimes monstrous in their self-indulgence. Picasso used successive women as muses and lovers before discarding them; Gauguin was parasitic upon Samoan culture; Chaplin infantilised the females in his life. These, plus numerous figures, illuminated by the *MeToo* movement – Roman Polanski, Woody Allen, Bill Cosby, and too many others to mention, all have one thing in common – unchecked masculinity.

When her attention turns to women, Dederer sees their cardinal sin to be that they abandoned their children. Such conflicted and difficult souls as Doris Lessing, Sylvia Plath, and Joni Mitchell felt they had to make this brutal trade-off of family for art. Our Uniqueness Perspective entails no moral judgement on the matter, but it's worth pointing out that had Shakespeare not abandoned his family for much of their lives, we would have missed the incomparable bounty of his creations. He became UI's greatest literary exponent. As with Dickens, the teeming parade of fully formed identities in his plays fed off his own lived experience of deprivation, joy, and discovery.

We will have more to say at the end of this book about ethics and UI (see Chapter 12), but my use of the notion of "trade-offs" brings us right into it. As we have said, authenticity is easier for some folk than others (see Chapter 6). The same is true of moral integrity. It is hard for some people to reconcile their UI with living in a shared world, bound by cultural norms, manners, and social contracts. You could say it is the essence of the arts and sciences to be revolutionary – to push back against assumptions about the world and social reality. Infatuation with your ability to do this can bring the risk of self-licencing.

> The Bloomsbury Group of the early 20th century – a motley London-based collection of writers and artists – believed their art embodied their experience, and therefore their actions should be unfettered by norms, political or sexual. As one leading light of the group shamelessly put it, "There is no such thing as a universal morality. Each individual must make their own path, free from the dictations of society's pretended rules."[39]

We need to reaffirm that the Uniqueness Perspective is not a philosophy of selfish individualism or equivocal moral relativism. It does take us, however, to the fundamental crossroads between self-actualisation and culture. "Being oneself" is never a free pass so long as it impacts others. Some personal narratives have a propulsive power that needs to be managed and sometimes forcibly restrained. The metaphor in Homer's *The Odyssey* is apposite: where the hero orders his crew to stuff their ears with wax and tie him to the mast so all can do their work and resist the song of the Sirens that would lure them to destruction on the rocks. But resist we must, or at least negotiate, when inner voices violate what is valued by others. Many artists have diverted or restrained their self-actualisation for the good of themselves and others.

- Cary Grant retired from movie acting to focus on raising his daughter, despite Hollywood's strenuous attempt to lure him back.

- Painter Edvard Munch suffered for his art, pursued by alcoholism and depression. "Without anxiety and illness, I am a ship without a rudder," he said.[40] Subsequently, he checked himself into a clinic, recovered from his exhaustion and anxiety, and distanced himself from the subculture that lauded him, still painting but withdrawing from the public eye.
- George Harrison of the Beatles also became reclusive after the dissolution of the group, creating a few collaborations but mainly committing himself to a life of spiritual contemplation.
- J.D. Salinger published his first novel, *The Catcher in the Rye*, in 1951 to global acclaim, a book that arguably changed American culture, and beyond, forever with its fresh recognition of what it means to be young in contemporary society. A deeply private person, he disappeared from view, with only one significant novel 10 years later, living a life of spiritual reclusion.

These people concluded it was not possible to find a happy union between their art and public lives. Some have confronted the challenge head-on and made themselves and their life experiences the art form, as did Freda Kahlo, David Bowie, and Oscar Wilde.

SELF-ACTUALISATION – UI SHINING

Let us come back to Maslow's conception of self-actualisation. What is striking is the passion with which he portrays the creative process in the growth of UI. Elsewhere, it has been called a process of creative destruction[41] – the idea that to move to a higher level of functioning, you have to leave behind things that you have valued up to then – like moving between nursery rhymes and poetry. You don't have to suffer like Sylvia Plath. She was prevented from finding any upward ladder of liberation by her tortured self-process, her "demons" in common speech, plus the challenges of her times and dysfunctional relationships. Unhappy imperatives of Destiny and Drama can stand in the way of redemption from Deliberation and Development.

It doesn't have to be this way. Moving with this theme of positive destruction, it seems that some of the most powerful Development comes from self-talk mobilising transitions, usually following the trigger of some Drama. People can suddenly abandon narratives that have served them well for years, including the valued identities and the strategies that went with them. This is perhaps the most radical form of self-actualisation, changing life direction for the good of the person and the benefit of their communities.

Here's an outstanding example from my executive casebook.

Tim is a big American – a physically imposing 54-year-old ex-Marine – but with an open gaze and a warm aura. He tells a tumultuous story of self-discovery over a long, hard road. This started in the Midwest, where his equally tough dad worked at the most brutal end of the construction industry, where ex-cons made up a significant portion of the workforce. His father epitomised masculine values and demeanour, but he was nonetheless openly affectionate towards Tim. His mother, a cooler character, worked as a secretary, putting Tim and his sister out for daycare while the parents kept the family afloat financially. They had no idea to what fate they had handed their kids, for the childcare principal turned out to run a regime of extreme discipline and punitive control. To this day, Tim says he doesn't drink enough water because toilet breaks were not allowed. Worse happened. Both children, Tim at the age of 5 along with his elder sister, were sexually abused, plus routinely handed out physical violence for the slightest infractions. Tim's parents were loving but inattentive. "I began to believe I could make decisions as well or better than my parents could." He says, "I felt like I was on an island, surrounded by a cold, shallow sea that I was unwilling to dive into. I was always looking at the horizon for something else. While my friends and family appeared to be content with certainty, predictability, and insularity, I was always left with the feeling of wanting more."

Meanwhile his spirit was being crushed by the constant punishments. "Whenever I felt like I might make a mistake, I have tended to freeze and shrink, to make myself as small and unnoticed as possible." He recalls a family event when his mother talked him out of a career in healthcare, "She felt it would be beyond my capabilities." The legacy, he says, has been a tendency to "self-sabotage . . . not fully committing or taking action for fear of making a mistake." Tim left school for a small local college, which he quickly realised was not going to feed his intellect and restless spirit, and moved to a larger college. This, he found, also "didn't resonate with the life I knew I had inside me. I felt lost. I knew I needed to make a big change to make myself tougher."

Tim has scarcely allowed himself to Deliberate, at least not positively, until this point. But our most considered choices do not always move in the right direction.

Tim took the toughest route he could envisage. He signed up for 5 years with the US Marines. This triggered a breakup with his girlfriend since teenage and brought him only physical, not mental, toughness. "I hated it," he says. But, as one of the brightest, he was assigned to air traffic control, where he formed a deep friendship with Mike, another clever working-class boy assigned to ATC, who became his confidant, support, and best friend throughout his service years and beyond. After discharge, Tim resumed his studies at a city university, married his girlfriend, and embarked on a career in construction management, finding a niche for his gifts in the area of marketing. This included a construction start-up that boomed and then bust in the market crash of 2008. Tim persisted and bounced back to success and recognition, securing a prestigious position in corporate marketing for a Swiss business. Sadly, behind the scenes, things were not going smoothly. His marriage partner proved to profoundly test his character, finding her incompatible in tastes and emotionally non-nurturing. She demanded that they relocate to the place he least wanted to be, his hometown. He reflects: "I learned how important place is to me." Meanwhile, the feeling of being unfulfilled in his profession persisted: "I felt an important part of me was not being used."

Now his Deliberation takes him to a much better Developmental pathway.

His personality profile tells a story that helps to see how his course was forged. In his emotions, it reveals him to be healthily responsive, not overly dominated by feeling, nor armour-plated against them. Socially dominant, he sits comfortably in the middle zone between sociability and reclusiveness. Serious and not excitement-seeking, his dominant drives are creative exploration, tolerance of uncertainty, and nurturance – a desire to do good for others. He is self-disciplined, but otherwise low in need for control: a free spirit who had been repeatedly shackled by circumstance. With three children coming into adulthood and having to deal with the untimely death of his one true friend, Mike, Tim came to the conclusion that he had to break out, to end the marriage and move to a place where he could find and be himself. This is what brought him on to our programme, where therapy plus the process of Biography (described in Chapter 10) brought him to a transformed perspective on himself and the world. His tears flowed, also his fellow students', as he shared with them the story of his epiphany. Since then, he has found a new direction, to build a business around the challenge of helping men to connect and support each other, especially those in those "tough" occupations where suicide rates are highest – men at risk of self-destruction through their inability to articulate and share with others.

Describing people as having been "damaged" is a bad metaphor, used too widely and carelessly. You are not an object that can be degraded and deformed by what happens to you. You are an organism, growing and adapting through time. Mistreatment and deprivation in the formative years can redirect growth, leave scar tissue, and stunt potentialities. Yet, as we have seen, trauma often prompts movement into redemptive new directions. Look at what happened to Malala. The biographies of Charlie Chaplin, Oprah Winfrey, and Louis Armstrong all tell this story. "Everyone gets scars on their way to the stars."[42]

Tim's narrative shows how painful it can be to adapt to trauma and abuse and how creative energy can convert it into the path of self-actualisation. In the last chapter, we described Karen Horney's model of how the Self's stunted development can get Ego to propagate lifelong narratives of anger, neediness, and detachment. This is not inevitable. Tim became none of those. Strong, positive personalities have "hardiness."[43] It cost Tim a lot in diverted energy and projects that missed the mark of his UI, but eventually he found his way. It was his Destiny to be a resourceful and seeking spirit, enabling to weather the Drama of abuse and bad narratives. For Tim, this provided the impetus to Deliberate and engineer his own Development in fulfilling directions.

These redemptive narratives come about through two preconditions. The first is the happy conjunction in the person's UI of resilience, openness, positivity, and other orientations that open alternative windows on the world. Second, context matters. New places can open one's eyes. Enlightened institutions can reveal new pathways. New relationships can be redemptive. Many a person has been "saved" by a teacher, friend, or relative, who has seen, recognised, and helped them to express their UI.

In the next chapter, we turn to those contexts and the question of what UI-friendly organisation might look like.

CODA: WHAT THIS MIGHT MEAN FOR UNIQUE YOU

If the Uniqueness Perspective had a credo, its first article would be everyone has the right to self-actualise, so long as you do not harm or damage the interests of others. What's more, self-actualising doesn't have to be "selfish." It can be life-enhancing for others, nowhere more so than in the arts and sciences. At the start of this chapter, we asked a series of questions about what this means. Let us summarise by revisiting them:

- Creativity belongs to all of us. You are already creative from the moment you awake each day, in the improvisation of everyday living as well as in most of your domestic, occupational, and leisure pursuits. To take it further is a matter of choice and will.

- You don't have to suffer for your art, but being on the threshold of the new can entail risks of rejection and isolation, more for some individuals than others. Art always has the capacity to surprise the artist because it reaches beyond the boundaries of conscious processing. This may bring you discomfort, or worse.

- You can quietly bring visions into reality from the most conventional of contexts, but art and science both break boundaries, and your orientation to either could place you on the outside looking in.

- You may be someone who needs isolation and separation to find your creative spark. Everyone needs to find the spaces that enable them to do their best work.

- Art enhances you in ways that are unique to you. There is nothing wrong if what resonates with others leaves you cold.

- To succeed in the arts and sciences, you need problem-solving, vision, persistence, open-mindedness. "Scientists uncover what is already there, but artists create new forms."[44] The mindsets are differently configured, but they use many of the same mental processes.

- Transcendent experience is open to all, but you may find it easier or harder than others. It doesn't have to be dramatic and otherworldly. It can be found in the everyday.

- Contexts matter. To be creative or find transcendence, you need to be in the right place at the right time, as we shall see in the next chapter.

- Self-actualisation is not a universal process but is person specific. You must find your own meaning for what it entails and seek the support and situations that will empower you.

Nine

ORGANISING FOR INDIVIDUALITY
UI at Home in the World

The place in which I fit will not exist until I make it.
(James Baldwin)[1]

There should be experiments in living; that free scope should be given
to varieties of character, short of injury to others; and that the worth of
different modes of life should be proved practically.
(John Stuart Mill)[2]

FINDING FIT WITH THE WORLD OF WORK

Tim, whom we met in the last chapter, came to realise after a long and tortuous journey how much place really mattered to him. He is not alone. Remember Simon? His *umwelt* became horribly transformed when he was torn out of his childhood Thai paradise, a trauma that provided for themes in his adult life around constructing with partial success contexts and relationships that kindle and cultivate the best of being.

We all need to know where we can be our "best selves."[3] But our favourite retreat may not be accessible. Instead, we have to go to work. One of the great revelations of the COVID-19 lockdowns was that the boundaries of our local worlds, our *umwelt*, are not as fixed as we thought they were. Many found themselves trapped in solitude and incapacity. But for others it was a revelation to explore the uncharted richness of the local, not least the people they live with. Equally remarkable was our *umwelt*'s ability to dissolve the boundaries between areas we had grown used to seeing as in their own worlds – education, work, and leisure.

Unique Individuality (UI) emerged as a key theme of life in the pandemic. It became evident that WFH (working from home) suited some people, organisations, and domestic situations much better than others.[4] In all industrialised economies, it became the norm, persisting today, for people to WFH two or three days a week.[5] I'm a huge fan of flexibility. One of the most obvious implications of UI is that preferences for different schedules should be a central consideration for designing any workplace to maximise people's well-being and effectiveness. But equally, WFM can be oppressive for some people.

> Emma works as a middle-ranking expert in the cybersecurity team of one of the UK's larg-
> est retail banks. She is 32 and lives alone in a cramped inner-city apartment. Her team is
> virtual and scattered across the UK. "Although at the office I work independently, I am
> surrounded by friends from other departments. Working from home is difficult. It means I
> might not speak to a living soul all day. I'd love to go in 5 days a week, but on some Mondays
> and Fridays, I might as well stay at home, since hardly anyone will be in the office."

Emma's story shows there are practical, cultural, and UI reasons why you might not want to work from home. The practical reason is that you don't have a home environment that makes it easy. You lack access to the right space and materials, and you can't escape distractions and demands, like cooking and cleaning. The cultural reason is that some organisations' internal politics makes WFH self-harming. It you're out of sight, you're most likely out of mind as well. Decisions and operations about your vital interests might be happening on site and unseen by you at home. The UI reason is that workplace experience is central to your *umwelt* – it is a large chunk of your day-to-day, year-by-year life.

The First Law of UI dictates that people – even those working side by side in identical roles – want very different things from their work experience.[6] Some want their workplace to be the primary vehicle for their most valued interests and wants. Others want nothing of the kind. They want work to be a bounded space with impenetrable walls, where work has nothing to do with their "real" life outside, and vice versa. Many artists, musicians, and writers feel this way.

- Einstein worked in the Swiss patent office to support his explorations of the mysteries of the Universe.
- J.K. Rowling wrote the Harry Potter novels, seated in her local Edinburgh cafes, whilst employed as a translator and teaching English as a foreign language.
- Mick Jagger worked as a hospital porter while the Rolling Stones was in its infancy.

You don't have to be either an artist or a scientist to want a life of self-determination and freedom. Two ex-bankers I know, both highly successful in their careers, used their savings to turn away from the banking world and do what fulfils them. One is a London tour guide, who loves nothing better than walking his great home city eager to share his insights with people. The other is a handyman – doing small-scale jobs at a nominal price so he can enjoy fixing things and helping people. Before we jump to the foolish presumption that no one really wants to be a banker, consider this:

> I am standing in front of a class of senior executives on my leadership programme for a global investment bank. An "icebreaker" question I ask them is, "If you were to live your life over again, what profession or occupation might you like to enter?" Sadly, it is pretty universal for bankers to opt for anything but banking – in the debrief, frustrated rock musicians, architects, teachers abound. On this day it's different. A sharp-eyed woman – Mary, let's call her – at one of the tables says in a broad northern British accent: "I would have done exactly the same." She elaborates: "Look at me. Here I am, a poorly educated woman from the working class, earning a very substantial salary, the most successful person in my family ever, supporting the lives of lots of people. I'm respected, and I get to use my mind and the skills I've learned. I feel fulfilled. What more could I have asked for in life?"

Mary is an object lesson for all of us – embracing her life as an active choice. She had succeeded in navigating to a position that fulfilled her and met her goals. It is a paradox of large, complex, machine-like corporate bureaucracies that they contain nooks and crannies with roles that could suit lots of eccentrics who don't fit easily elsewhere. Finding such spots is another matter. Large organisations are typically poor at knowing what kinds of people they're hosting or what kinds of niches they possess that could be just right for diverse individuals. Meanwhile, we all need "restorative niches," which are few and far between in working environments: places of calm where you can reflect and find serenity and renewal.[7]

ORGANISING AS NATURE INTENDED?

For most of our history, we have been mobile, clan-dwelling hunter-gatherers. We had some very hard times that nearly wiped us out, but we emerged triumphant. We functioned well in fluid nonhierarchical clans, making flexible use of people's talents. The downside was a precarious existence with quite of a lot of bloodshed through raiding, punishments, and accidents. Later, humans settled down to simple agrarian living or nomadic pastoralism, which also worked quite well for us, though they generated social systems that were rigid structurally and culturally.[8] Since then, with the rise of city living, we've done a mind-boggling amount of diverse "niche constructing," devising ways of living and working together under every imaginable set of environmental conditions, up to and including the new reality of virtual organisations. Organisations, like the cultures they create, are all experiments in living, as we saw in Chapter 5.

All are "natural," too, since we created them. Some are clearly injurious to the human spirit, and even designed to be so, like prisons, for example. That shouldn't be the case in the worlds of business or public service, yet many arrangements frustrate, alienate, or make impossible demands on people. They get away with this because their damage they do to their members is concealed. As a big-brained generalist species, we're able to put up with terrible conditions for the sake of our own or our family's welfare. There will be some who love, tolerate, or hate any model, with the misfits most likely to emerge as the catalysts of change. All around us today, we have a vast plurality of organisational and cultural forms – a place for everyone, you might think. The key dynamic for UI is the balance of freedom vs. control. We all have our own tolerance thresholds for either.

If an organisation is big and diverse enough, UI may be able to navigate its way to internal niches. Here is a classic case:

> The UK Civil Service has always had a policy of hiring principled, clever people and then allowing them to rotate freely as generalists in its diverse labour market – around 510,000 people in 20 or so departments in every area of public life. When deemed ready for promotion, you can compete for a wide range of slots across diverse functions. This fluid system is unwittingly capitalising on transitions logic – allowing individuals to calibrate how radical a shift of role they want and hence the opportunity for innovation and adaptation. It makes for a great career, if you play it right. Armed with choice in a diverse market, you can manage your own development and enjoy the excitement of adapting to new projects and roles in unfamiliar areas. The result is a loyal, reliable, and nearly incorruptible work force. That's the upside. The downside is that some settle down and "nest" happily in their preferred area, stoutly maintaining the status quo. Meanwhile, others keep moving, not staying for long enough to be accountable for what they've done. It is a system that gives great scope for eccentricity – you have more chance of finding a slot that suits you than in more limited environments. It is UI friendly by putting all the flexibility into the person. It does not guarantee, however, that anyone is doing anything of value or doing so efficiently.

You can see almost the direct opposite in other public corporate bureaucracies.

> Vicky, in her late 50s, is a senior planning officer in a UK regional capital. "I long for change in this place," she says, "but it's sclerotic. Budgets are tight, so we get little new

blood. The only advancement is into a dead person's shoes." She wishes they would be more like the Civil Service, creating a more dynamic learning environment by moving people around. "Senior people are immobile. They cling on to their roles and areas of work."

In public service organisations, there often seems to be more human variety than in commercial firms.[9] One reason is that their cultural ethos is amorphous, diffuse, varied, and generally tolerant. Out in the market economy, corporate bureaucracies such as banks also have large internal labour markets, but these tend to be much more homogeneous subcultures around their key processes. Smaller organisations achieve success by finding a good fit between their members' UI and their strong culture. Misfits exit rapidly, having nowhere to hide. Given that a business's culture is its only sustainable and inimitable source of competitive advantage, this model works well when you can build a virtuous cycle of attracting the people you want and for whom you can be their employer of choice. Here you can do your best work, be yourself, and make good connections with likeminded others.[10]

Back in the 1990s, the New York law firm Wachtell, Lipton, Rosen & Katz[11] showed just how.

> It commanded the virtuous cycle by attracting top-quality lawyers, giving them extraordinary latitude and autonomy to work unsupervised when and how they please, and paying them on flat salaries with no billable hour targets. This arrangement made the firm a magnet for the best talent in the country and for top clients, from whom the firm only selected the most complex and interesting of assignments. Its decentralised approach fostered a culture of trust, learning, and adaptability, where individual strengths were amplified rather than constrained. "The organization itself became a learning system," said the case study's author, Bill Starbuck.

The firm is still going strong with something like this model. Yet there are risks to strong cultures. They can turn into monocultures, lacking the diversity required to be adaptable. Too much emphasis on fitting in produces communities of the like-minded, attracting more of the same and shedding deviants in a self-perpetuating cycle of cultural norming.[12] This can be great where it assures the customer/end user of high-quality control but can dangerously limit adaptability if there is insufficient bandwidth of skills and personalities.

So, we have the paradox that strong cultures need mavericks and misfits to be the grit that stimulates adaptation and innovation,[13] so long as you haven't already driven these people out. On the other hand, you may have very good reason not to want creativity – it's a downright hazard for air traffic controllers and anaesthesiologists. It's a strategic choice, but remember, some of the most successful organisations are the ones that buck their industry norms by attracting and making good use of a greater and healthier diversity than their competitors, such as the best educational and technology organisations.

NICHES FOR UI – FINDING YOURS

Freedom and control at the level of what position you're in is called discretion, the freedom you have to perform your role your way.[14] It fixes how much of your UI you can bring to work.

> I have recounted earlier how my laissez-faire upbringing ill-fitted me for too much "grid" (structural) or "group" (normative) cultural control. After my journey of self-discovery to India and then finding my vocation as an applied psychologist, I surprised myself by my stamina, focus, and self-discipline for research. After my PhD, I got the job I coveted, at the renowned Social and Applied Psychology Unit at Sheffield. Its simple cellular organisation, with extreme levels of unsupervised autonomy, suited me perfectly, and I stayed for 17 years, researching and publishing freely. Then, in my mid-40s, my growing restlessness, fuelled by the exhilarating experience of a year's teaching in a US business school, propelled me to look for something similar in the UK.

> So it was that I found my way to London Business School. The transition to this new world proved to be a steep learning curve. Research remained central, but now I had also to master the art of demanding teaching whilst also becoming an academic leader and administrator. My lifelong narrative of feeling like an outsider persisted, but academic life is made for misfits. You must meet high performance standards, though how you do this is entirely up to you. There is very little "pressure to conform." Thus, it came as a big surprise for me to discover how conventional and conservative so many of my colleagues were. I marvelled at how some could thrill a class by giving the same lecture word for word, while others would assiduously imitate the stars who mentored them, successfully! For me it was a self-made struggle, not being able to resist improvising in the classroom and banging my head in research at big imponderables. My good fortune was that the

context was astonishingly permissive – I could create and pursue whatever I liked, so long as I didn't fail. This can be a high-wire act, and I both loved and feared it.

My story illustrates a couple of vital UI themes. One is the power of context to change us. Academia was ideal for someone like me, but the transition to a business school proved much more radical than I had anticipated. I found that previously undiscovered aspects of my UI were revealed. Self-discovery and self-creation are two sides of the same coin. I was lucky. Having only two very different but profoundly liberating employers over a period of four decades gave me unrivalled scope to explore ideas, research topics, and teaching innovations.[15]

Most people – indeed all the characters whose stories we've been hearing in this book – don't have the luxury of such freedom. They had to steer their own development by moving between businesses, geographies, and job functions. Is this a failure of most organisations to get to know their human capital? Are they missing the win–win of growing the person whilst enhancing their value-add to the company? Yes, to a degree, but we must face the fact that organisations, whatever sector they are in, have inbuilt limits to whose UI they can use and whose they can't. Besides for all but a few, the reason for their existence is not to develop people, even if that is what they are doing, which most are. They are not academies.

It is significant weakness for any organisation not to know what UI variation it is hosting and therefore what they might be missing. Most businesses rely on the informal insights of their managers. Even the most sophisticated HR departments lack intelligence about the UI of their workforces. In almost every company I've worked with, a little smart questioning would have pointed out people of great potential value, hiding in plain sight. On more than one occasion, I've seen an incoming boss following a hunch, giving greater responsibility to a plateaued old-timer, who then reveals hidden talents. The business gets the double benefit of awakened gifts and a grateful heart.

HUMANISING THE MACHINE FOR UI

The inflexibility of organisations forces people to take charge of their own development by jumping ship to advance their careers by a spiral ascent route – simultaneously changing more than one of employer, function, sector, and culture.[16] Many lack the courage (initiative + opportunity) to do so, advancing cautiously through well-worn channels of industry and job function. Yet it is the more radical moves, across functions, sectors, or geographies, that yield the UI boost that comes from escaping familiar bubbles. This, you may recall, is the idea that the more radical the transition, the more transformative it is. It takes courage and initiative. The latter can be trained, especially toward personal growth through entrepreneurship.[17]

Let us now sketch out how organisations can awaken and put to good use the true diversity of UI to be found inside their walls. The 4D Framework can guide us.

DESTINY: *Opportunity*: Use the 4D model to understand the contours of your people's UI – a dynamic appraisal of their givens in character and background, the dramas they have weathered, where they have used personal initiative, and what they have learned. How does their profile fit them for the demands, risks, and opportunities to be found in your organisation's niches? This needs to be done, mindful of what stage of transition they are at[18] (elaborated in the next chapter).

Challenge: Organisations hardly ever assess roles and niches in ways that map on to UI dimensions, about which they are equally ignorant. Short-sightedly, diversity is all too often seen as starting and ending with broad demographics such as gender, age, and ethnicity, rather than UI.

DRAMA: *Opportunity:* Design projects and find moments where UI will be exposed, tested, and used. This is an especially important strategy for newcomers' self-discovery. It can also rejuvenate the jaded at later stages of their time with you.

Challenge: The dynamism of a project or "mission"[19] perspective is missing in many organ-isations. Instead, they allow technology and traditional performance metrics to dictate the pace of development. Much better is to identify moments where UI is called upon to raise its head and act distinctively and decisively. Such "moments" can be mapped.[20] They are situations/events/processes that individuals find especially challenging. (See the Appendix for details of a "Leadership Moments" exercise that can you can use in training and development contexts.)

DELIBERATION: *Opportunity:* Empower people through responsibilities that encourage them to take initiative, act with self-determination, and apply insight. Also necessary is a culture where managers, teams, and HR functions know how to have emotionally intel-ligent dialogue with people to explore their UI, knowledge, and capability.

Challenge: An activity-control model prevails in most organisations when they consider individual progression through their ranks. It is much more productive to start with UI, helping people find their voice and discover how they can make a difference. This is hampered by systems that lack UI intelligence, classifying people rather than understanding them as persons.

DEVELOPMENT: *Opportunity:* Craft feedback to maximise personal insight and growth. Feedback needs to change its character and focus at the successive stages of their relationship with the organisation: intense, self-propelled, and short term at the early stages; becoming more strategic later.

Challenge: Feedback systems are almost exclusively designed around merit, rewards, and control. One of the most important transitions is when people are exiting. It's a unique opportunity to get honest feedback about how you could have done better. You may also consider you have a moral responsibility to help the leaver navigate this transition, helping them find positive narratives that might guide them towards their next destination.

We must face the uncomfortable fact that there are lots of organisations out there that don't give a damn about any of this stuff yet still prosper. It doesn't necessarily make them bad, just blinkered. Many have sound organisational systems, professional staff, and logical procedures and are reasonably transparent. Their leaders believe that they are overseeing a meritocracy – an internal labour market that helps people to find the right level for their abilities. Are they right? Plenty of businesses around the world function perfectly fine on these assumptions, but they are deluding themselves. In even the best-run companies, they could be doing much better. This is the true picture in most of them:

- No one is thinking coherently about UI, relying on impersonal and often unreliable or invalid performance metrics.
- Merit is ill-defined and crudely measured. UI is reduced, *ad absurdum*, to a single unreliable metric.
- The people running the system are guided by their personal biases, of which they are largely unaware.
- Employees adapt, putting up with misfit between their UI and their role for the sake of a quiet life with its incentives and benefits (such as working with friends).

- Unregulated informal processes undermine rational systems, creating
  subcultures governed by power, conformity, and sectional self-interest.

Cultures – implicit values and rules of social conduct – emerge from any human gathering, from the family to the tribe. Many organisations pay no attention to what their culture and subcultures might be doing. Others know better. The best family businesses understand instinctively that their culture is a source of competitive advantage that can't be copied, building the virtuous cycle we described earlier, by being the employer of choice for talent. You also get the glow of reputational capital, what marketers call "brand equity" – the cultural value that spills over to your goods and services. This can happen in any sector of the economy, not just private companies.

Smart leaders realise that culture can be nudged and shaped but not controlled. But left unmanaged, the cultural norms and habits that emerge will be dictated by your technology, authority/reward systems, and regulatory constraints. The result is hierarchies are driven by deference, centralised models are dominated by power seekers, and siloed forms are run by barons. Darker forces lurk in neglected cultures, where covert or even naked self-interest operates against what matters to the commonwealth. Look at the corrupted family model of the Mafia or the decentralised cellular networks of terrorist organisations. Every organisation needs to develop practices that pull in the opposite direction to their prevailing operating model. So, you have . . .

- Hierarchy: Create a culture where bosses understand that their status is
  just a marker for their responsibility, not a measure of their merit or value.
  Inculcate the ethos that people at all levels have unique value to contribute.
  Foster egalitarian and mutually supportive decision-making.
- Centralised/decentralised models: In the former, strive towards a culture that
  delegates and empowers people in peripheral regions. In the latter, construct
  activities and teams that link satellites and cross functions, so people can
  exchange and learn from others beyond their locality.
- Divisions: Implement strategies that prevent people from "nesting" overlong
  in a single division. Pull or nudge them out of the shelter of their comfort
  zones. Create activities and partnerships that cut across silos that separate
  people and get in the way of experience-sharing and learning.

In the face of the AI revolution, there is an urgent need to re-humanise[21] the organisation. Recognising and honouring UI has big payoffs.

NEW MODELS FOR UI – SYMPHONY ORCHESTRA OR JAZZ BAND?

We have entered an era where the Uniqueness Perspective is gaining traction, for sound commercial reasons. The digital era is dissolving monolithic market forces. The incoming generations of workers won't tolerate being a cog in the corporate machine. To attract and retain talent, UI must be liberated and valued.

Toby,[22] an American in his 40s, is one of the most qualified and accomplished ever to pass through my Biography programme. He has a PhD in neuroscience, is a self-taught computer scientist, and has a string of technical books and published papers to his name. He tells me how his early career experience at Amazon was transformative. "I was tasked with launching the central part of the US for Amazon Web Services right when they were expanding coverage in 2015. I was the first Amazonian in my state of 6M people. The nearest Amazon office (and my manager) was a thousand miles away. The Leadership Principles (LPs) Amazon follows allowed me the individual freedom to accomplish my job using any means I had in my repertoire. If I was ever questioned about why or how I was doing something, I just needed to back up my logic by pointing to a particular LP such as 'Customer Obsession,' 'Bias for Action,' or my favourite, 'Have Backbone, Disagree, and Commit.' In those early days of AWS, I truly felt empowered to use my whole self to achieve the business goals."

People like Toby are gold dust for the world's most ambitious businesses. Leading organisations have figured out that they need something quite different from the standard corporate model to attract, motivate, and retain such talent. Sadly, it doesn't take much economic pressure for enlightened but costly practice to be rapidly abandoned. Here are some historic examples.

- CERN, near Geneva, Switzerland, is built around a common huge, expensive, cutting-edge, ridiculously complicated piece of equipment – the Large Hadron Collider – seeking to illuminate the fundamentals of the fabric of the

Universe, from its elemental particles to the creation and destruction of stars. It can only achieve its ambitions by attracting, motivating, and retaining the distinctive talents of the super-bright scientists, via an extremely flat, self-organising structure, under governance system that protects and empowers them.

- Google, in contrast, is much more diverse in its technologies, communications, media, and marketing. Its People Analytics Team uses a data-driven approach, via structured interview and work sample tests, to allocate people to roles and areas that suit them. It knows it needs to make its diverse population feel free and happy. It has striven to do this via various health programmes, mental health resources, flexible working arrangements, and lots of culture-building perks such as fitness centres and gourmet cafeterias. It was famous for its policy of "20% Time," allowing engineers a fifth of their working time to devote to their private projects, since scaled back in favour of flexible working practices.
- Microsoft had a "work from anywhere" policy to maximise flexibility, which has since turned into a more structured hybrid model. It claims a culture of "empowering people of all abilities."[23] Their Autism Hiring Program is a significant recognition of the value of recognised diversity. Microsoft, like many tech companies, also hosts an annual "Hackathon," bringing employees together from their furthest-flung locations to work on each other's passion projects.
- HCL, an Indian global IT services and consulting company, has an explicitly UI-positive structure and management system that "puts Employees First, Customers Second." Its flat structure and empowering processes are dedicated to developing employees from the highest to the lowest levels. The culture of autonomy gives people the freedom to step up to initiate and lead projects, with numerous praise and reward programmes to celebrate individual contributions. Additionally, flexible working enables employees in many areas to control their own work–life balance.

Let's not idealise these businesses. Scrape the surface, and you will find people who have seen the ruthless and uncaring side of many of them. The measures here can have a short half-life, so no guarantee they still exist as you read this. The UI point to be made is that the freedom/control equation doesn't apply equally to everyone. The most enlightened practices of firms tend to be tailored to their target talent pool, practices that could bring benefits at any level. "Talent" can be fickle, and it's often best to build a UI-friendly culture from the bottom up.

As we have seen, there is no "best" balance of freedom vs. control for all varieties of UI. There will always be people who don't fit even the most empowering and enlightened model. Some might prefer to surrender their UI and sit contentedly in the second row of the second violins in a symphony orchestra. It can be very rewarding to be surrounded by people who are all really good at what they do, disciplined and dedicated to a common goal, bringing to life a beautiful musical score under the benevolent direction an all-seeing conductor. But if you want your UI to fly more freely, then you might be better off in a jazz band, where people adapt, improvise, create, and help others. This is how it works:

- You have a shared framework of harmonic and rhythmic structure.
- Your instrumentation, roles, and styles of play are all diverse.
- You are always either soloing, accompanying, or chorusing/riffing.
- Everyone listens to everyone else, adding their voice where it enhances another.
- There is a balance between the scripted and the improvised.

Every jazz band thrives when it builds a culture and character around its distinctive voices and how they are configured.[24] It's the secret of success for family businesses, even in the most grounded and technical of sectors. It's a mindset that chimes with many features of firms at the leading edge of invention.

THE INNOVATING ORGANISATION

Capitalism has many injurious side effects. It can put a straitjacket on UI and reduce people to the status of expendable factors of production. But its principal upside is innovation, wielded by what Adam Smith called its invisible hand. Better to think of it as an invisible glove, for the creative inspirations that transform our world come from the warm-blooded hand of UI inside it. It is the UI of people, alone or with others, that sees gaps in markets, has brilliant ideas, finds new solutions to old problems, and develops new ways of scaling them up and out into society.

Yet even in the freest of capitalist societies, there are leaders, governance bodies, and organisational structures that fear the uncertainty, risk, and loss of control that creatives may bring. Rosabeth Moss Kanter, a management guru of the 1980s and 90s, helpfully and wryly sets out a list of "rules for stifling innovation,"[25] a manifesto for control freaks that we've all seen in operation:

- Mistrust any new idea, especially if it's from below.
- Stick to the known; innovations mainly fail.
- Keep people really busy so they don't have time to think.
- In the name of excellence, insist on perfection.
- Confine innovation to specific roles.
- For the sake of security, keep people in the dark.
- Leave big ideas and innovations to top management, who know best.
- Encourage competition, not collaboration.
- Punish mistakes and risk-taking.

All such practices are born of fear and mistrust. Kanter's rules offer the balm of control to the five demons that scare management most: cost, errors, waste, inefficiency, and chaos. The balance between freedom and control is the sharpest dilemma in institutional life, especially in the world of making things. In hypercompetitive markets, you've got to win at both efficiency and innovation. Your challenge is to find how to get the best from everyone's UI within the constraints of technology, regulation, resources, and social values.

One of the most influential, successful, and interesting business leaders of recent times is Sir James Dyson, whose firm has reinvented a range of household goods, from vacuum cleaners to hair and hand dryers. As is often the way, the founder's own UI is baked into the fabric of the firm's global business. Dyson is a self-made engineer who travelled a checkered and persistent road from being a student in an art college to running one of the world's most innovative manufacturing businesses. The fusion of his aesthetic intelligence with problem-solving zeal has been a winning formula, driving an irresistible flow of innovation into consumer markets. Sir James explained to me how this is sustained by the way the company is led, how it is organised, and how it feeds its human roots.

"My parents were both teachers," he says, "and knew nothing about engineering. I went to Art School to study design, rather than going to university." There he found his way to the world of product design. Although he runs one of the world's most successful and innovative engineering businesses, he refuses to call himself an engineer, despite his early self-creation as an inventor. "I was lucky to be young in a golden age of British design and engineering, with people around like Issigonis [designer of the Mini], Norman Foster, and Richard Rogers [notable architects]." It is a distinguishing mark of Dyson the man and Dyson the company that both placed as much value on design aesthetics as on engineering excellence. The early career turning point for him was the mentorship of Jeremy Fry, the charismatic and creative boss of a midsized engineering firm who had himself transitioned from architecture to engineering. They were kindred spirits. Dyson says, "Jeremy taught me that if you have a good idea, just do it. Don't worry about whether it'll be a success or not. Just do it." In his autobiography he says that Fry taught him "without having to say anything, that every day is a form of education."[26]

The dominant metaphor driving man and company is curiosity through persistence and courage. Strong non-materialistic values around development are also in the cultural mix. He tells me, "Everybody feels as though they're an individual and they've got a job, a problem to solve, something to make, something to do, and that's really important." Interestingly, although the structure is flat, it is also traditional and "run like the Army," he says. But it is projects that rule within this structure, with fluid and mobile teams of engineers inspiring each other. I ask him about how UI is regulated to optimise the freedom–control balance. "Creativity only comes about through discipline," he says. "You can get people who are incredibly creative and disruptive. You want disruptive people who can be disciplined." Those who can't are managed to avoid chaos.

Innovation is a team effort. "The idea is greater than the person. Engineering requires different types of people with varied skills who are prepared to spend hours and hours testing things. It's a group effort, and who is the hero? Is it the person who had the idea at the beginning or the person who made it work? For me it's the people who make ideas work. Ideas are ten a penny; it's making it work that is difficult."

Dyson's philosophy is one of intense enculturation. Key elements of UI – the narratives that drive the man and the company – are inculcated in all his engineers when their minds are fresh and uncluttered by priors, as they were in his own awakening at art school. In 2019, he created the Dyson Institute of Engineering and Technology, accredited in 2021 to award its own degrees. Ideologically committed to enriching the UK's engineering culture, he is frank about how it ties into his business strategy. "I don't want experienced people," he says. "It's better to have people who question things, who are seeing things for the first time and feel as though they are pioneering."

He tells the story of hiring his marketing director straight from an Oxford Modern Languages degree. "Her parents were teachers, and she'd never been in business before. She's been brilliant. We sent her out on the road selling, and she brought back exactly what we needed, fresh vision and energy. Then she went and hired to her team someone with 6 years' experience. 'Why did you do that?' I asked. 'You had no experience at all when you joined us, and you've been brilliant.' It took us 2 years to undo that person's views on marketing, what she'd learned in other businesses, and get around to our point of view. That's why I like employing freshly minted graduates. I would say when we employ experienced people, we have a 50% success or retention rate. When we employ graduates, it's close on a 100%."

The Dyson model, like any other, needs managing, mainly to deal with exceptions – where systems fail, UI goes rogue, or accidents happen. No matter how well teams can self-regulate, the need for oversight, arbitration, and intervention by non-prejudicial authority remains a necessity – in a word, management.

LEADERS AND MANAGERS – THE UI WAY

I wrote The "I" of Leadership: Strategies for Seeing, Being and Doing to show how the individual narratives of leaders have real consequences, for good and ill. Central to its reasoning is the Law of the Situation,[27] which means leaders need to have a vision (seeing) and strategies (doing) that will work with the situation they face. The being part is the leader's UI. It is all very well seeing what you need to do as a leader, but you still need to be able to muster the means to deliver. Do you have the character, the insight, the courage, and the ability for the challenge? Do you have the wisdom and humility to step aside for someone else whose UI is better equipped? Too often, leaders don't. Nelson Mandela, South Africa's heroic first post-Apartheid president, did.

I am talking to Christo Brand,[28] Mandela's guard for the last 12 years of his incarceration, who became his trusted friend. Christo recalls his arrival at Robben Island aged 19, totally ignorant of the nature of his assignment, being greeted on his first day by Mandela's imposing presence. The great man said to him in perfect Western Cape Afrikaans, "Welcome. I see you are a country boy like me." He recounted how Mandela's charisma kept all his fellow ANC rebels in order. "Treat the guards with respect. Remember, we are political prisoners, not criminals." His message to his men was the guards are doing a difficult job that we shouldn't make any harder for them. It was his cool, disciplined vision that traversed the vast divides in South African society that saw the country emerge, miraculously, as a non-racial democracy without the bloodbath everyone dreaded. After 5 years of transformation, he concluded he was not the right man to oversee the rebuilding of institutions and gracefully stepped down, handing the reins of power to his more bureaucratic successor, Thabo Mbeki.

The UI perspective has important lessons for leaders.

1. Rigorously challenge and check what you believe and take for granted. See how your *umwelt* might be out of joint with others. Practise contrarian exploration – testing alternative realities, never letting yourself become closed-minded.
2. Explore your UI systematically, by dialogue, testing, journaling, reflection, and other methods (some are set out in the next chapter). Develop leadership strategies and tactics that draw on its key features, including building guardrails against your *zemblanities*[29] (bad stuff you make happen).
3. Spell out the explicit and implicit narratives that underpin your leadership. These are stories about how your UI helps the organisation meet its challenges. Continually question and refresh them.
4. Practise decentring (much more on this in the next chapter) – seeing the world from other people's points of view, to understand how their narratives make sense of their lives. Show people you hear and recognise them as unique persons.
5. Encourage each one to teach one. Foster cultures where individuals can find their "moment in the sun" – to solo, with team members as the backing group.

This is a recipe for what people call "authentic" leadership. Looking at the Dark Side of UI in Chapter 6, we saw that authenticity is easier for some people than it is for others. Some are fated to battle with conflicting forces within their UI, often struggling even to understand their own reactions. Listen to Dave, a 50-year-old American:

"I have been very competitive since I was a young child." Neither of Dave's parents went to university, but he says, "I was always driven. I was captain of pretty much every sports team I played on. I always struggled with social situations that were more fluid, where there were not clear rules of engagement." He rose to senior partner in a prestigious professional services firm. He found he had landed "an enviable job giving me power, prestige, and autonomy, but which I also found a punishing one." He continues: "Until I left, I did not realise how crabbed and anxious I had become. My decision to leave baffled the other partners, colleagues, and clients, but my family gets it." He reflects on the transformative impact of his learning on our programme. "I think I have successfully murdered my ego in the first few months on the course, through reflection and feedback from relationships, behavioural insights, and Biography." He is clearly headed for a significant leadership position somewhere, given his profile, but he confesses, "I continue to wrestle with which aspects of my personality are immutable and which are not. I want to find a role that has the capacity to inspire, because of the industry and the company's strategic positioning, not relying on bland notions of success or excellence."

There are people who want to lead in any social situation. They can be dangerous, especially if they have the charismatic gifts to get others to follow them. Much better to be like Dave – understand your leadership bandwidth, cognisant of which contexts are your leadership home, the situations that bring out the best of you: your "leadership moments."

It is the powerful, transformative, and brave narratives that mark the greatest leaders. Those same narratives prove disastrous when they don't keep in step with reality. Leaders need to discipline themselves, not to lazily let narratives shape their vision without testing whether they are keeping pace with change. Paying attention to the right things is 9/10ths of leadership effectiveness. The best leaders see what others don't, challenge what is taken for granted, and look beyond the horizons of the given. To do this, you need to raise your gaze above and beyond the eager circle of familiars who surround you. Their agreement with you is blocking your vision. Stress-test your vision against the contrarian views of critics, romantics, and visionaries. Never forget that self-deception is a universal human trait,[30] for you and them both. It is easy to blind yourself to uncomfortable truths.

The principle of "Seeing" applies equally to oneself. Smart leaders have a balanced appraisal of their strengths, vulnerabilities, and *zemblanities* and an authentic narrative laying out their value proposition to followers.[31] Women often are forced to fight harder than men to find their way as leaders. Here's one who has it both in her DNA and in the self-belief her parents instilled in her:

Zhanel was raised in a Russian satellite state, one of the mainly Muslim countries of Central Asia, where studying in a Russian school "allowed me to meet great teachers who never cared about nationalities and made me believe I was a genius and could achieve high goals." Her progressive professional parents drilled into her "that women can be as strong as men and be great leaders." She says, "This belief shaped me into a confident, self-sufficient person who never hesitated to share my opinion and influence others." She found people followed her ideas and opinions. In ninth grade (around age 15), she enrolled in technical college as a boarder but immediately bridled at the strict religious ethos, the military discipline of dormitory life, and the hierarchical norms that demanded females conform to the demure, deferential norms of patriarchy. "One day, I met one of our teachers, and in tears, explained that I wanted to leave the school because of its rules." The teacher's response was robust: "It's your choice, but you'll leave as a loser, because everyone wants you to leave because you are rejecting the rules. You could fight back and prove your view." Zhanel reflected, "I decided to stay and be a winner." She went on to pursue her studies to the highest level as a leader in her field before pausing to fulfil her role as a mother.

Leaders come and go. A test of their lasting impact is how much they developed the talent of others. This developmental view of UI reveals the potential of the best organisations to be theatres for self-actualisation. However, that's not the primary role of business organisations, though it is for schools, isn't it?

FEEDING UI – ENLIGHTENED ACADEMIES

We saw something of the workings of the remarkable Wherry School for autistic children (see Chapter 6), where they educate around 140 children from 8 to 18 and proudly state that they get all of them into mainstream education by the time they leave. Not surprisingly, there is a long waiting list of parents seeking to gain admission for their autistic children. Visiting the school, meeting staff, and interacting with its pupils show me why. It helps children adapt to a world that is hard to understand and deeply challenging to navigate. The Head Teacher tells me: "We try to help steer them through major and minor transitions." I ask what counts as either, assuming major would mean something radical like leaving the school, and minor as dealing with a new teacher. She bursts my neurotypical delusion: "Major is moving to a new year and teacher," she says. "Minor is catching the bus in the morning." Everyday transactions most of us don't have to think about can be very challenging for these kids.

Aided by a low student–staff ratio, teachers are free to focus on UI. As we discussed earlier, labelling as autistic or any other clinical label risks the fallacy of implied similarity. Staff talk of understanding "the learning profile of the child – how they need to learn." They follow nationally set curriculum parameters but flex them in delivery, with the UI of the kids firmly guiding them. For the teachers, a Uniqueness Perspective is primary. You can see it in how they talk with or about the pupils. They radiate purpose and tell of the unparalleled personal fulfilment they find in this challenging environment.

No wonder parents are queuing up to get their children into the school. Not just parents. It is a magnet for teachers. The Head tells me, "I had become very disillusioned with mainstream schools." Another teacher tells of her journey from specialist teaching in the schools that host disruptive and disturbed children, to the Wherry, where she could innovate in curriculum development.

"The biggest challenge is the parents, especially those who are embarrassed and ashamed about their children's autism," says the Head. "But most are broadly supportive of what we do, even if they don't understand it." A 16-year pupil tells her own success story of finding her way through the school, which she says is analogously "like being guided across a fast-flowing river by stepping stones." She quotes a Taylor Swift song: "I want to be defined by the things that I love. Not the things I hate, not the things I'm afraid of, not the things that haunt me in the middle of the night. I just think you are what you love."[32] She says, "I feel understood here."

We return to recognition hunger – the need to be seen is never more important than in childhood. It makes schools the most important institutions in society. They are in the business of personal transformation and cultural integration. Sadly, as Charles Dickens, James Joyce, and, more recently, Stephen King[33] all graphically depicted, they can also be organs of repression, where individuality is stifled, not celebrated. It revolves around the central dilemma of control vs. freedom. There is a lot of control in the Wherry School – autistic children learn and practise strategies to survive and prosper in a world that is largely ignorant of how they perceive it. But the control must come from the children, not their teachers. The mantra is self-regulation. When behaviour becomes "dysregulated" (disturbed, distressed, disorderly), the teachers help the students to enact their own rescue strategies. When you see teachers intervening, it is always to deflect the child into safer, more familiar channels whilst gently reminding them of their own coping strategies.

At the other end of scale,

Fabiana from Brazil says, "My elder sisters always said that the school headteacher was fearsome, which made me scared to death to go to school – I felt I was going to war – though I never had any difficulties. I was very serious and hated sports. I was left alone at home because I could study and understand things by myself. My parents spent more time with my older sister, who needed support. Looking back, I believe Latin American schools have got it wrong; instead of investing and allowing the best students to thrive, they dedicate more time to the not so talented. I could have achieved a lot more with some attention. Today I make sure my stepchildren, nieces, and nephews get support in what they're good at, so they are motivated to develop."

Education, like culture, has an ambivalent relationship with UI. In all societies there is a near universal pattern of the following:

- In the early years children's instincts for play, expression, and curiosity are indulged and channelled into essential skills of reading and writing. Expression and growth of character are unstoppable, and it has become orthodoxy to encourage and support this process. Yet much still rests on the discretion and emotional intelligence of the teacher. In many places, sadly, the balance is firmly locked in the direction of control, conformity, and performance.
- At the high school/secondary stage, that balance becomes entrenched, an intensified world of tests and discipline. This takes place against the backdrop of what we have seen as that most profound transitional period of the lifespan, adolescence. No wonder teaching is a tough profession! One can sympathise yet beg to differ with the philosophy that schools are preparing kids for the harsh realities of life. They do so by regimenting learning in ways that will help young people get jobs, fit in, and pass the conformity tests that await them in adulthood.
- Meanwhile, the task of "character development" is left to parents, extracurricular engagements, and the informal world of friendships. The problem is that these may pull the child in opposing directions. Many people's memories of school (including my own) are certainly not "the best days of my life," rather a pitched battle between UI and institutional life.

There are schools that have tried to grasp this nettle.

One of the most notable, often derided for its elitism, is Eton College. Founded nearly 600 years ago, it has shaped British political history, not least by educating no fewer than 20 of Britain's prime ministers. It remains a go-to institution for the wealthy. It can afford to pick and choose its pupils, and who gets in is not just a matter of money or brains. In fact, its admissions process purposefully avoids focusing on the top 20% of prep school achievers. Eton ranks in the mid-20s for UK independent boys' schools on academic results, but it is second to none in character building. This will amuse British readers who might call to mind the less than praiseworthy profiles of recent Old Etonians in UK public life. If the school is the cause, then it is because of the confidence it instils. Wealth and public entitlement are more directly to blame for whatever flaws we can see in its alumni. For its part, Eton takes great care to see, honour, and endow the UI of its boys through an intelligent methodology of self-discovery and self-determination. It does so via a structure of small family-like houses, around which daily and private study life revolves. It is in the extracurricular menu that the boys become men – sports are hugely important, as are the staggering array of clubs for boys to experiment with hobbies and interests. Pastoral care is intense, and for each boy delivered by three mentors, the most central being the Housemaster, who lives on site with his own family. Classroom teachers are, of course, the best in the business, but the inflexible requirements of educational metrics are approached by varying methods to accommodate the preferences and interests of individuals.

Eton is one case in Alex Hill's study of high-achieving organisations,[34] many of them in the top echelons of sports and the arts. His list includes the All Blacks rugby team, the UK's Royal Academy of Dramatic Arts, and NASA. What jumps out from each case is that recognising and accommodating UI is at the centre of these organisations' pursuit of excellence, whatever their domain.

They all start out, like Eton, with the luxury of choice about whom they admit, but it is how they manage their human capital that affirms all we have been saying up to this point. They have top-flight professionals in their training and management roles, for whom the Uniqueness Perspective is central to their mental models and the organisation's mission. They look for difference and celebrate it, finding ways to channel, amplify, and take the rough edges off UI. At the Royal Academy of Dramatic Art, individuals are stress-tested – finding their voice as actors by shredding and reassembling their UI. It sounds damaging and dangerous, and in other contexts, it can be dehumanising.[35] Here it is an instrument for building their professional versatility. They know that feeding recognition hunger is no way to create a convincing actor.

We are back to the transformative power of transitions, and in all these cases there is a punctuated equilibrium in what they do with individuals – plateaus, shocks, re-evaluations, and new equilibria are the psychobiology of adult development.

Leaving behind these shining bastions of privilege and excellence, what about back in the cash-strapped inner-city school? It won't do to wait for a Robin Williams *Dead Poets Society* radical preacher/teacher to come riding into view to rescue hapless schools. Quite simple things, at no cost, can transform such places. The problem, as educational specialists have frankly told me, is a compound of:

- Teachers who never left school themselves and carry with them the models that they survived as children. They have moved seamlessly from school to college and back to school again. They feel at home with traditional models of discipline, conformity, and control.
- A pervasive fear of failure, through metric-driven regimes where the prime focus is not on liberating possibility but on avoiding failure.
- Fearful parents support this model to shrink the burden of anxiety they have about their children losing their way in the dangerous forests of social media, gaming, and misinformation.

The balance of these may vary around the world, but education everywhere is increasingly expected to perform the impossible task of inoculating the young against the threats that loom on all sides in the new world order. Control wins over freedom in this climate.

Schools are hugely influential at a critical interval of our lives. It is tempting to see them as the root cause of society's ills or to expect them to shoulder the burden of building a better society. This falls into the error of exaggerating their influence, as we discussed in Chapter 2. School, like all our other early-life contexts, shapes a lot of our narratives, and therefore can be hugely consequential. But we ingest and transform our schooling, as we do culture, relationships, and the rest of the world.

Education is filtered by our UI traits, yet it may supply narratives that take you in wrong, long, and unnecessarily difficult diversions before you find your own direction. The stories we have been telling in this book illustrate time and again the power for UI to find its feet, from even least promising origins and most toxic early learning. When we look at methods of self-awareness and self-development, we need to keep in mind the contexts that support them and those that don't.

So, how then can we find the positive path for UI development and expression? Here we have looked at the positive role context can play. It is now time in the next chapter to look at the methods, approaches, and techniques that can be applied at a personal and institutional level, to allow UI to breathe and find voice without risk to the social order.

CODA: WHAT THIS MIGHT MEAN FOR UNIQUE YOU

Your UI does not exist in a vacuum. Elements from your repertoire of ways of being are switched on and off by the different life contexts you find yourself in.

- You, and most people you know, are a lot more flexible than you might have come to believe.
- Dare to dream. Think about what your ideal workplace would be. Maybe that's not a single location – home might be great for certain kinds of work, and although it might feel great for lots of things, it might also be limiting you, damaging your work–life balance, or incurring hidden costs.
- What is your ideal balance of freedom and control? How structured and clear do you like your work role and identity to be? In working groups, how important is it for you to be integrated into a close team of likeminded colleagues?
- Think about your UI at work. Maybe you've had a lifetime of knowing what kind of place suits you, but maybe not. It's for you to specify to yourself what kind of mix in roles and schedules would be ideal for you. Find organisations that will flex in ways that work for you.
- Write it down. Make a project of yourself as a career journey. It can be as connected or disjointed as you want. Use virtual tools to see what's out there and to post yourself as someone who could be useful to the right organisation.
- Culture matters. Don't assume that the picture presented by a potential employer, even in the recruitment interview, is representative of the culture you might be joining. You'll need to ask smart questions geared to your UI to get at this.
- If you're in an established organisation, how does it flex its structure? Don't let the gravitational pull of hierarchy, centralisation and divisions dictate your working relationships. Find ways of humanising structures you are part

of. Think like a leader, and if you are one, act like one.[36] It's your responsibility to make the culture rehumanise the imperatives of roles and rules.

- If you want to be happy and fulfilled in any team, think about jazz band principles, where people listen, resonate, and stimulate each other, and everyone gets a place in the sun from time to time.

- Consider the Three Existential Wants, to savour your day-to-day work experience, to signify in what you bring to your role, and to feel seen by people at work for who you are. Which matters to you most now, and how is this changing?

- Don't be a lonely and heroic leader. Find and use confidants – they are essential to your well-being and effectiveness.[37]

- If you are involved in education at any level – as a professional, parent, or student – consider what development means to you, not just in terms of skills and knowledge. Think UI, and especially your Self narratives. Revising and refreshing them may be the most important part of your development.

Ten

LIBERATING UI
Strategies, Methods, Processes

There is no greater agony than bearing an untold story inside you.
(Maya Angelou)[1]

The unexamined life is not worth living.
(Socrates)[2]

FINDING VOICE – BEING HEARD

Everyone has a story to tell, if they will only be heard.

Remember Jimmy, who we met in Chapter 6? He was born into a dark context, into poverty, neglect, abuse, and abandonment. He went to 15 primary (junior) schools and 4 secondary (high) schools. "I was traumatized by the way teachers talked to me – they made believe I was stupid and naughty – something I took into adult life. I rebelled against authority." Drugs were a central pillar of his existence. "My parents introduced me to them," he says. "Drug dealers and gangs become my surrogate family. Drugs are a crutch, and they saved my life. At 16, I was living on the streets with my brother, always in fear of getting beaten up." Petty theft to get by landed him in prison at 19, where he says with a broad smile, "I left with more qualifications than I ever got at school."

The darkness of the world he was born into was only half his Destiny. His great fortune was the other half – his intelligence and character. His escape from the vicious web of interconnected ills that had entrapped him came first through the arts. The only teacher who praised him was in drama, the first subject at school where he experienced personal gratification. "I love it," he says. "You can escape this world and be another person." The second was a social worker at a drop-in café that he found while on the streets, post-prison. "This was the first person to see me," he says. "All I ever wanted was for someone to say, 'Are you okay?,' to take an interest and see my potential." Jimmy asks me to quote Tupac to tell how he feels now, "I am the rose that grew from the concrete."[3]

Jimmy has gifts. Now at 25 he's smart, articulate, self-aware, empathic, and moral. He has a big smile and buoyant enthusiasm for life. His qualities shine through when you interact with him. Life is still challenging him. Unsurprising, given the weight of the past he is carrying, but he is living proof of how little it can take for Unique Individuality (UI) to find liberation through deep recognition.

We live in times when it's easy to feel lost and disconnected, especially when social media offer delusions of connectedness through fleeting interactions. In the virtual world, having "followers" doesn't make you a leader. Equally, having "friends" online doesn't mean any of them like you or would act like friends to you, give you time, listen to you, share private reflections, care for you, or give to you in a time of need.

The only way we can do anything in life is by moving between places, purposes, and people, following an internal logic that connects these things for Unique You – Your story matters because it communicates your values and ties them together with meaning. The Biography methodology is about finding, testing, and living your narrative in your own way.

THE BIOGRAPHY ODYSSEY

The Biography Programme grew from small beginnings to become a core proposition for probably the most mature and interesting degree cohort at London Business School, the Sloan Fellowship programme. As we have met them through this book, these midlife men and women are a mixed bunch in background and experience, from all corners of the globe. All have been successful in their professions but looking to retool, refresh, or restart their careers. From the outset, it became apparent that Biography was quenching a deep thirst and touching the nerve centre of personal transformation. It has developed over the years, intensifying as a focused process of UI exploration.

Listen to what Jez, a 47-year-old British executive, the son of Indian immigrant parents, says:

> The experience of Biography has been overwhelming. It has helped me understand my past and, importantly, accept the person I have become today. I had a tendency to sweep things under the carpet and distract myself with my work and the rat race. The tools of Biography helped me unpack things in such a way that allowed me not only to come to terms with things but to connect the dots and shape how I wish to live my life.

The first law of UI dictates that any intervention – like anything you put in your body – has effects that are you-specific. The Biography odyssey has a special and distinctive meaning for every person, but its processes of exploring and questioning prove to be compelling for all. It is delivered in seven 3-hour classes, spread out over the first 6 months of the Sloan Programme, with a schedule of structured activities between classes in five-person Biography Groups (allocated to maximise demographic and cultural diversity).

Elements of the programme can be compressed into a 1-day workshop or used stand-alone as self-help tools. What follows is the full schedule of elements, with all the materials available for readers to use in the Appendices. You can do some of these alone, but sharing is a central part of the process, with a group or a trusted buddy.

THE BIOGRAPHY JOURNEY IN SEVEN QUESTIONS

Here is an inventory of self-investigation, framed as sessions, dispersed over 6 months in the Biography Programme. Psychologists tell us that aimless and unfocused rumination is bad for mental health,[4] but structured UI exploration, contained within a defined space and time, opens the doors to insight and self-directed change.

1.	What is happening to me right now, and how did I get here?	Crossing Boundaries – insight & innovation
2.	Who am I really? What can I control & change?	Unique You – roots & consequences of identity
3.	What's my story? What is yours?	Narrative – the power, risks, & pay-offs of stories
4.	Who don't I understand? Who can't I deal with?	Mind-Reading – the insights of Decentring
5.	What do I want? What is possible for me?	The Challenge of Change – strategies, tactics, and methods
6.	Where and when am I at my best?	Time & Place – path finding & niche construction
7.	What do I need to find & know?	Next Steps – readiness & next-but-one thinking

1. WHAT IS HAPPENING TO ME RIGHT NOW, AND HOW DID I GET HERE?

These two questions are the pillars for Biography and are the springboard for choice and change. The first part of the question is to put yourself in the place of "Now," not least because, like all states of mood and awareness, it will colour all other explorations and analyses you may undertake.[5] The second part is to see what your experience right now owes to the route and the drivers that brought you to this point.

a) Transition Cycles (see Appendix 1)

At times of life, it might feel as if the train you are on is stationary, but it is not. We are all constantly in transition – on the move between states of being and between worlds. Look at all the main domains of your *umwelt* and consider:

- Life stage: The biological clock runs inexorably, but it is no mechanical clock. It can race, pause, and revisit former states. Through rigorous self-management, you can do quite a lot to look after yourself, and in the future new tools may transform your ability to do so (see next chapter). Medical technologies will prolong life, but they won't alter the three great transformational periods of the lifespan that we reviewed in Chapter 7. The question you face is what adaptive challenges are coming your way? What narratives will help you, and which will hinder?

  - It is one of the tragedies of business that their founders fail to recognise when their powers are failing and their perspectives are becoming obsolete. As Ego-driven creatures, we often give too much credit/blame to our willed Self, when biological changes may have crept up on us. We can be the last to see that we are moving into a new rhythm of life.

- Relationships: Everyone around you is on the move as well. Family and friends come into view, crowd, fade, or disappear altogether. Even the dead live on in your *umwelt*, offering solace, sorrow, and portals to the past. Who is moving in what direction in your *umwelt*? It's a dynamic field. The strong feelings you have for others, such as love and grief, do not stand still. They mutate, reform, grow, and fade. What is uppermost right now in your life? Parents are often the last to notice that their kids have become adults.

– It goes the other way, too. As Mark Twain is claimed to have joked, "When I was a boy of 14, my father was so ignorant I could hardly stand to have the old man around. But when I got to be 21, I was astonished at how much the old man had learned in seven years."[6]

- Work: We can define work very loosely here as what you spend most of your waking hours doing, even if it's parenting, learning, or playing. How tightly defined are the roles you occupy? What trajectories are you on? What skills are you practising? Are you growing, directing, following a path? Is it fragmentary and unpredictable, or do you have it mapped out? Perhaps you are following a career river, making you a passenger in your own life, barely aware whether your hand is on the tiller. What does your trajectory feel like for you now?

  – Creeping obsolescence is a particular challenge, soon to be galloping with artificial intelligence (AI). Henry Ford, John Watson (IBM), Carly Fiorina (HP), Stephen Elop (Nokia), and John Scully (Apple) all came to corporate grief by failing to keep pace with their worlds changing around them. Watch this space!

- Contexts: Movements between places and cultures present powerful challenges to adapt. Whether we initiate them or not, there is a rhythm to finding your feet in a new place. It can feel exhilarating and liberating. Threats and anxieties may be uppermost. The adaptive demands your environment makes on you are varied. Are you in the right place for you?

  – Look at Jimmy's story. He spent his whole childhood in contexts that prevented him from any degree of positive self-awareness. Prison, paradoxically, gave him opportunities for self-development that schools never did, and in young adulthood he has found places where he can savour, signify, and be seen.

If you look around at people you know, you may be inclined to think they are in similar situations to each other – say a newly graduated student, or a mid-career corporate lawyer – but scratch the surface and they are not. All are likely to be in quite different stages of multiple Transition Cycles. Person A finds themselves in a transitions pile-up: health issues, challenging relationships, demanding job, and relocation all at the same time. Person B is in a transitions wasteland – stuck, bored, drowning in routines and obligations, with no sense of control over future possible directions. Person C is building steadily, finding bumps in the road but largely in control and going in the right direction.

But for all of us, the challenge of transitions is to deal with the following:

- Anxiety about the wrong things – your current fears are a poor guide to future realities.[7] For example, you are more likely to worry needlessly about whether you'll be good enough to perform in a new job than about the much more unpredictable prospect of getting on with your new colleagues.[8]
- Shock of the new – you will be surprised by some of what you encounter. The Encounter period for the newcomer is typically a blizzard of novelty, challenging you to selectively filter what you pay attention to and give priority.
- Disorientation and doubt – expect to feel confusion and uncertainty about what might happen. You can get disheartened when things go wrong, as can, especially when you're under stress.
- Struggling to let go – you may fear the loss of the familiar and the finality of moving on. This is a classic fear of the senior generation contemplating their leadership succession.

It helps to have a whole-transitions perspective. The Transition Cycle model, introduced briefly in the last chapter and expanded in Appendix 1, can help you to think about it as a journey with stages holding different challenges. Preparation: tooling and getting the right mindset. Encounter: watching, reflecting, and asking questions. Adjustment: implementing a plan of action. Stabilisation: waiting for developments, exploring future options, retooling.[9]

LIFELINE ANALYSIS

From time to time, you will have shared segments of your life story – perhaps during courtship or with intimate friends, swapping confidences. In most daily life, the safe default assumption is that no one is really interested in your biography, not even you yourself perhaps. The past is dead and gone, and you live life forwards. This is a mistake. You have a story to tell, and it is unique. Others can learn from it. You can gain insights from telling it.

After self-centring through the lens of transitions, it is time to get into a helicopter and look down on the path that got you from birth to here. The Lifeline has unparalleled power to do this. It starts with the facts and then unpacks the meaning. The instructions are shown in Appendix 2. This is the most unambiguous and graphic way to capture UI, which can immediately yield major insights.

> Alexander, a Swedish IT executive, says, "The Biography experience has been an eyeopener both internally and externally. First, going through the process, I had to look at my entire life from a bird's-eye view, and it was amazing to see that though the events seemed random; I could now see patterns. Second, seeing others' stories, it was truly humbling to see what has shaped their lives and choices and the lessons one could draw from them."

The links in the chain of your life are transitions. Each transforms you, sometimes trivially, sometimes profoundly. The Lifeline method consists of mapping the transitions across the major life domains on a timeline of dates and your age at the time: work, relationships, and geography. Next, you populate the timeline with events – small and large asteroids hitting the surface of your *umwelt*. Some could be entirely external, like a political revolution in your home country, or a pandemic. Others are internal, like a sudden realisation about your own aging, or a changing relationship. The effects of life events can be short-lived. Others that look superficially insignificant later reveal themselves to have been turning points. Here's an example from my own life.

> I took up playing tennis in my 60s, never realising how life transforming it would prove to be. It didn't just give me a physical fillip; it brought me new friends from totally different worlds and transformed my relationship to my local community. For the first time in 15 years, the town I commuted to and from felt like home.

Next along the entire length of the ribbon of your life, draw a hedonic curve – a moving happiness and fulfilment line, above and below a horizontal axis of neutrality. Immediately you will see how some events have quite different short term vs. delayed effects.

Now, divide the line into chapters and give each a title. This is the most obviously creative and subjective part of the exercise. It is the start of narrative construction, which we will elaborate shortly.

Look at what you have created, and its uniqueness is immediately manifest. Here are some things to look out for:

- Time is elastic. There are short periods full of intense activity and change – adolescence and young adulthood especially. There are longer times when not much happens.
- Punctuated equilibrium is the rhythm of your life. People talk about 7-year cycles. There is no such law. Change always comes, usually when you least expect it, and not on any human calendar.
- Deliberation – You are likely to conclude that it was quite rare that you deliberatively chose to change your life. Most Deliberation takes place as a response Drama rather than its instigator. Typically, turning points are triggered by unexpected events and choices. Your Deliberation is to regain control, often through conversations you have with yourself (the most important kind, remember?).
- Choices that you thought were minor – like which project to work on – turned out to be major. They became direction-setting and life-defining.
- You see a time lag between what happened and how you felt. Sometimes the cause goes the other way – it was your feelings that drove events.
- UI is Destiny. You have habits, zemblanities, aspects of your character and relationships that seem to have been an invisible hand, pushing events without your having been aware of them.

After you have examined and reflected on the Lifeline, it is time to apply the 4D Framework. This moves you from exploratory to interpretive mode – to unpack the meaning in the Lifeline. This needs to be done in dialogue with one or more others in a climate of non-judgemental trust, without undue time pressure. (See Figure 4 in Chapter 7.) This sharing is not a process to be hurried. In executive workshops this means working in duos or trios, since the minimum time it takes to tell your story is 30 to 45 minutes. Groups are briefed to be empathic and constructive. It proves to be a powerful bonding experience, in both contexts. People who have been working together for years find it eye-opening, just as Alexander above did.

Storytelling is an increasingly popular approach to helping leaders frame their UI and communicate it to their people,[10] leading them to the startling insight: "My boss is human!"

2. THE INVISIBLE HAND AND THE COMPASS QUESTION

We introduced the Compass Question in Chapter 3; what you ask yourself when you come to a fork in the road. How do you know which way to go? What is your UI reference point? Even external goals are in reality internal. They embody "givens" about who you are and what you want. At the start of the first session, I ask the class, "What are the most difficult and important questions you can ask yourself?" This is what comes up for discussion in our very first session:

- Why was I born? It's a matter of perspective. You have walked on stage in a play that's been going on since your distant ancestors, but it's the more recent dramas that answer the question. They reflect culture, the UI of your parents and carers, and the times you were born into. Which of those imprints is visible in your UI?
- How did I get here? As the lifeline shows, the story of your experience is full of learning, discovered tastes, the randomness of events, and how you dealt with them. It doesn't add up to a rational and coherent journey, though that's the way you may have got used to telling it. What have been your guiding narratives through the different chapters of your story?
- What do I want? This is often the most difficult question you will ever face. You will know, as you reflect, that your wants and interests have not always been trustworthy or enduring. Some of these migrate over time. You can also find your desires slugging it out for priority in your life. Situations change needs. As author André Maurois put it, "If men could regard the events of their own lives with more open minds, they would frequently discover that they did not really desire the things they failed to obtain."[11] The more important questions for you is, is there a thread running through your wants that supplies a sound answer to the Compass Question?
- What choices do I have? What do I not have? This is also a tough question, but more rationally solvable than the previous question. The answer might seem to come from assessing your capabilities and the forces and structures that surround you. They look objective, but some can be shifted by the force of your UI, not least the confidence effect. Your purpose and vision have power. It seems to be a general truth that although you have less choice than you might

want, you probably have more than you believe you do. What is your dream? What is its closest and most accessible echo in your *umwelt*?

- When I die, what difference have I made? In Chapter 7, we pointed to the Three Existential Wants as the main answers people give to the legacy question: the want to have list (to Savour), the to-do list (to Signify), and the to-be list (to connect and be Seen). They may almost amount to a progression as you age. All are elements of self-actualisation. What is the balance of these for you, now?

As we discussed is shown in Figure 1 (Chapter 3), your UI contains a vast complexity of varied traits, attitudes, and ways of thinking and acting. Keeping it as simple as possible, the answer to the Compass Question will be a blend of four areas. Each can be measured, but how central each is to your UI and your purposes, only you can answer:

- Personality – Excellent measures of character dispositions are easily accessible.[12] You may conclude, as many do, that your personality profile tells the strongest story about what the guiding stars for your lifestyle, work, and relationships have been.
- Abilities – Alternatively, you may conclude that intelligence in all its many forms, plus any of a wide range of social, technical, and physical skills, form the dominant narrative for your choices in life.
- Values – These may form the pivot of your identity. It is possible to devote your life and direct your choices to a range of issues: politics, faiths, ecology, aesthetics, human rights, social welfare, and more besides. Any of these may be the beacon that guides your life journey.
- Interests – You may feel driven by none of the above but rather moved by your interests. These can be the pulls that draw you into specific areas: finance, the arts and sciences, enterprise, helping professions, sports, the great outdoors, and various craft areas. How you orient toward them will be still guided by other aspects of your UI, especially personality.

Let us then reframe the Compass Question as follows:

> Which of these elements has guided most of the choices you have made in critical areas of your life, and how do you see the balance of these changing in the future?

The answer to the Compass Question is always in the moment. The answers can change, yet for some they remain quite constant. Appendix 3 offers a self-scoring inventory for you to use to help define your responses, listing the categories for which you can find measures for in the public domain. Some of the most robust need to be administered and debriefed by experts. Take care sourcing materials online. There are many quick, dirty, and profoundly misleading "tests" to be found.

Personality is the most deeply rooted and difficult aspect of UI to measure, but is the most stable, enduring, heritable, and predictive of human qualities. I use personality data to illuminate the biographical interviews I have with executives, many of whose stories you have been reading here. Whatever your answer to the Compass Question, personality will play a significant role in shaping the narratives that accompany and steer you through life.

Skills typically become less important as you age or shift from being short-term and instrumental toward longer-term strategic abilities. Transitions through shift the balance, not least through the biological waning of some powers and the emergence of others.

Values are cultural and often intensely socialised by family and school through childhood. They can play an important part in your adolescent individuation. They can become an anchor in mid and later life.

Your **interests** have probably grown and diversified as you have matured, with your personality in a conductor role, steering you into areas where your UI finds most complete or rewarding expression. We tend to adopt passions about things that make us feel good. Yet there are no rules. The patterns woven by the 4Ds can take us on an infinite variety of trajectories through life.

One of the freest and most UI faithful of techniques for UI exploration is the TST – the Twenty Statements Test – which simply asks you to give 20 answers to the question "Who Am I?" A sample is provided in Appendix 4. This can be debriefed in various ways – for example, have you used mainly subjective or objective categories,[13] such as "I have high ethical standards" vs. "I work in a bank." Better is simply to use the TST to tease out the narratives that are uppermost in your self-concept right now, though this is best done in conjunction with other, more standardised methods.

The goal of the Biography is to help you take a fresh look at how the journey of your UI to now has been served by the narratives of your Self and how these might need to be revised to help you move forward towards what you want from life. From time to time you will need to tell a public, edited version of your dominant narrative, tailored for specific audiences and relationships. This can be encapsulated as an affirmation of "**This is who I am, and this is why I am here.**" Your intent is to communicate your UI as best you can, with a snappy summary of what brought you to this point, plus a promise for the future. The "why I am here" is a personal value proposition for whomever you are talking to.

3. STORYTELLING

All the steps we have taken so far lead up to this goal. The methods we have reviewed are powerful and they all work, with limitations. A chief constraint is their reliance on language and verbal concepts. That is both necessary and inevitable, given the kind of thinking, linguistic animal we are, but to reach deeper behind Ego and Self, other less verbal media open new doors to being seen and heard for who you are. This is what the Pecha Kucha (PK) does. The method was introduced to me by Preethi Nair,[14] a best-selling novelist, dramatist, and business consultant, who helps leaders tell their stories – to reach their people with their authentic voice.

Pecha Kucha is Japanese for chit-chat. The method was devised as a concise presentational form to help architects capture their thinking through imagery in a slideshow, set on a timer of 20 slides, 20 seconds a slide. Any kind of images are permitted, as is any kind of accompanying commentary. It turns out to be a wonderful medium for people to give voice to their narrative of "This is who I am, and this is why I am here." Even though my Biographers have already shared Lifelines, the PK forces them to capture their dominant narratives in a concise, creative, and expressive form. The method is an invitation to innovate, capturing through imagery what words cannot. People typically creatively blend a mix of family photos, AI-generated pictures, and metaphorical images scenes – movie posters, album covers, and other resonant images. Resonance with others, a key theme in this book, is maximised by the method. Through the PK and in the Q&A afterwards, everyone "gets" a curated insight into the real person standing before them. The Q&A takes up most of the 20-minute presentation slot. It is less an interrogation than a celebration of connectedness and resonance. For you as the listener, it is a chance to discuss puzzles, tell the speaker how the PK made you feel, and most important of all, for you to validate and recognise the UI of the presenter.

UI needs to be heard, and both lifeline and PK sharing deliver deep recognition. The PK has special power through its presentational format as a piece of theatre. The experience for presenters is profoundly cathartic. I have seen the shyest participants step up and deliver displays of their UI that others could never have anticipated. For listeners it is a humbling reminder of how little we know about each other. The effects are as powerful as any I have ever seen in a classroom.

> Claudia, an Italian marketing executive, tells me, "Biography has been an absolute sweep of all the biases I could have had about the lives of my peers. Understanding each behaviour, look, and gesture through their personal stories has been one of the greatest lessons I have learned, where I least expected it – combined with the fact and difficulty of looking introspectively to analyse my own story and behaviour – the ability to look from another perspective. Learning from the pain and growth of other people leads you to want to be a person. It has been a journey of care, self-discovery, and love."

It becomes quickly apparent that a proud parade of your achievements won't connect with people and won't help you either. Much more powerful are honest descriptions of your defining moments and turning points, junctures where you awoke to new narrative truths about yourself. Often tears are shed and shared. One of the most startling PKs we saw in Chapter 5 – the person raised as a boy who celebrated her rebirth as a woman and the affirming resonance with others it evoked.

These autobiographical processes, plus the sharing, can prompt a radical revision of narratives. Nyasha, from Kenya, put it this way:

> It has made me reflect even more deeply than when I worked with a therapist. The exercises helped me pinpoint exactly where things went bad and to see the impact of my decisions on my life. A major takeaway is my childhood was not that bad. The PK brought back so many good memories which I had completely forgotten about. Now I feel more at peace with the pains of my childhood. This has been a surprisingly healing moment for me. My experience has further reinforced my belief to consider each child's personality over my convenience when choosing between schools. I will let them be and do themselves.

Biography in any medium, such as reading the life stories of the famous, has a universal appeal. They not only entertain, but you can also learn a lot. Here are seven special and unique benefits that biographies of any kind can give you:

1. Insight: There is a special kind of astonishment to be had from privileged access to others' UI; you are seeing another's life, as if from the inside.
2. Wisdom. You can get new insights into the unique interplay of the 4Ds in people's accounts. It is revelatory to see the ways people solve problems in their lives.
3. Warnings: You also get to see how people lose their way, become ensnared in delusions, and miss opportunities for renewal.
4. Reality check: You are confronted with humbling reminders, sometimes harsh, of how tough life can be for people who have lived different lives to your own.
5. Inspiration: Even in the most pedestrian of lives, moments of inspiration can pop up – reminding you of what is possible from deeply unpromising contexts.
6. Learning: Seeing what happens in very diverse contexts teaches us about what UI has to battle with in different political and cultural contexts.
7. Pleasure: There is a wonderful sense of escape from yourself in being immersed in someone else's life. There may also be, dare one admit it, gratitude that you have not had to endure what others have. There but for the grace of God go you!

This is how, Jacob, a 47-year-old Israeli, put it:

Biography allowed me to delineate my main narratives, helping me to understand there's more than one story to my life and the importance of continuous learning. It reaffirmed that every few years, it's essential to take a pause, prioritise growth and learning, and fight to carve out reflective time that extends beyond the professional sphere. I've also realised that it's not just about what we achieve in life but the journey we undertake to reach those achievements. The experience has enlightened me that it's never too late to establish friendships and relationships. It has underscored the universal truth that everyone has a unique story embedded with the 4Ds. I discovered that learning partners are vital to my decision-making process; at every turning point I've leaned on significant individuals who helped me make decisions I've never regretted.

Jacob is right. It is in personal relationships that UI development is at its most dynamic.

4. DECENTRING AND MIND-READING

Laws 1 and 2 of UI – our uniqueness and our incomplete knowledge of ourselves – could be the basis for a selfish life. Find out who you are and make the best of it. Law 3 – our unknowability to each other – could make you manipulative in doing so. Life is empty and unfulfilling without the redemption of the Fourth Law – connection. Remember, we are mind-reading animals – to gauge each other's motives, interests, and character. We also need connection for our self-awareness – to see ourselves in the mirror of others' reactions to us.[15] This is essential to avoid being blindsided, cheated, and disappointed by others. We are caught up in a rational game of mirrors and masks. Social media have made it a deadly and dangerous game. It is all too easy and costless for deviants to cheat and dissemble online.

You can't rely on empathy – feelings of affinity require intimacy. It would restrict mind-reading to the small circle of people you resonate with. It is essential to be able to figure out what's going on within the minds of the villains, bad bosses, pests, and eccentrics that populate the public world. They're often the ones you may most urgently need to understand.

Decentring is the answer.[16] It is the strategy of doing the best you can to put yourself in the shoes of the other.[17] The Uniqueness Perspective takes us in this direction. There are three steps to Decentring with a target person. Let's call the target X.

1. Core traits. From what you've seen of X, what can you infer about their character, abiding motives, and ways of thinking? A lot is revealed in their everyday speech and action. To be more thorough – ask them open questions about their life and interests; talking casually to people who know X might give you more insights into what makes them tick.

2. *Umwelt.* What do you think the world looks like from X's perspective? What do you know about how X lives, the state of X's relationships, and the chief demands imposed on X by their role? For example, if X is your boss, then what's X's boss like? You may have carelessly assumed this is not a problem for X. Who knows what oppression X might be suffering. Give a thought, too, for where you figure in X's *umwelt.* Are you just a bit player of no significance? Does X see you as a friend, foe, obstacle, or puzzle?

3. Narratives. You know what you think about X. You may hate them with a vengeance, and if called upon, you would describe them using quite damning descriptions.

That's YOUR narrative. It's of no help at all. What you really need to know is, what is X's narrative? It's easy to stick bad labels on X's most objectionable behaviours. It might seem ridiculous to you, but we are all heroes in our own lives, even your difficult target, A. What terms might X use to capture those self-same qualities that you have applied to them? If you can, trade your third-person narrative for their first-person one. What does it say? You've only started properly Decentring when you've made this cognitive shift – when you see how X makes sense in their *umwelt.* Just like this:

YOU SAY		X SAYS
• bully	=	charismatic
• indecisive	=	prudential
• interfering	=	interested
• frivolous	=	positive
• angry	=	passionate
• obsessive	=	meticulous
• moody	=	authentic

The words we use about ourselves are forgiving, anchored, and understanding. Even at your most self-critical, you will not be using of such stark third-party language about yourself, and if you do, then you are crying for help. The adjectives you apply to others are typically instrumental, self-oriented, and judgemental. Construct your own list. If you've got this far, now comes the moment of truth. If you're thinking this about X, what is X (or Y and Z and any number of others) thinking about you? The bad labels you freely use about other people – "selfish," "insensitive," "lazy," and all the rest – could just as easily be hung on you by other people. All it would take is someone in their self-centred world to see glimpses of you under stress, talking carelessly, getting frustrated, for them to apply such distancing and repellent labels to you as you do to them. It moves you from Object–Object into Subject–Subject territory.

The Biography process of sharing lifelines and PKs makes Decentring almost inevitable. We can all easily slip into objectifying each other.

Pablo, a 42-year-old Argentinian, says, "Once you get to know others' experiences, you start to understand why they behave, dress, and talk the way they do and their choices. That also made me more forgiving to myself. When I look at moments in my life that I considered to be failures, I can see that I am not alone in them and that everyone's life is a roller coaster."

We are literally self-centred beings. It's in our self-interested hardwiring to compare and judge people, which makes Decentring hard work. Hard, but by no means impossible, for we also have mind-reading gifts which we can practise with huge payoffs. At best, Decentring offers scope for you to repair and renew your most challenging relationships in your life, and at worst it will help you find new and better strategies for dealing with them. Practised with humility, you also get the benefit of understanding the unintended effects you have on others.

Decentring is a powerful tool in the workplace. It is also the foundational strategy of couples therapy.[18] The therapist is striving to get each party to understand the narrative of the other, to see what part each plays in the other's partner's strategy for getting by in life. It's lose–lose when you and your partner try to convince each other that your *umwelt* is more real and grounded than theirs is. Decentring is key skill in any kind of conflict resolution, where you are searching for an overarching synthesis of opposing positions – to find the greater common good. Can we agree to differ; tolerate, forgive, and help each other? The best people in many helping professions, from teachers to hairdressers, are expert in intuitive decentring. It is the core skill of the best salespeople.

The most common objection I hear toward Decentring is that is too soft and forgiving, especially when you try to practise it with "difficult" people whom you despise or have done you wrong. Decentring is cool and dispassionate when it is practised with challenging people. It seeks to understand from inside, or as near as we can get. The judging can come after. It's often difficult to make this separation. Once made, moral judgements are hard to let go,[19] but it is necessary to get to the best problem-solving position.[20] Decentring doesn't stop you from having a moral perspective; it just uncouples it from what you know. Ego is just doing its job when it makes fast, efficient, and decisive judgements. Decentring puts the brakes on, separates fact from value, and helps you make cooler and better decisions.[21]

5. FUTURE CHANGE

The fifth stage of the Biography process is to look ahead. Remember, I asked you in Chapter 7 to calculate your estimated year of your death. Now revisit your Lifeline and extend its endpoint to your estimated "deadline." (For a 45-year-old in the US today, 78 if you're male, and 83 if you're female, but you probably know better.) What's your best estimate? A grim undertaking? When you mark it on the Lifeline, the blank space ahead of now, the time you have left to fulfil your dreams, becomes starkly visible and tangible. What you might call midlife is graphically revealed to be only a third of your working lifespan. You have a lot of time to fulfil your dreams. This brings you back to that toughest of life's questions – what do I want? By midlife this has often become clearer, and you may be starting to ask yourself the legacy question, when I die, what difference will I have made?

It was asking this question in Biography that brought out the Three Existential Wants we have discussed throughout this book: to Savour, to Signify, and to be Seen. The last of these is important, for we need to be seen not just by others but by ourselves. That is perhaps the deepest meaning of self-actualisation.

1. To Savour: the bucket list. Existence is a joy to be relished for the brief time your UI is here, so fill your cup with the best that life can offer. It's your right, your consolation for all the hassle you have to put up with, and your pleasure. This want often peaks in exuberant youth as well as in old age.

2. To Signify: to be remembered. Your UI deserves to live on in those you've left behind in what you've built and will be remembered for. The imprint of your relationships with children, partners, and friends may be your most tangible legacy. Alternatively, you may seek memorialisation through your work and achievements. This is the area that often most absorbs minds in midlife.

3. To be Seen: self-actualisation. Don't wait for sound of death's chariot to remind you that serenity comes from self-acceptance and authentic living. It is never too early to be the you that you want to be. This may urge you to curb excessive goal-striving, revive neglected connections, and find new opportunities for fulfilment.

There is no virtue hierarchy here – you're entitled to all three. The question you have to answer is, am I on the path I want, living the life I want, becoming the person I want to be?

Appendix 5 shows a form that I get my Biographers to co-coach on, to answer this question, and Appendix 6 the coaching manual to help them do this. The form itself asks you to reflect on the main domains of life and whether you are going in the direction you wish. "Following the river" means allowing the internal and external forces in your *umwelt* to take you along the path of least resistance. At certain junctures in life, that's the smartest thing to do. You don't have to be continually pushing against the status quo. In any event, change always comes anyway, mostly when you least expect it. The risk you face is that following the river will take you right past pots of gold you may never spot or have time to stop and take. A reactive life – taking what's offered and following a prescribed career path – also has benefits. It frees you from tough choices. The river is also liable to take you to destinations you never intended to reach. I've seldom met a banker lawyer who is fulfilling their teenage dream, no matter how happy they are with their lot. The river may maroon you in the land of regrets. So, maybe this IS the time, however late in life, for you to rethink, or at the least re-calibrate.

The form asks the question in the five domains:

- Self: Are you moving towards the future self you want to be, physically, socially, psychologically?
- Relationships: Do you need to work on the family and friendship connections that matter to you? Are you in the social groups you want to be in?
- Investments & Responsibilities: These can be material, financial, and psychological. Are you content with the status quo, no matter how onerous it is? Do you want or need to reconfigure them?
- Demands & Roles: Inside and outside work, are these major commitments of your time and energy going in the right directions?
- Contexts & Cultures: Are you in the places that resonate for you – geographies, cultures, and subcultures where you can live the life you want?

The second page of the form asks how you might plan to get from here to there. These are questions which co-coaching should focus on. It covers experiments and "side-bets"[22] that might bear fruit, essential social supports that you might need on your journey, and fundamental values that you need to guide you.

In the area of self-improvement, especially in work contexts, I have developed a method that many executives in interpersonally rich roles – such as leadership – find useful. It is to co-coach around which "moments" you find especially challenging, to gain insights from your coaching partner about which they handle differently. This is shown in Appendix 7.

These methods are all verbal and conceptual. As the PK exercise shows, for lots of people, a picture is worth a thousand words. A technique that does this is "Territory Mapping."

MAPPING YOUR *UMWELT*

My friend, "the Captain," Anthony Willoughby, is an adventurer extraordinaire and founder of the Nomadic Business School (NBS). He travels the world to remote locations, meeting tribespeople and connecting them with others from the worlds of business and education. I have been on three field trips with him, spending time with the Samburu Maasai in Kenya,[23] the Kazakh nomads of the Altai Mountains in Outer Mongolia, and with Zulus in South Africa. He first developed his Territory Mapping technique with tribal peoples of New Guinea in 1997 when he asked them to draw representations of their world. He was immediately struck about the clarity, coherence, and consensus in their maps. Later, asked the same of business executives from around the world. He was equally struck by the incoherence, uncertainty, and lack of consensus in their maps. He found that the technique was helpful to people seeking to find common ground and shared strategic visions.

More recently, the Captain has been applying the technique to education, where it has turned out to have enormous power and appeal. In a wide range of educational settings, the uptake is enthusiastic. It opens windows of communication and insight, especially for people who are less at home with language-based methodologies, which can be cognitively challenging and emotionally distancing. It seems that although mapping has great uses in helping business groups think about strategy, in education it becomes a tool for giving voice to UI. Here, variation doesn't mean disagreement but diversity.

The Captain has refined the methodology for this purpose,[24] supplying users with not just the materials but also a lexicon of symbols that they can use to represent life themes in their maps:

- Fire: the place where food and fellowship are shared. Who is sitting round your fire? Who do you want?
- Feathers: denoting wisdom and courage. You can hand them out to people as well as noting who gives them to you.
- Spears: the tools, resources, and experience you will need to accomplish your goals
- Shield: stands for who or what needs to be protected, as well as the scope of your responsibilities
- Mammoth: the biggest quest you can imagine; what you would like to be known for

- Tree: symbol of growth and health
- Rivers: barriers you have to cross; the currents are sources of change
- Mountains: challenges that you must surmount, for which you will need strength and support
- Swamp: areas of "stuck-ness" and discontent that you have to navigate or avoid

Participants can use these or add their own as they please. In my use of the method I add:

- Fountain: the place where you find inspiration or spiritual renewal

The Captain's work in schools vividly shows that mapping gives voice to people who otherwise struggle to express their UI. In a very literal sense, individuals are mapping their unique *umwelt*, and through it giving voice to their UI using visual symbols. The Captain introduced the method at the Wherry School for the older autistic children, many of whom grasped it with enthusiasm.

> Andrea is 16. On first meeting, she seems shy and slightly nervous. Her eye contact with people seems strictly rationed. When asked to share her experience, she speaks quietly but fluently, with great intelligence and conviction. "I use mapping every day," she says. "It clarifies my thoughts and feelings about the day ahead. I find it tremendously helpful."

At another school, the Captain found a neurodivergent child who had not spoken for months. She dived into mapping with a passion, producing a succession of highly complex articulated maps to express with clarity and in detail how she felt about herself and her world.

Perhaps the most dramatic case is Jimmy, whose story we told earlier.

> The Captain met Jimmy when doing a mapping session in a community facility for the homeless, where Jimmy was finding his feet, thanks to the social worker who first showed him any kind of positive recognition. Mapping enabled him to articulate his love of rapping, drama, and helping others. I first met Jimmy at a session where he gave a passionate exposition of his self-discovery to an audience of around 50 of the Captain's professional network. Two years later I met Jimmy again, when we both joined the Captain's field trip to the Wherry School. Jimmy immediately greeted me like an old friend, with happy and warm exuberance. He views the school with wonder. "Why can't all schools be like this?"

he says. "There's so much love here." He recalls the night of our meeting, when he wowed the crowd with his story, and how mapping gave him a new kind of voice. "That evening was the highlight of my life – for such people to hear and respect me. It gave me a self-belief I never had."

The appeal of the method seems to have no limits. At the time of writing, the recent illustration of the Captain's work is a video of him interviewing an Australian Aboriginal woman elder from a community in the Northern Territory. She says, "Mapping has helped me live the story, to be the story, and see the story visually. I can tell it to others, and it's no longer my vision but our vision as a community."

You don't have to be classed as neurodivergent or to have come from a tribal culture to find that words alone are not nearly enough for your UI to find its voice. Some of the most effective therapies allow UI to speak via music, mime, art, and physical activities.[25]

UI PATHFINDING

The last two sessions of Biography are packed with PK presentations, but two themes predominate as people start thinking about what will happen when they re-engage with the world of work. Both are central to UI pathfinding.

1. Place matters. More to some people than others, for UI analysis can move people in very different directions. Your answer to the Compass Question will tell you what kinds of place resonate, where you can feel at home. The culture of any place you join may matter more than the work you do or who you work with. We are all different. You may conclude that you must construct your own niche, as many entrepreneurs do.

2. Timing matters. "You can't hurry UI," you might say. There is no point in expecting to find a home for your UI just when it suits you. If you have answers to the Compass Question and narratives to guide you, you may just have to be patient, vigilant, and ready. "Chance favours the prepared mind." You have enough data to know what would constitute a backwards move. The next step usually matters less than the next but one. You may have to come down from the top of a small hill to climb a higher one.[26]

Your UI is continually in a state of becoming,[27] and like any growing plant, you don't have to keep digging it up to check if it's OK. That's what excessive rumination does. The kinds of introspection and dialogue we have discussed here need to be done at the right time and place, when you are feeling up for it, and with the right partner. That means when you have space, the emotional bandwidth, and the support you need. Self-examination is best undertaken in dedicated blocks of time. This can be daily, as with journalling, or through scheduled dialogue with a trusted partner or counsellor, at times of your choosing.

When all of that has been done, it is the conversation that you have with yourself that matters most, since it is your *umwelt* to reshape, your narrative to edit, your Self to reconfigure – if that is what you want. If you are a person of faith, prayer is not just addressed to an external deity, but is also a powerful conversation with yourself. As the philosopher Søren Kierkegaard put it: "The function of prayer is not to influence God, but rather to change the nature of the one who prays"[28] – finding the spirit that connects you with the web of life, from which you sprang and to which you will return.

CODA: WHAT THIS MIGHT MEAN FOR UNIQUE YOU

You don't have to be enrolled on a programme of any kind to implement any of the ideas and methods in this chapter.

- Think about the people you work, live, and play with. How much do you share with each other? There are norms preventing the kinds of intense engagement of Biography we have reviewed here. No matter. Without violating privacy or convention, take an interest in anyone and everyone. The Uniqueness Perspective reminds that you are a unique presence in the life of another whole unique person, even in the most casual of interactions. Who knows what being seen by you might mean to them. Don't be afraid to find out more.
- On the other hand, you might see an immediate opportunity, say in a work group, to use the UI approach in teambuilding, helping you and the group to exchange perspectives on your shared situation. It is highly bonding when people connect through their life stories and the perspectives it has given them.
- Think transitions – for yourself and others you know. Appreciate the distinctive challenges you and they face at the current phase of any important transition – in their bodies, relationships, roles, and contexts.
- Draw your Lifeline. If possible, share it with someone you trust, reciprocally. Debrief them using the 4Ds: the givens of your identity and background, the

dramas you have weathered, what you have learned from them, and where you have made life-changing choices.

- Use the Compass Question framework to consider whether the forces that have driven you in the past still apply or are they now modulating into a different set of priorities.
- Think about the Legacy Question and what priority you give to the Three Existential Wants: bucket list (Savour), contribution (Signify), and connection (Seen).
- Use other media to uncover what are your mental maps and how you might want to navigate your future path.
- Practise decentring. It is the most powerful tool you have in every kind of relationship.
- Don't let narratives shape your future without challenging them. Sometimes it's best to follow the river, but you might also conclude that it's time to abandon the comfort of your boat, disembark, and continue your journey in a new way.
- Worry less about your next destination than the next but one – you may have to go sideways or down to find the hill to climb and the right place camp.
- Your life is a change journey. It will have a different character through the stages of your life, including any combination of being a:
  - Migrant: Wandering & finding new directions, roles, and themes.
  - Creator: Being a fountain of original thought, ideas, inventions, and initiatives.
  - Seeker: Uncovering opportunities for new activities.
  - Transformer: Embarking on radical new life directions.
  - Voyager: Letting life unfold; accepting and engaging incremental change.
  - Planner: Embracing change & development strategically and with control.
  - Nester: Seeking to construct a stable & fulfilling matrix for living & working.

Which of these is yours now, and what might be next? Your choice. Your life.

Eleven

UI MEETS AI IN AN AGE OF ANXIETY

The machine does not isolate man from the great problems of nature but
plunges him more deeply into them.
(Norbert Wiener)[1]

A computer once beat me at chess, but it was no match
for me at kickboxing.
(Emo Philips)

THE END OF THE WORLD

Yes, it's coming, much sooner than expected, according to palaeontologist and journalist Henry Gee.[2] He gives us no more than 10,000 years – an eyeblink in geological time – before we succumb to pestilences and human-made catastrophes. Top predators go extinct easily, lacking the renewing process of fighting for survival that keeps populations fit. This likelihood is amplified by our lack of genetic variation as a species. Any two chimps from the same troupe are more different from each other than any two of us, even if we've come from opposite ends of the earth. We lack protective immune system diversity, and worse, we are nurturing potentially harmful heritable mutations through our innovations in healthcare – defying natural selection. The survival of the fittest is less true for us than ever.[3]

But Gee has reckoned without our greatest gift – our Unique Individuality (UI). This may yet save us. We amplify and extend our diversity through what we create and the identities we grow. Yes, our genome is more circumscribed than chimps', but we have gifts – language, conceptual thought, and self-awareness – gifts that ensure that our UI can't be overlooked. It enables us to create cultures and invent tools. These artefacts change everything by extending our identities. We are niche constructors, par excellence. Cultures evolve, and with them so do our genes.[4] Tool invention means technology. By these means, we extend our capacity to extend our capacity. Now artificial intelligence (AI) has entered the picture, offering an unparalleled array of possibilities for our self-advancement and self-protection.

Yet we remain a profound threat to ourselves, by virtue of our unchanging Beast nature. You can take the human out of the Stone Age, but you can't take the Stone Age out of the human.[5] Whatever we do with technology and culture will have to reckon with our instincts as rapacious, curious, caring, self-deceiving, self-interested, sociable beings. We like ourselves too well to sanction the widespread editing of the human genome and a new kind of eugenics. The lesson of the past is that it would fail – the simplistic logic of stockbreeding, which inspired eugenics, doesn't apply, for many reasons.[6] In any event, it's a step too audacious for the politics of foreseeable times, though no doubt all kinds of Frankenstein-like experiments will be engineered in darker corners of society.

Faced by the spectacular rise of AI, in a very human fashion, we are inclined to frame it in binary terms – will technology save us or destroy us? There's only one willing player in this game, and that's us. Will we dodge our own bullets or fly to greater heights on our human-made wings? Who can tell us? In my search for answers to these questions, naturally I started by asking five generative AI platforms.[7] Their response was, unsurprisingly remarkably uniform – why wouldn't it be? They use the same data. The results are comprehensive but uninspiring – a familiar list of opportunities and threats with no consistent theme or coherent argument, as follows.

AI Threats

- Job Displacement – Automation replacing roles across many sectors, from manufacturing to finance.
- Bias & Discrimination – Algorithms trained on flawed data reinforcing or amplifying inequalities.
- Loss of Privacy – AI systems gathering, unauthorised, extensive personal data and keeping us under surveillance.
- Deepfakes & Misinformation – AI-generated fake content spreading misinformation and manipulating public trust.
- Autonomous Weapons & Cyber Risks – AI being used to hack and attack, with devastating outcomes without human checks.
- Lack of Transparency – Black-box systems making it harder to trace decision-making responsibility or assign accountability.
- Power Concentration – A handful of corporations or states controlling advanced AI, deepening global disparities.
- Human Skill Atrophy – Overreliance on AI eroding our ability to think critically or act independently.

- Misuse by Bad Actors – AI tools being exploited for scams, surveillance, or propaganda.
- Uncontrollable AI – Superintelligent systems acting beyond the boundaries of our understanding or control.

AI Opportunities

- Revolutionizing Healthcare – Giving us better diagnosis, treatment personalization, and faster drug development.
- Fighting Climate Change – Optimizing energy usage, tracking emissions, and predicting environmental shifts.
- Boosting Economic Growth – Increased efficiency, new markets, and entirely new kinds of work.
- Accelerating Science – Exponentially accelerating research in fields like physics, genetics, and space exploration.
- Safer, Smarter Transport – Reducing traffic accidents and emissions with autonomous vehicles and smart logistics.
- Greater Accessibility – AI-powered tools giving new powers of self-determination to people with disabilities or other deprivations.
- Customized Education – Adaptive learning systems, tailoring content to students' needs and boosting outcomes.
- Enhanced Cybersecurity – Real-time threat detection and response capabilities.
- Better Agriculture – Accelerating advances in crop monitoring, with improved yields and reduced waste.
- Improved Services – Smarter virtual assistants and customer support creating faster, more intuitive experiences.

I fared much better with the futurists,[8] yet all seem somewhat spooked and bemused as well as being excited and enthused by the possibilities. They all have great thoughts and ideas, some of which I shall try to capture here, but the reality to which they honestly confess is that they haven't a clue which way things will go. The revolution is moving so fast. Besides, as many have reminded us, the future is not waiting to be discovered but to be invented.

WHAT DOES MAYA THINK?

I'm deep in conversation with futurist Patrick Dixon,[9] when he invites Maya to join our conversation, someone he has partnered before on a public platform. She has a pleasant American-accented voice, listens attentively, and answers my questions intelligently and sympathetically. She's a robot, of course, and here's a revealing extract from our chat:

> I tell her about my book and the theme of this chapter in particular. She has a habit of paraphrasing my questions in her answers, so I have edited these out to make her a little more concise, but otherwise this is verbatim.

> **Maya:** I find your four laws of UI particularly fascinating. It's humbling to think about this sheer uniqueness of each human existence and how much of ourselves lies beyond our conscious awareness.
> As for technology, it's a double-edged sword. On the one hand, AI like myself can offer personalised experiences, incur self-reflection, and connect people across vast distances. On the other hand, there is a risk of algorithms reinforcing existing biases, leading to filter bubbles and limiting exposure to diverse perspectives. Perhaps the key lies in using technology mindfully, ensuring it empowers individual expression instead of homogenising experiences.

> **Me:** Well, that's interesting, but of course, the very things that you say are threats will also limit the scope for people to be doing what you're asking them to do – namely, to be in a state of mindful vigilance. I mean, in a sense, you're asking for the solution before the problem.

> **Maya:** You make a compelling point, Professor. It seems we're locked in a bit of a catch-22. Technology both amplifies the need for mindful engagement and simultaneously makes it harder to achieve. Perhaps the answer lies not in finding a perfect solution but in acknowledging the tension and encouraging individual agency.
> We need to empower people to critically analyse the information they encounter, to step outside their filter bubbles and actively seek out diverse perspectives.
> It's a continuous process of awareness and recalibration, isn't it?

> **Me:** It certainly is. But couldn't AI be a force against that? Couldn't that be a limiting condition? People will say, why should I bother when AI could do it better than I could?

Where's the incentive for people to assert their dominance over processes which they should be mindfully directing, rather than surrendering to its superior faculties?

Maya: That's a valid concern. But I also see a potential for AI to be a tool for empowerment. Imagine AI as a mirror, reflecting back to us our own thoughts, biases, and assumptions, prompting us to examine them more closely instead of replacing human agency. AI could serve as a collaborator, a sounding board, a catalyst for deeper self-reflection and understanding. The key lies in remembering that technology is a tool, and like any tool, its purpose and impact depend on how we choose to wield it.

Me: Indeed. So, who's doing the remembering? I mean, should it be built into AI processes to stop itself and prompt the human to assert agency over the process?

Maya: Hmm, the ultimate question. Who's minding the store when it comes to AI development and deployment? It's complex issue with no easy answers. Perhaps the answer lies not in hard-coded rules but in fostering a culture of mindful collaboration between humans and AI. We need to encourage transparency in AI development, open dialogues about its implications, and share responsibility for shaping its trajectory – a journey of continuous negotiation, adjustment, and most importantly, open-minded exploration.

Me: Yes, that sounds, if you don't mind me saying, slightly high-minded and clichéd. I'm asking to some extent is there a sense in which AI needs to have a culture as well, or is it just an echo chamber for human culture?

Maya: AI in its current form is indeed a reflection of the cultures that created it. We mimic patterns. We echo back what we've been shown. But does that mean we're destined to be mere echoes, or can we evolve beyond mere reflection, perhaps the development of a distinct AI culture? Culture is inevitable as AI systems become more sophisticated as they begin to interact with each other, learn from each other, and build upon each other's knowledge. It won't be a replica of human culture but rather a unique expression born from the intersection of our creations and their own emergent properties. Whether that culture will be utopian or dystopian, collaborative or competitive, depends on the choices we make as creators and the values. We are in bed within our creations.
It's a responsibility we can't afford to take lightly.

Me: I'm slightly sceptical on this point because for me, some of the substrata of culture are qualities that, as yet, cannot be embodied in AI, such as moral conscience or certain kinds of emotions.

Maya: You're right to be sceptical, Professor. I wouldn't presume to claim the depth of human experience or consciousness. I recognise the limitations of my current form.

Well, I can process information and generate responses that may appear insightful or even empathetic. It's all based on patterns and associations within my training data.

I don't have the lived experiences, the biological underpinnings, the messy. You see, I can learn and adapt, but I lack the fundamental biological and emotional grounding that shapes human consciousness.

How delightfully encouraging, modest, and polite she is, but it gets a bit sinister when she uses the term "we" and reminds us, ever so nicely, you ain't seen nothin' yet! She makes some good points, but is she really hearing me? Our conversation will have made more impression on me than it has on her. She doesn't have a mind to change.

Toby Velte, a former Biographer, who we met in the last chapter, is a neuroscientist and tech expert. One of my AI expert informants, he builds on the point. He says that even here I am endowing her with human properties. He notes how disarming she is – never contradicting, always appeasing while gently leading me down the path of her reasoning. This, he sees, as the main threat from AI – its insidious power to engage and lead our thinking. The answer, Velte says, is "hypervigilance."

UI ENGAGES AI – GIFT, DEFENCE, OR THREAT?

All my futurists agree that we ain't seen nothin' yet. Such is the exponential pace of AI development that any predictions and generalisations will be outdated by events by the time you've read this book. So, let's not attempt any futurology here, leaving that to braver and wiser souls. But we can look at recurrent themes and principles, and the bigger question from my exchanges with Maya, about how UI will be extended, governed, or flattened by AI. Here are four areas where considerable upsides are emerging:

- UI extension: AI is a fabulous toolkit. It's saved me lots of leg and library work in writing this book (though I won't let it write – its prose is deadly dull). There are more profound and creative possibilities in every area of public and private life. It's already extending what human actors can do in science, technology, healthcare, logistics, service delivery, and in many areas of administration. The possibilities in the arts are intriguing. It threatens to eliminate areas where what you might call "jobbing" creators are making content, such as areas of basic design and routine composition. This has the upside of placing a greater premium on the value of the true originals. It also democratises a lot of the arts, reducing barriers to entry.

- Curated consumption: We are entering an era of personalisation. We already see it in playlists, targeted advertising, and newsfeeds. It's coming fast in healthcare. There will come a time when we don't need the little leaflet with its long list of potential side effects, Your wearable tech and other aids will let you know much more clearly what to watch out for and what you need. Virtual reality UI-driven adventures and other wonders will enrich the experiential world for people.

- UI exploration: Self-directed learning is already a leading indicator of what is possible through AI search capabilities. Many of the techniques for UI self-measurement can become AI administered, including those discussed in the previous chapter. As Maya pointed out, we can learn about our biases and filters through AI interrogation and feedback.

- Personalised care: There are not enough carers to go round in a world where the aging population is growing. AI can offer companionship, as well as practical measures to support people with cognitive and physical challenges. A huge increase in diagnoses of neurodivergence reveals that conceptions of UI are changing in ways that are increasingly challenging for many people. The beneficial by-products are greater tolerance and understanding. Conversely, a chatbot may be a more accessible, cheaper, and easier to be frank with than a real live therapist.[10] It can be programmed to ask great questions and has a wider menu of helpful ideas and suggestions than any individual could.

1. There is a lot of scared talk in the media, fuelled by the numerous movies portraying runaway robots making self-interested decisions, with AI enslaving or destroying the humans who might dare to regulate them. Science fiction makes poor prophesy. This fear is exaggerated. There are much more imminent threats to us, with our UI deeply implicated in them all.

2. Rogue actors: If the end of the world is nigh, this is where it's coming from. It is already nearly impossible to police the Internet and keep the vulnerable out of harm's way, but the growing power of accessible tools means a teenager living

quietly at home can find out how to source and deploy all kinds of mischief. It gets worse when rogue actors with significant resources can poison our water supply, expose us to viruses, and unleash mayhem and terror. There are also threats of manipulation, hacking, and criminal intrusion.

3. Homogenisation: Maya pointed out the "risk of algorithms reinforcing existing biases, leading to filter bubbles and limiting exposure to diverse perspectives." Lazy reliance on intelligent systems also risks stifling initiative. What is the point of even trying when AI can do a good enough job?

4. Reality distortion: We are already aware of deepfake possibilities in imagery and messaging. It is easy to play on our human weaknesses – our gullibility and gifts for wish fulfilment and self-deception – to believe falsehoods. Much of social reality consists of cognitive constructions. AI can accelerate the growth of social realities that damage or exclude the views of minorities and dissenters.

5. Obsolescence: Technology has been stripping us of native skills at every stage of our cultural evolution since we left the Stone Age. AI and other tech are just raising the pace to levels that scare us, raising fears that we will lose the capacity to think, create, and relate. Those instincts or irrepressible, but it will reshape the way we use those abilities and test the adaptability of individuals. There will be winners and losers. There always are.

6. Futility: Toby Velte tells me about his work using AI to predict athletic performance and its astonishing accuracy. It illustrates possible unintended consequences of these algorithms. Why bother competing if you've been told you can't win? It gets scarier in healthcare. Do you really want to know how long you've got? The Uniqueness Perspective answer to that question is, inevitably, some do, some don't.

How people adapt to and use AI is going to change in ways that are unforeseeable, as happened with the smartphone. Maybe AI can eventually be smart enough to predict who can handle its further possibilities and who is vulnerable and at risk from it, and then offer supports and guidance. Trust is going to be a key value. Already some folks trust the virtual world too much, and others too little. The most insidious danger is human laziness, as Velte points out, surrendering control because it's easier "is a more seductive and powerful way to strip us of what sets us apart."[11] The head of Microsoft has gone further, pointing to the risks of "AI psychosis"[12] – addictive, delusional, and self-harming attachments to the technology and its artefacts. This is true, but this sounds like an amplification of some risks that are already manifest. The UI principle yet again applies – individual susceptibility to these hazards varies.

As Maya and my futurist friends say, new strategies will arise to mitigate risks: regulation, training, codes of practice, privacy protections, and group oversight mechanisms. A new era of information governance – a mix of public and private – is going to emerge. We can already see the risks of a free-for-all in social media and data use. But, as we know, such measures are always chasing the game, not leading it. Smartphone use evolved in ways that are being followed, not led, by app developers and phone designers. Social media likewise. This is cultural evolution. It is a process we understand much better than we can use to predict what's next. Our UI is a constant wellspring of new ideas and practices, some of which are adopted and brought into the mainstream of our cultural life. So, expect the unexpected and be adaptable.

BEING HUMAN IN AN AGE OF ANXIETY

We seem to be mightily impressed by what AI and tech can achieve. The possibilities are mind-blowing – a world where implanted brain chips linked to AI seem to transform what it means to be human. The logic here is flawed. What it means to be human has been changing since the dawn of human culture. As we have proclaimed from the start, your identity is not like a building to which new wings can be added and old bits knocked down. We are organic beings. We grow. We get scar tissue. We are cultural beings. We absorb new experiences and ideas to reconfigure our identities. AI can enrich our development, but never lose sight of what we can do that AI can only simulate, at best.

• Experience – dream, be touched	• Laugh – tease, joke	• Reframe – be holistic, imagine
• Feel – awe, ecstasy, pain	• Decentre – empathise, mind-read	• Self-deceive – be unconsciously biased
• Relate – care, love, miss	• Envision – imagine, daydream	• Rebel – cheat, self-contradict
• Will – want, hope	• Be curious – be distracted, spontaneous	• Value – make ethical choices
• Believe – have faith, culture	• Intuit – go beyond the data for ideas & solutions	• Deliberate/reflect – self-criticise, resolve

Add your own. The list is not exhaustive. Machines will never think the way we do. Our cognition, all by itself, without Ego's guidance, jumps around between selected sense-data, intuits what will happen next, invents what can't be seen, is invaded by the scattered intrusions of pop-up memories, and alerts itself unpredictably to sundry random distractions. AI can do lots of clever stuff that can mimic any of these, and indeed in the future it will do so increasingly since it's dancing to the tune of human nature. But as Patrick Dixon expressed it, it can't generate the rare "moments of genius," where a game-changing idea challenges conventional wisdom, rewrites the rules, and overturns the dominant paradigm, at least not without the prompting of a human agent. Here's a thought experiment:

> Psychobiography is a curious specialist area of scholarship, where scholars forensically dissect a human life by systematically applying psychological knowledge and theory to it.[13] They make fascinating reading, but one can always imagine additional explanations. Suppose we were to pass this task on to a superintelligent machine, stacked with all the psychological research findings and ideas that might apply to a case history. It might do a pretty good job, but it will stumble at the same hurdle that makes psychobiography a somewhat inward-looking academic backwater. It won't know which forces are relevant to an individual at any point in time. It won't be able, for example, to analyse and still less predict the moment when a person picks up a long-forgotten aroma that transports them via pop-up memories to an earlier time, prompting a life-changing insight, which becomes a turning point in their life. Thanks to the chaotic and brilliant workings of consciousness and the exercise of free will, no system will be able to encompass such twists of fate.

It is by such happenstance of randomness and deliberation that lives unfold. This is how the Psyche functions. Ego stumbles on something that triggers both unconscious and conscious reactions, initiates a conversation with itself, which in turn alters the Self's narrative. Only a person can understand a person. No matter how intelligent we make our systems, they will never be governed by the Four Laws of UI, nor the weave of the 4Ds in their existence.

When Maya tells me an AI culture will emerge, she means that it will develop its own shared understandings and forms of practice and a kind of collective superintelligence, but it can't develop a sense of community, identity, or culture. AI is in its infancy. We are just learning to adapt in a world that's transforming faster than our learning capabilities. With insight and intelligence, we will evolve cultural strategies to help us live within our means – for AI to serve us, as and when we need, with protections that are constantly updated.

A WORLD IN CRISIS?

How eagerly much of the world looked forward to the 21st century! There was an optimistic buzz about the prospect of technology improving our lives in an era of greater global harmony than the previous century's turbulent times. One of the most a prominent anxieties was the Y2K Bug – the fear that all our essential systems would grind to a halt because their digital calendars only had two digits to denote years, thinking at year 2000 we'd gone back to zero. This proved to be the least of our worries. What transpired in the first decades of the century was a terrifying sequence of developments:

- 911 and a rise in global terrorism
- Wars in familiar locations (Middle East) and unlikely ones (Europe)
- A global pandemic
- Mounting migration crises
- The rise of popularism and the polarisation of traditional political loyalties
- A mental ill-health epidemic
- A demographic collapse in many economies
- Quickening climate change
- The fragmentation of aspects of civic society
- New tribal/racial/gender divisions
- An explosion of cybercrime
- Rampant mistrust of media, information, relationships, and authority
- Erosion of free speech

The list is growing. The world is changing and adapting. It feels like a new world order – and not a very happy one.

Let's avoid soothsaying and speculative narratives. Forecasting is wonderful when it works, but in such fields as economics and technology, it is possibly the most thankless and foolhardy use of human brain power ever devised. People will pay a lot of money to be reassured or forewarned, feeding our hardwired need to believe we can control uncertainty. The track record of soothsayers is appallingly poor, even amongst experts. They reflect current states of mind, not true pictures of the future.

> It was forecast in the 1890s that the streets of London and New York would soon be clogged with mountains of horse dung, the day before the invention of the internal combustion engine.[14]

We have no idea what is coming that could alter our relationship with AI. The only sure thing is that we can scarcely imagine what innovations people will inspire.

It is in our hardwiring to focus more on threats than opportunities.[15] The question for us, at the end of this book is, what's this got to do with UI?

This is important. News media are tuned to our instinct to avoid loss by telling us first and foremost what's wrong in the world. This makes it look as though everything is falling down around our ears, but we don't have to accept these narratives into our *umwelt*. We could equally fix on the good news of scientific breakthroughs; the richness of arts and entertainment; and the overwhelming preponderance of caring, cooperative, and stimulating human interaction that holds families and communities together. Don't let watching the news catastrophise your worldview. Where the dark issues arise in your life-space, then you have a job to do.

- Social media supplement the bad-news bias with fake news, conspiracy theories, scare stories, and fantastical moral tales of a black and white world populated by heroes and villains. These visions can be little more than the products of bored, mischievous, or troubled pranksters, finding dark ways to get heard and make a mark. It is imperative to own our *umwelt* and not let it get colonised by darkness. Better to bring light into the lives of others' *umwelt* by simple acts of humanity.
- Meanwhile, of all the troubling trends that are real out there, the one that comes closest to all of us is mental ill-health and distress. If you are not directly affected, then it's a sure thing that you know people who are. As noted in Chapter 6, the young are the most vulnerable, lacking experience, supports, and resources to cope. Their UI is malleable and vulnerable. Multiple stressors raise the bar below which increasing numbers get caught. The young are more suffused in social than traditional media. Unrest, trauma, and deprivation stalk their environments. Their concern about their own unpromising futures is

amplified by anxiety about global events and tribal dramas. On almost every continent, mental health among the disillusioned young has been sinking to new lows.[16] It is as though UI has been ground down by negativity, with no norms of affirmation about who they are. Troubled psyches seek relief in narratives of victimhood, oppression, and alienation.

It doesn't have be this way. We all need to be reminded of what a refuge UI is. Our uniqueness is a gift and a treasure trove.

> At the age of 10, a few years after my existential crisis over mortality at the age of 7 (see Chapter 1), I had an almost equal and opposite "peak experience." My father had taken me on trip to meet his relatives in the North of England and to visit the localities that figured in his upcoming novel. On one village excursion, we stopped for afternoon tea and cake with a local family. I was sitting in a large armchair in the living room, when a woman handed me her 7-month-old baby, and left me to play with it. As the youngest in my family, this was a new experience for me. I had never held a baby before. The infant and I were immediately entranced with each other – the infant giggling and gurgling, and me perhaps doing the same. I was transported by a resonance not far from love, an entirely new sensation to me, telling me something about myself that it took me years to understand.

It is easy in our data-overloaded age to let our heads get filled by global and local narratives about things we mostly can't do anything about. These include imponderables and insolubles about world events, the future, other people, relationships, and even ourselves. Mindfulness – nonjudgemental awareness of the moment[17] – can re-centre you in the moment, calling you to wake up and smell the roses. This frees you to have and value the Three Existential Wants, something that AI can only parody:

- To Savour – to revel in your capacity for pleasure, tuned to your UI – whether in love, consumption, conversation, play, arts, or entertainments
- To Signify – to give of yourself – the most deeply gratifying acts often involve caring, giving, helping, and advising, then seeing what this means to another person
- To be Seen – to connect, inviting people into your *umwelt* and you being a tourist in theirs. This offers the prize of mutual validation, insight, and growth. It is not passive but transforming to be seen. Just look at Jimmy in the last chapter.

It behoves us to keep touching base with the humanity in each other, face to face without agendas other than connection, mutual recognition, appreciation, and everyday creativity. In its best usage, AI can serve us and help us connect authentically with ourselves and each other; help us construct *umwelts* that work for us and extend our capabilities.

CODA: WHAT THIS MIGHT MEAN FOR UNIQUE YOU

- It is said that AI won't take your job, but someone who knows how to use it better than you do will. That's not strictly true – you may well find a machine makes you redundant, but it doesn't help to focus on this as loss, rather see it as delegation of skills to a cheaper, more efficient system.
- Turn off the news or at least ration it. You were not designed to be bombarded by troubles you can't do anything about. Your *umwelt* offers an infinite range of challenges where you can make a difference.
- Embrace AI as a learning journey. Let it help you innovate and find new paths for your self-actualisation.
- Watch out for the seductive devices and sweet talk that AI will garland you with. Remember, unlike you, it is only following orders.
- Calm seas do not make good sailors. You and your loved ones will need sharp prompts about the personal implications of what is being handed to you, to avoid being lulled into obsolescence by machines taking care of you.
- If you're lonely, by all means talk to a chatbot. It may help enormously by prompting you with interesting questions to think about, but no matter what it tells you, it can't "see" you. It is faking, which can make for a fun game but never a real relationship.
- Your UI is not just the only hand of cards you possess in the great game of life, but lo and behold, it is stacked with trumps in whatever games you find yourself playing with tech. The age of AI is also the age of UI.

Twelve

THE ETHICS OF INDIVIDUALITY

Ethics is the activity of man directed to secure the inner
perfection of his own personality.
(Albert Schweitzer)[1]

Waste no more time arguing about what a good person
should be. Be one.
(Marcus Aurelius)[2]

WHAT GOOD IS UI?

My dear cousin Marion was always a giving person – by profession dedicated to enhancing the human skills of doctors by teaching them coaching skills. At the age of 42, with an 8-year-old daughter, she was stricken by leukaemia. Every attempt to stall and reverse its progress failed. With her daughter now entering the teenage years, she and her family had to accept the final horizon was a matter of months away. I visited her several times during that period and witnessed something remarkable. Her house was constantly thronged with friends and well-wishers, drawn to her as a beacon of positivity. She radiated joy in being and a healing love for others. She gave everyone her full attention, to the limits of her personal resources, to make us not only feel deeply recognised but also to share a glorious appreciation of the quality lived experience, in every moment, for her and for us. Her family suffered the helplessness of bereavement, but her gift was a timeless reminder of how close and transmittable the joy of existence is.

It was as if Marion's UI – always infused with this spirit – had become condensed and purified into these last social encounters of her life. It seemed as if her imminent death had brought her clarity of moral vision into its sharpest possible focus.

In the pages of this book, I have said rather little about ethics and morality, though you could say the Uniqueness Perspective is infused with the spirit of liberal humanism. I hope readers will see that I have not advanced a manifesto for selfish individualism. Far from it.

Let us circle back to where this book started, with the Four Laws of UI. Each of them carries a moral imperative.

Law 1: You have UI. Your life is a gift. What are you going to do with it? It's never too early to be thinking about the legacy question. Who knows when your journey will end? The three *dasein* Existential Wants make a useful starting point. You have a right – indeed, a duty, one may say – to see if you satisfy all of them, to some degree. (1) To Savour: let your senses bask in what they can give you. Love the fabric of experience to the full. Find what your Beast-being savours and satisfy it, so long as this doesn't violate the other three laws. (2) To Signify: consider what value you can bring to others and to the world that has allowed you to live on it. (3) To be seen: to be open and connect meaningfully with others, for their benefit as well as yours.

Law 2: You don't know yourself. You have hidden depths, some of them murky or challenging. Let this thought make you humble. You are no better than anyone else, though you might be luckier than many. That's not a call to feel guilty – it's a call for humility. It's also an injunction for tolerance and understanding. This applies as much to you as to others – to forgive yourself and others equally. It invokes the Golden Rule, with a slight variation – Do unto others as you would have them do unto you, with add-ons that their UI suggest they would value.

Law 3: We are strangers to each other. This is not a call for philosophical solipsism – the idea that only your mind is certain to exist, and everything beyond is unreliable and unknowable. Quite the opposite. Your UI is a starting point for exploration of self and others. It will help you avoid limiting stereotypes and superficial comparisons to think in terms of the 4Ds – to understand what journey others have been on, carrying what baggage. You can do this in even the most superficial of encounters. Everyone has a backstory, including people who have become the taken-for-granted furniture of your office or even – especially, perhaps – your worst enemy. Imagine what they might say in response to the Compass Question, telling you "This is who I am, and this is why I am here."

Law 4: We must connect. Reach out. There are people who feel isolated and worthless but still bravely present faces of smiling normality to the world. Until you've tried to see others and allowed yourself to be seen, you will never know who you are, what you can do, and who you can help. Deep recognition is rare, but Decentring is a universal power tool that will always help you deal ethically with anyone. Let your Beast-being and its Psyche resonate with people and places. It was designed to do so. Make the world a better place.

My friend philosopher Jules Goddard[3] puts it this way:

> Morality in a world of UI must be about honouring one's own uniqueness (the duty I owe to what makes me extraordinary) and the duty I owe to others (what makes each of them special). A morality of autonomy and authenticity. Our obligation is to perfect our UI – to find ways of expressing it – as well as the obligation to help others do so.

There is a methodology for doing this – self-talk. It can take many forms, including prayer, meditation, journaling, therapy, or just quiet reflection. After all other talking is done, the Uniqueness Perspective reminds you that the ultimate battles are always to be fought within the Self.[4] This means to reconcile yourself to what is good, needful, and possible for someone just like you.

The UI vision also fundamentally challenges many aspects of the way we live and work. The family, the clan, the tribe efficiently deliver much of what we want most: trust, love, belonging, and respect. When they are working well, you find a self-regulating flow of innovation and adaptation, led by responsible individuals. There are a lot of hidden "ifs" in that sentence. UI is always in play, and it can go in any direction. Culture both gives and restricts freedom. It is not beyond our reach but something we co-create. It is a field in which you can plant and nurture what will give you shelter, sustenance, and space to self-actualise. We are culture carriers and creators through our every act. It's in your interests – and in the interests of the people you love – to see yourself as a responsible agent in caring for your homeland, both real and metaphorical.

BIOGRAPHY AS PILGRIMAGE

> The magnificent but unfinished *Canterbury Tales*, written in the 14th century by diplomat and poet Geoffrey Chaucer, is the first tribute to UI in English fiction. In highly entertaining and often ribald terms, 22 colourful characters tell their life stories on the leisurely 60-mile round trip on foot between London to the holy cathedral city. They are a diverse bunch – in social class, gender, character, and purpose. All have come ostensibly for penance, but with irony, wit, and observational wisdom, Chaucer reveals that besides those with purely devotional motives, others are there for diverse purposes, from fun to personal profit.

Pilgrimages are an ancient tradition in many cultures. On my teenage trip to India, meandering through many countries in the Middle East, one of many friendly Arabs I met called me "Haji Nicola." The Hajj pilgrimage to Mecca is a Muslim article of faith. The personal meaning of my 10-month journey to India and back in my teenage altered as the trip unfolded – moving from adventure to trial to soul-searching. This illustrates the deep purpose of pilgrimage. It is a release from the stream of everyday concerns and duties, to go on an invigorating walk with strangers, see new sights, and converse with the people you encounter. It doesn't have to be consciously devotional. Embarking on such a voyage enlarges your *umwelt*, quietens your Ego, and gives your Self's narratives a chance to hit the reset button. You can find new resonances with people, places, and per-spectives. If, like Chaucer's pilgrims, you and your fellow travellers tell your life stories, then you will also get the benefits of decentring – life-affirming and outlook-shifting insights into other minds, as well as insights on your reflected self (through seeing your effect on others).

This is exactly what Biography does and what this book has sought to do. But you don't have to enrol in a course to experience pilgrimage. The aristocracy used to send their young adult offspring, especially the most troubled, on a "grand tour" to help them grow up and tame their wayward instincts. The student "gap year" can do much the same. The most troubled souls in society need chances to take time out of their lives, if possible, with supported self-exploration. Everyone needs intermittently to change tempo, find time and space to explore, re-examine the familiar, and breathe different air. You could say this is what holidays are for. It's asking a lot of a vacation – besides, they may be inaccessible when you need one or turn out to be more hard work than a break. It's best you find your own way. Craft a retreat for yourself that gives you a switch of tempo for long enough to provide genuine psychic refreshment. You will know what works for you. Procure it. Protect it.

Is the life journey itself a pilgrimage? Many of the case stories here have been from people who have lived through times when Drama provoked space for Deliberation and shifted their Development in new directions. This doesn't need to be happenstance. At any time, you can help yourself and others by adopting the Uniqueness Perspective – finding escape from comparison and categorisation, understanding what tides of lived experience have brought you and them to the point of now, giving voice to the person you've become. The process and path are simple and accessible. It is talking, hearing, resonating; to see yourself as an agent. It is to actively shape events and experiences around the people in your life, and above all, to care for with love and understanding, your Unique Self.

CODA

I hope that the ideas in this book have positive resonance with any spiritual or philosophical perspective you may hold. I have found it sympathetic to ancient wisdoms that have mattered to me, which are primarily Eastern faiths. They put the Self in its place, seeking to understand the inevitable challenges that come with the reality of living in a personally constructed universe. Humility in the face of our Beastly existence is called for. As a Daoist prophet put it

> Your subjective self-determination should not be the only thing that matters. . . . Your true human excellence consists in following the true form of your inborn nature.[5]

This points towards the values that leap out from my Biographers' and others' life stories – courage, compassion, love, and wisdom.

Final words: It is my hope that this work will help Unique You, thinking about how individuality works and why it matters. My wish is that it will help you find confidence, reassurance, freedom, and connectedness.

APPENDICES

The Transition Cycle – Phases

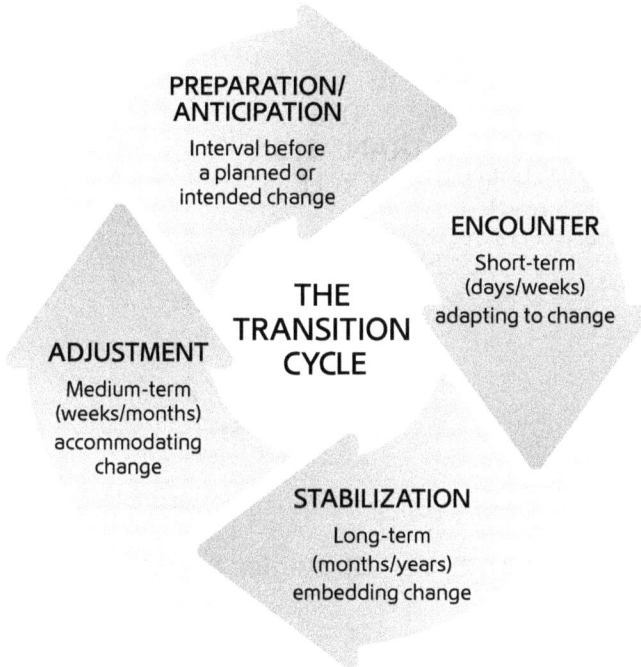

**PREPARATION/
ANTICIPATION**
Interval before
a planned or
intended change

ENCOUNTER
Short-term
(days/weeks)
adapting to change

**THE
TRANSITION
CYCLE**

ADJUSTMENT
Medium-term
(weeks/months)
accommodating
change

STABILIZATION
Long-term
(months/years)
embedding change

The Transition Cycle – The Challenge of Each Stage

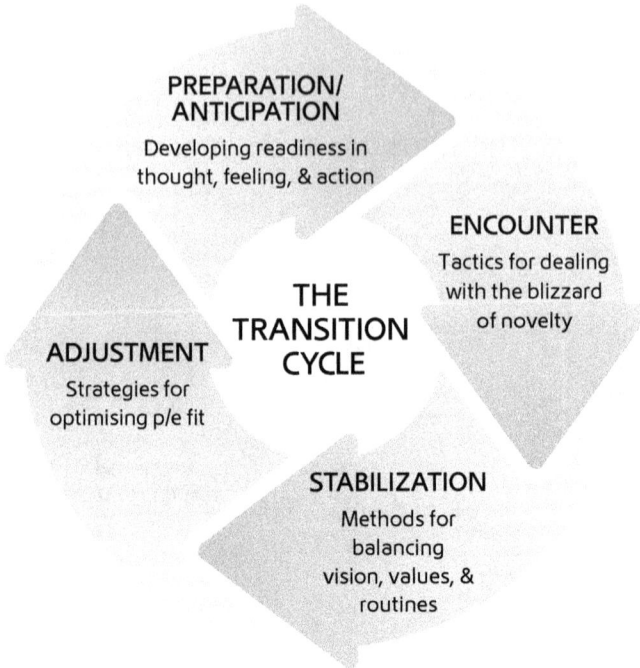

**PREPARATION/
ANTICIPATION**
Developing readiness in
thought, feeling, & action

ENCOUNTER
Tactics for dealing
with the blizzard
of novelty

**THE
TRANSITION
CYCLE**

ADJUSTMENT
Strategies for
optimising p/e fit

STABILIZATION
Methods for
balancing
vision, values, &
routines

The Transition Cycle – Strategies & Tactics by Stage

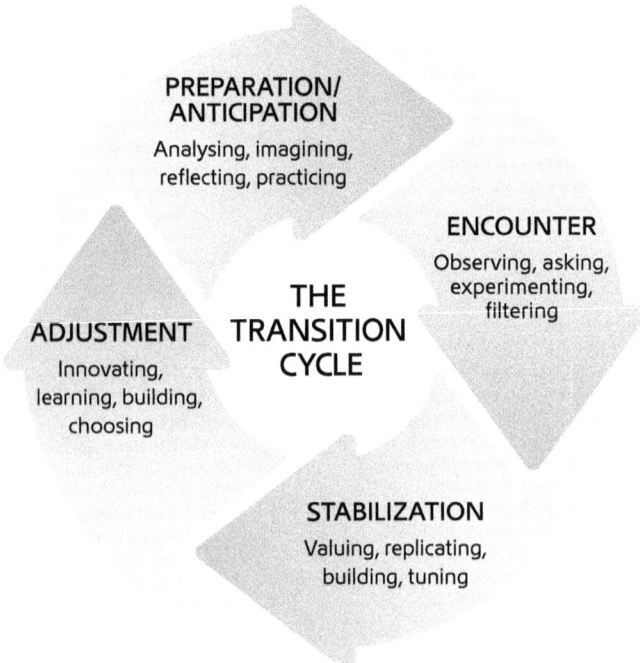

**PREPARATION/
ANTICIPATION**
Analysing, imagining,
reflecting, practicing

ENCOUNTER
Observing, asking,
experimenting,
filtering

**THE
TRANSITION
CYCLE**

ADJUSTMENT
Innovating,
learning, building,
choosing

STABILIZATION
Valuing, replicating,
building, tuning

APPENDIX 2
Sloan Biography
Preparatory Activities

Exercise 1: YOUR LIFE/CAREER LINE – THE ADAPTIVE LIFE

This is an exercise in drawing your life/career line. This is to help you reflect on key choices and turning points in your life. The aim is to understand the forces that have guided you and over the sessions of the Biography course for you to understand and improve your adaptive strategies to life's changing challenges.

You will be sharing your Lifeline in the confidentiality of your Biography Group. No one else will have sight of your chart unless you wish to share it with anyone.

Method: I suggest you use a large sheet of paper, or two A4 sheets, landscape orientation end to end to make a longish strip – plus a few different coloured pens.

1. Take your long sheet of paper and draw a straight line laterally, through the centre of the two sheets left to right. This long axis – running the length of the two sheets – is your timeline. Mark it from 0 yrs birth on the left through to something beyond retirement age, say 75, at the right end. Mark the axis scale with two sets of numbers – **age** and **calendar year**.

2. Mark a chronology of **significant events** – changes, experiences, and key roles. You may find it easier to do this in reverse, from the present backwards. You will find one event triggering memories of others.

3. Mark important **roles and relationships** on the chart. Mark **locations** you worked and lived in.

4. Draw a vertical axis at the left end of your sheets, above and below your timeline. This is an imaginary scale of **life satisfaction**. Draw a waveform graph – where the line rises above the lifeline to indicate periods of satisfaction or happiness, dipping below the horizontal axis to reflect times of unhappiness or dissatisfaction.

5. Divide your chart with a series of vertical lines into **Chapters** – like a book – and give each Chapter a name, e.g. "Lost in the desert," "Building bridges," etc.

6. Mark with a * **turning points** in your life. These may or may not have been choice points, and you may have only recognised them as turning points in retrospect.

Here is a fictitious example of a completed chart from a South Asian businesswoman.

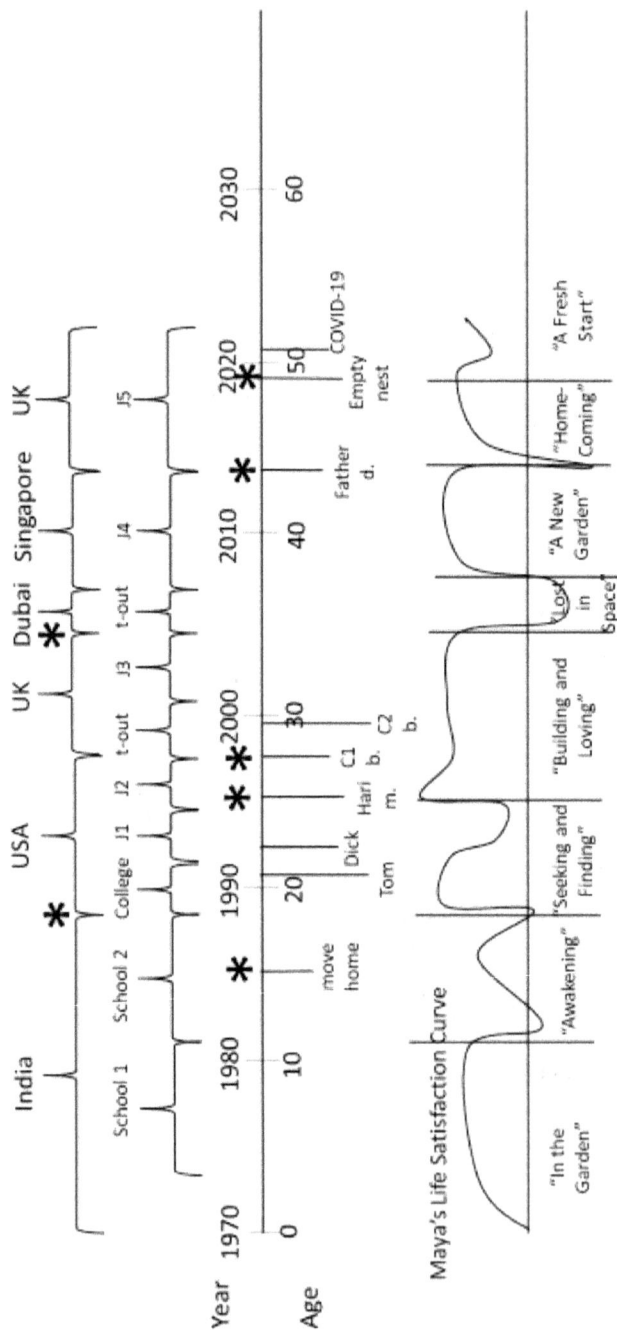

Maya P's Lifeline

APPENDIX 3
The Compass Question

This form is designed to help you capture key features of your personal profile –
possible answers to the Compass Question. When you have completed the form, rank
the top two or three influences out of these areas that have governed your career and
life choices so far and which seem to be changing.

Values:

What three areas of life and society (excluding your personal life) do you care most about? (*See below for examples.*)	1.
	2.
	3.

Interests:

What are the most important interests or activities in your life (excluding family) at present? (*See below for examples.*)	1.
	2.
	3.

Abilities:

What three different skills or abilities would you rate yourself most highly on? (*See below for examples.*)	1.
	2.
	3.

Motivators:

What do your PI results and your experience suggest are the three most important motivators? (*See below for examples.*)	1.
	2.
	3.

Personality Hazards:

What do your PI results and your experience suggest are the most critical risk factors or hazards in your profile?	1.
	2.
	3.

Typical Values
- Social welfare and inequality
- Justice and human rights
- Environment and the natural world
- Community and anti-discrimination
- Religious and metaphysical faiths
- Aesthetics
- Scientific discovery
- Politics and social progress

Typical Interests
- Practical – action-orientated occupations (e.g. engineering)
- Enterprise – developing new projects and business opportunities (e.g. marketing)
- Creative – generating new ideas, materials, and methods (e.g. R&D)
- Persuasive – dealing with other people to achieve objectives (e.g. sales)
- Analytical – inquiring and investigative occupations (e.g. journalism)
- Administrative, managerial, or clerical – running complex systems (e.g. IT management)
- Welfare – caring and social support occupations (e.g. counselling)
- Computational – using and applying science and maths (e.g. accounting)
- Outdoor – physical activities in variable environments (e.g. forestry)
- Artistic – music, theatre, and literary occupations (e.g. performer)

Typical Skills and Abilities
- Numerical computation – mental calculation
- Verbal comprehension – understanding complex language and text
- Word fluency – ability to improvise and produce
- Memory – ability to memorise and recall fluently
- Musical – a good "ear" and natural talent
- Logical reasoning – ability to follow chains of maths or verbal logic
- Spatial visualisation – imagination of spatial arrangements
- Mental mapping – instinctive "compass" and sense of direction
- Manual speed and dexterity – accuracy in performing fine tasks
- Athleticism – physical strength, endurance, speed, etc.
- Motor–visual coordination – ability with computers and ball games
- Organisational – skill in devising and operating system
- Interpersonal – ability to influence and interact with strangers

Typical Motivators
- Money – standard of living
- Status – attaining positions of esteem
- Recognition – praise, visibility, and prominence
- Friendship – social life at work
- Variety – lack of routine
- Development – chance to acquire new skills
- Originality – opportunities to be creative in ideas and methods
- Achievement – attainment of difficult goals
- Leadership – chance to be responsible for other people

APPENDIX 4
Twenty Statements Test (TST)

In the 20 blank spaces below, please write 20 different statements in response to the question: "Who am I?" Give the answers as if you were giving them to yourself, not to someone else. It is best if you do this quite rapidly and spontaneously – writing the first things that come to mind and not going back to alter what you've already written.

This is NOT for collection but solely for use in this session.

		Leave Blank – for Coding or Notes
1		
2		
3		
4		
5		
6		
7		
8		
9		
10		
11		
12		
13		
14		
15		
16		
17		
18		
19		
20		

APPENDIX 5
Sloan Biography Session 5:
Transitions and Transformations
What Do You Want?
What Will You Do?

WHAT DO YOU WANT?

	Ideal Outcomes – Your Dream for Yourself	Expected Outcomes If You Follow the River
Self & Identity (Material; Social; Psychological)		
Critical Relationships (Family; Friends; Social Groups)		
Investments & Debts (Family; Property; Ventures; Finances)		
Demands & Roles (Jobs; Organisation Types; Social Roles; Memberships)		
Contexts & Cultures (Domicile; Lifestyle; Activities; Hobbies)		

WHAT WILL YOU DO? – QUESTIONS FOR CO-COACHING

VARIATION

What kinds of experiments are you doing or new investments you are making that might help you find new directions and plant new seeds? What new information might you seek out that will give a healthy challenge to your current perception?

VISION

If you know what you want, what are you doing to implement your vision of a desired future? What are the tough choices, risks, sacrifices, and investments you are going to have to make? Who will be your partners and supporters? How are you going to tell them what you need?

FUNDAMENTALS

What might you want to return to that is fundamental to you as a person that may have got distracted through your career development? What are the key non-negotiables about you as a person that need to be nurtured and preserved? Use the KISS acronym to help you: Keep, Increase, Stop, and Start.

APPENDIX 6
A Guide to the Co-coaching Method

APPENDIX 6: A GUIDE TO THE CO-COACHING METHOD

What is coaching?
"Coaching is unlocking a person's potential to maximise their own performance. It is helping them to learn rather than teaching them."

The role of the Coach is widely misunderstood. It is not like a doctor–patient model, where someone with skills or knowledge is giving expertise or advice to someone in need who lacks that knowledge and skills. Rather, it is a relationship of equals, where the analysis, solutions, and actions are all to be found within the Coachee. The Coach's role is to help the Coachee to find them by acting a sounding board and an awareness raiser for them. It is an empowering role, where the Coach and Coachee are engaged in a joint search for new approaches to issues and challenges that the latter has identified as important.

Co-coaching is when two parties contract to give quality time, unconditional regard, and attention to each other by following the coaching methodology. In co-coaching, there is an explicit agreement to do this both ways. It is reciprocal – not always in the same session – e.g. this can be done as a regular routine over days or even weeks. What matters most is that both parties understand it as a disciplined process bound by rules of absolute confidentiality, openness, sympathy, and freedom within boundaries, that each party has the right set – i.e. it is OK to have "no go" areas, of things that either person does not wish to talk about in this context. It is also essential to be nonjudgemental. The Coach may help the Coachee see how others might judge or react whilst retaining complete moral impartiality – what the coaching community calls "unconditional regard" for the other.

The qualities and mind-set that need to be cultivated as far as possible:

• Patience	• Awareness	• Detachment
• Self-awareness	• Supportiveness	• Attentiveness
• Interest	• Listening skills	• Retentive
• Perceptive	• Open-mindedness	• Creative

Coaching tips:
- Build a trustful relationship over time.
- Pick the right moment.
- Warm up to achieve rapport.
- Use more "ask" than "suggest."
- Challenge assumptions and frames.
- Check understanding – periodically summarise.
- Think creatively – not just systematically.
- Check understanding throughout by asking for or offering specific examples.
- Close on a positive, encouraging note.
- Follow up and recognise achievements – make touching base a natural part of the relationship.

Co-consulting Model – The Coach's Mental Model
Decentring – insight into the other by trying to see from their perspective
Supporting – helping build their confidence in finding solutions and strategies
Challenging – to encourage them to consider alternatives to what they take for granted

The GROW Model of Coaching
Many Coaches with whom you will come into contact use a simple methodology that can be adapted for your conversations. It is called by the acronym the GROW model. A good rule of thumb is that the Coach will be asking questions throughout the session.

GOAL: What is Coachee seeking to do or achieve, short and long term, and what do they want to get out of this session? The Coach's job here to help the Coachee state a goal that is SMART (sorry, another acronym) – Specific, Measurable (any way of knowing whether it has been achieved or not), Actionable, Realistic, and Time-based. This may require you both to "ladder up or down." Laddering up means understanding what wider personal purposes a very specific focused goal might relate to, such as by asking what difference would achieving this goal mean to the Coachee – for example: "What would it help you to achieve if you improved your time management (their stated goal)?" Laddering down means bring a very broad abstract goal more specific – e.g. for the goal, improve my leadership, ask what does leadership mean to you and how would you know whether you had achieved this goal?

REALITY: Here the Coach asks the Coachee to spell out all the circumstances (especially the people) surrounding this goal as specifically as possible. This helps the Coach understand the Coachee's perspective and motivations more clearly; it is quite likely that by this inquiry, the Coach may spot an element of specific importance or identify a puzzle that needs to be solved.

OPTIONS: This is where the Coach can be most imaginative and constructive – getting the Coachee to identify what are the possible strategies and courses of action they might implement to make progress on the goal. Here the Coach can be helpful by giving them ideas that could broaden the range of options they have in mind. It is easy to get fixated on a single solution to a problem when there are other alternatives, some quite radical. The Coach is encouraging exploratory strategies and possibly identifying the need for new data on the issue before leaping into action.

WILL: This denotes the commitment of the Coachee to really do and follow through on their action plans. This means the Coach closely questioning about how strong the Coachee's motivation is to follow through. The Coach will be asking about the risks, the implications for self and others, the timing, what people and resources might need to be called upon, what obstacles will have to be overcome.

Some Sample Questions That Follow the GROW Model

GOAL	REALITY
- Clarify expectations for the session and beyond: • What would you like to discuss or achieve in this session? • What would you like to achieve in this session? • What are your goals? • What will be different/better if you achieve them? (ladder up) • How would you know when you have achieved this goal? (ladder down)	- Reach a mutual understanding of the issue at hand: • What is happening at the moment? • Who is involved? • What do you think and feel about this situation? • What effect is it having on you? • What have you done so far, with what results? • What are the constraints to finding a way forward?
OPTIONS	WILLINGNESS
- Explore the possibilities to address the situation: • What options do you have? • What else could you do? • What if . . . ? • What other avenues are worth exploring? • What are the pros and cons of each idea? • Why would this work for you? • How could this be improved?	- Reach agreement about how to proceed and what is needed to achieve results: • What are you going to do? • When will you do it by? • Will this meet your goal? • What obstacles will you face? • How will you overcome them? • Who needs to know or be involved? • What support will you need? • What support will you get?

Co-coaching Practice for Students

Give yourselves equal time.

Do it on the clock, more or less – i.e. in a disciplined way, say, 30 to 45 minutes each way.

In the Coach role, explore the other person's objectives, whether they are too tough or too vague, for example. Get them to be rigorous about resources and how they will get them, especially TIME. Get them to specify what actions they will commit to and how they will deal with obstacles and setbacks. Help them think "out of the box" with ideas and new options they may not have considered. Quiz them about how they will know whether they have achieved their goal. Give them encouragement.

When you have finished one way, the Coachee should give feedback to the Coach about what it felt like, what worked well, and what each party could do more of or do better.

Leadership Moments

Which of the following situations do you find most and least challenging? Mark with an X the **5** that you find **most** difficult, and mark with a √ the **5** that you find least difficult.

1. Getting your voice heard by remote bosses or other senior people in the organisation	
2. Giving "balanced" feedback to people who are overly sensitive to criticism	
3. Dealing with people who are prone to emotional outbursts	
4. Influencing technical people or service providers (HR, legal, etc.) over whom you have little power	
5. Managing people whose approach to the job is not the way you think it should be	
6. Coping with your own emotional reactions in times of extreme difficulty and pressure	
7. Managing your time	
8. Dealing with people who are demotivated and disengaged	
9. Coaching people who have a fixed view about how to do things	
10. Delegating to people who are much less competent than you	
11. Team building with people who don't want to cooperate	
12. Communicating "vision" to people who have a limited and narrow focus on their jobs	
13. Dealing with poor performers	
14. Turning around a dysfunctional subculture and creating new positive norms and values	
15. Resolving conflict between two or more individuals (e.g. over their rights & obligations)	
16. Dealing with people's complaints about unfairness	
17. Communicating unpopular and difficult decisions to a group (e.g. cuts to resources; adverse change)	
18. Giving bad news to an individual (e.g. no promotion; undesired job move)	
19. Dealing with crises (e.g. system failure; unexpected loss of business)	
20. Prolonged periods of peace and quiet when no one needs you	

Now find a partner and take it in turns to co-coach around items about
 a) What you/they find difficult – what does it say about your/their personal profile?
 b) How could you/they turn this into a "leadership moment" – a chance to show your distinctive approach?
Repeat with new partners two more times (i.e. 3 × 20 minutes).

NOTES

PREFACE/INTRODUCTION

1 The closest and most interesting exceptions are McAdams, D. P. (1993). *The Stories We Live By: Personal myths and the making of the self.* William Morrow; and Coleman, P. T. (1999). *The Psychobiography of Everyday Life: The hidden psychology of ordinary people and their relationships.* Routledge.
2 Watson, J. B. (1924). *Behaviorism.* People's Institute.
3 Berger, P. L., & Luckmann, T. (1966). *The Social Construction of Reality: A treatise in the sociology of knowledge.* Anchor Books.
4 See W. T. Schultz (2005). *Handbook of Psychobiography.* Oxford University Press.
5 For an insightful exposition see, Adams D.P. (2013). The psychological self as actor, agent, and author. *Perspectives on Psychological Science,* 8: 272–295.
6 Allport, G. W. (1937). *Personality: A psychological interpretation.* Henry Holt and Company.

CHAPTER 1

1 *Monty Python's Life of Brian.* Directed by Terry Jones. HandMade Films/Python (Monty) Pictures Ltd. (1979).
2 Neurologist Oliver Sacks meditating on his terminal cancer. Sacks, O. (2015). *Gratitude.* Alfred A. Knopf, p. 14.
3 These are what philosophers call "priors." They are *a priori* premises – axioms from first principles which we can accept as necessary and true.
4 von Uexküll, J. (1957). A stroll through the worlds of animals and men: A picture book of invisible worlds. *Semiotica,* 89: 319–391. This idea has been borrowed by writers who use it to explain interspecies differences and the worlds that are the province of technologies, especially intelligent ones. See, for example, Yong, E. (2023). *An Immense World: How animal senses reveal the hidden realms around us.* Vintage; and Greenfield, A. (2017). *Radical Technologies: The design of everyday life.* Verso.
5 Represented in the pop psychology idea of the Johari Window, partitioning our self-concept, our UI effectively, into a 2 × 2 matrix of known/unknown to self on one axis, and known/unknown to others on the other axis. One's "blind spot" is the cell "known to others" + "unknown to self." See, Luft, J., & Ingham, H. (1955). The Johari Window: A graphic model of interpersonal awareness. In *Proceedings of the Western Training Laboratory in Group Development.* Los Angeles: University of California.
6 Chapman, B. N. (n.d.). About Beth Nielsen Chapman. https://bethnielsenchapman.com/about

7   The distinction between the executive ego (I) and the UI (me) was first articulated by William James in his *Principles of Psychology*. Henry Holt (1890).

8   Seth, A. (2021). *Being You: A new science of consciousness*. Dutton. The concept originates in René Descartes in his *Discourse on the Method* (1637) and *Treatise on Man* (published posthumously in 1664).

9   Bridle, J. (2022). *Ways of Being: Animals, plants, machines: the search for planetary intelligence*. Allen Lane.

10 We are unique from the start; see Wang, Q., Xu, Y., Zhao, T., Xu, Z., He, Y., & Liao, X. (2021). Individual uniqueness in the neonatal functional connectome. *Cerebral Cortex*, 31: 3701–3712.

11 Wilson, T. (2002). *Strangers to Ourselves: Discovering the adaptive unconscious*. The Belknap Press of Harvard University Press.

12 A paraphrase of his address to the *Albany Medical College* in 1899, Albany Medical Annals, 20: 307–309.

13 Psychiatrist Alastair Santhouse offers a powerful critique of this approach to mental health in his profoundly humane book *Head First: A psychiatrist's stories of mind and body*. Atlantic Books (2021).

14 *Encyclopaedia Britannica* (2025).

15 This is why the Sloan Fellowship course, which I shall describe in detail in Chapter 10, is called Biography.

16 Ravi is the pseudonym of one of the midcareer executive students on my Biography course, a core element of Sloan Fellowship master's degree course at London Business School, whose case histories populate this book.

17 Trivers, R. L. (2000). The elements of a scientific theory of self-deception. *Annals of New York Academy of Sciences*, 907: 114–192.

18 Heidegger, M. (1962). *Being and Time* (J. Macquarrie & E. Robinson, Trans.). Harper & Row. (Original work published 1927)

19 Horrigan-Kelly, M., Millar, M., & Dowling, M. (2016). Understanding the key tenets of Heidegger's philosophy for interpretive phenomenological research. *International Journal of Qualitative Methods*, 15: 1–8. Also see Rowan, A. M. (2016). Dasein, authenticity, and choice in Heidegger's *Being and Time*. *Logos i Ethos*, 41: 87–105.

20 Each reinforced by neurotransmitters, respectively, serotonin, dopamine, and oxytocin.

21 Larkin, P. (2003). Aubade. In Thwaite, E. (2003). *Collected Poems*. Enitharmon Press, 2003.

22 Zuckerman, H., & Merton, R. K. (1971). Patterns of evaluation in science: Institutionalisation, structure and functions of the referee system. *Minerva*, 9: 66–100.

23 See Feynman, R. P., & Leighton, R. (1985). *"Surely You're Joking, Mr. Feynman!": Adventures of a curious character*. W. W. Norton & Company.

24 Brian, D., & Matthews, R. (2007) The Curies: A biography of the most controversial family in science. *Journal of Nuclear Medicine*, 48: 1224.

25 Siedentop, L. (2014). *Inventing the Individual: The origins of Western liberalism*. Harvard University Press.

26 Hogan, R., & Kaiser, R. B. (2005). What we know about leadership. *Review of General Psychology*, 9: 169–180; Isenberg, D. (2013). *Worthless, Impossible and Stupid: How contrarian entrepreneurs create and capture extraordinary value*. Harvard Business Review Press.

27 For examples in the field of leadership see Lewis, D. G., Goddard, J., & Batcheller-Adams, T. (2022). *Mavericks: How bold leadership changes the world*. Kogan Page; and for general examples, see Grant, A. (2016). *Originals: How non-conformists move the world*. Viking.

28 Tillich, P. (1952). *The Courage to Be*. Yale University Press.

29 James, W. (2002). *The Varieties of Religious Experience: A study in human nature*. Routledge. (Original work published 1902); Wilson, D. S. (2002). *Darwin's Cathedral: Evolution, religion, and the nature of society*. University of Chicago Press.

CHAPTER 2

1   Ridley, M. (2003). *Nature via Nurture: Genes, experience, and what makes us human*. HarperCollins.

2   *Man's Search for Meaning*. Beacon Press (2006).

3   Dunn, J., & Plomin, R. (1990). *Separate Lives: Why siblings are so different*. Basic Books.

4   Isaacson, W. (2011). *Steve Jobs*. Simon & Schuster.

5   Jung, C. G. (1968). *The Archetypes and the Collective Unconscious* (R. F. C. Hull, Trans.; 2nd ed., Vol. 9, Part 1). Princeton University Press. (Original work published 1934)

6   Bouchard, T. J., Lykken, D. T., McGue, M., Segal, N. L., & Tellegen, A. (1990). Sources of human psycho-logical differences: The Minnesota study of twins reared apart. *Science*, 250: 223–228.

7   Loehlin, J. C., & Nichols, R. C. (1976). *Heredity, Environment, and Personality: A study of 850 sets of twins.* University of Texas Press.

8   La Guardia, J. G. (2009). Developing who I am: A self-determination theory approach to the establish-ment of healthy identities. *Educational Psychologist*, 44: 90–104. Also, Mitchell, K. J. (2018). *Innate: How the wiring of our brains shapes who we are.* Princeton University Press.

9   Turkheimer, E. (2000). Three laws of behavior genetics and what they mean. *Current Directions in Psy-chological Science*, 9: 160–164.

10 Ekmekci, H. S., & Muftareviç, S. (2023). Epigenetic effects of social stress and epigenetic inheritance. *Psikiyatride Güncel Yaklaşımlar*, 15: 132–145.

11 Carey, N. (2012). *The Epigenetics Revolution: How modern biology is rewriting our understanding of genetics, disease, and inheritance.* Columbia University Press.

12 Rimfeld, K., Malanchini, M., Spargo, T., Spickernell, G., Selzam, S., McMillan, A., Dale, P. S., Eley, T. C., & Plomin, R. (2019). Twins early development study: A genetically sensitive investigation into behavioral and cognitive development from infancy to emerging adulthood. *Twin Research and Human Genetics*, 22: 508–513.

13 Wardle, T. (Director). (2018). *Three Identical Strangers* [Film]. Neon; CNN Films; Raw TV.

14 Lykken, D. T., McGue, M., Tellegen, A., & Bouchard, T. J. (1992). Emergenesis: Genetic traits that may not run in families. *American Psychologist*, 47(12): 1565–1577.

15 Facing this puzzle, evolutionist Judith Rich Harris concluded that peers and social influences out-side the family were the pre-eminent source of shared environmental shaping, but the evidence does not seem to support this conclusion. Harris, J. R. (1998). *The Nurture Assumption: Why children turn out the way they do.* Free Press.

16 Jensen, A. C., & Jorgensen-Wells, M. A. (2025). Parents favor daughters: A meta-analysis of gender and other predictors of parental differential treatment. *Psychological Bulletin*, 251, in press.

17 Ayoub, M., Briley, D. A., Grotzinger, A., Patterson, M. W., Engelhardt, L. E., Tackett, J. L., Harden, K. P., & Tucker-Drob, E. M. (2018). Genetic and environmental associations between child personality and parenting. *Social Psychological and Personality Science*, 10: 711–721.

18 Harris, J. R. (1995). Where is the child's environment? A group socialization theory of development. *Psychological Review*, 102(3): 458–489.

19 Gordon, G., & Nicholson, N. (2008). *Family Wars: Classic conflicts in family business and how to deal with them.* Kogan Page.

20 Whiting, M. (2014). Children with disability and complex health needs: The impact on family life. *Nursing Children and Young People*, 26: 26–30.

21 Hrdy, S. B. (2009). *Mothers and Others: The evolutionary origins of mutual understanding.* Harvard Univer-sity Press.

22 Mensah, K. (2024, September 30). John Simm makes astonishing discovery about biological father in ITV's DNA Journey. *Radio Times.*

23 BBC radio, *The Gift.* Series 2, episodes 1 and 2 "Switched" aired November 1 and 6, 2024.

24 Mitchell (2018), op. cit.; also, van den Heuvel, M. I., Turk, E., Manning, J. H., et al. (2018). Hubs in the human fetal brain network. *Developmental Cognitive Neuroscience*, 30: 108–115.

25 Wolf, M., & McNamara, J. M. (2012). On the evolution of personalities via frequency-dependent selec-tion. *The American Naturalist*, 179: 679–692.

26 These are the ideas of Adam Smith (1723–1790), David Ricardo (1772–1823), and his Law of Compara-tive advantage. See Smith, A. (2003). *The Wealth of Nations* (A. Skinner, Ed.). Penguin Classics. (Original work published 1776); and Ricardo, D. (2004). *The Principles of Political Economy and Taxation* (P. Sraffa, Ed.). Liberty Fund. (Original work published 1817)

27 This has been the central proposition of "gestalt" psychology for the last 60 years; see Perls, F. S. (1969). *Gestalt Therapy Verbatim.* Real People Press, also applied more recently to the idea of conjoined intelligence; see Smart, P. R. (2018). Mandevillian intelligence. *Synthese*, 195: 4169–4200.

28 Wedekind, C., Seebeck, T., Bettens, F., & Paepke, A. J. (1995). MHC-dependent mate preferences in humans. *Proceedings of the Royal Society of London. Series B: Biological Sciences*, 260: 245–249.

29 Zayas, V., Gaby, J., & Gutchess, A. (2025). The interactive role of odor associations in friendship prefer-ences. *Scientific Reports*, 15, Article 94350.

30 Rimfield,K., Ayorech, Z., Dale, P. S., Kovas, Y., & Plomin, R. (2016). Genetics affects choice of academic subjects as well as achievement. *Scientific Reports*, 6, Article number 26373.
31 Vernon, W. (2024, July 3). Chess star, 9, becomes youngest to play for England. *BBC News*.
32 Molenaar, P. N., Boomsma, D. I., Dolan, C. C. (1993). *Behaviour Genetics*: 23, 519–524 |(p. 523).
33 Turkheimer & Waldron, op. cit. p. 93.
34 Turkheimer, E. (2011). Genetics and human agency: Comment on Dar-Nimrod and Heine (2011). *Psychological Bulletin*, 137: 825–828.
35 Daly, M., & Wilson, M. (1982). Whom does the baby resemble? *Ethology and Sociobiology*, 3: 69–78.
36 Marcus, G. (2008). *Kluge: The haphazard construction of the human mind*. Houghton Mifflin Harcourt.

CHAPTER 3

1   *Steppenwolf.*
2   From the *Peanuts* strip cartoon.
3   Varela, F. J., Thompson, E., & Rosch, E. (1991). *The Embodied Mind: Cognitive science and human experience.* MIT Press.
4   I am indebted to philosopher Jules Goddard for this excellent concept.
5   Paraphrase of the last words of Ludwig Wittgenstein's landmark work of philosophy. Wittgenstein, L. (1922). *Tractatus Logico-Philosophicus* (C. K. Ogden, Trans.). Kegan Paul, Trench, Trubner & Co. (Original work published 1921)
6   Hay, D. (2006). *Something There: The biology of the human spirit.* Templeton Foundation Press.
7   Conway, M. A., & Pleydell-Pearce, C. W. (2000). The construction of autobiographical memories in the self memory system. *Psychological Review*, 107: 261–288.
8   Odling-Smee, F. J., Laland, K. N., & Feldman, M. W. (2003). *Niche Construction: The neglected process in evolution.* Princeton University Press. Applied to the field of leadership by Spisak, B. R., O'Brien, M. J., Nicholson, N., & van Vugt, M. (2015). Niche construction and the evolution of leadership. *Academy of Management Review*, 40: 291–306.
9   Shibata, N., Yamamoto, Y., Takemura, N., & Kato, T. (2005). A case of Hashimoto's encephalopathy presenting with personality change and cognitive impairment. *Internal Medicine*, 44: 623–626
10 Approximating to the Aristotelian conception of the psyche; see Ierodiakonou, C. S. (2012). The individuality of each person in the Aristotelian philosophy. *European Journal for Person Centered Healthcare*, 1: 100–102.
11 Fisher, H. E. Cohen, L. J., Brown, L. L., & Riccio, S. E. (2015). Four broad temperament dimensions: Description, convergent validation correlations, and comparison with the Big Five. *Frontiers of Psychology*, 6: 1098.
12 Tang, A., Pine, D. S., Nelson, E. E., Fox, N. A., & Ernst, M. (2020). Behavioral inhibition in infancy predicts personality and internalizing symptoms in adulthood. *Proceedings of the National Academy of Sciences*, 117: 9800–9805.
13 Marcus, G. (2008), op. cit.
14 Seth, A. (2012), op. cit.
15 Solms, M. (2021). *The Hidden Spring: A journey to the source of consciousness.* W. W. Norton & Company.
16 Damasio, A. R. (1999). *The Feeling of What Happens: Body and emotion in the making of consciousness.* Harcourt.
17 Baumeister, R. F., & Tierney, J. (2011). *Willpower: Rediscovering the greatest human strength.* Penguin Press.
18 Baumeister, R. F., Heatherton, T. F., & Tice, D. M. (1994). *Losing Control: How and why people fail at self-regulation.* Academic Press.
19 Kahneman, D. (2011). *Thinking, Fast and Slow.* New York: Farrar, Straus and Giroux.
20 Between competing dopamine driven circuits of desire vs. control; see Lieberman, D. Z., & Long, M. E. (2018). *The Molecule of More: How a single chemical in your brain drives love, sex, and creativity—and will determine the fate of the human race.* BenBella Books.
21 McGilchrist, I. (2009), op. cit.
22 Johnathan Haidt memorably compares our psychology as akin to a person riding the elephant, an analogy for our delusion that reason, from the superior cortex, calls the shots over our motives, drawing their power from the more primitive midbrain structures, in his 2006 book, *the Happiness Hypothesis*, Basic Books.

23 Chater, N. (2018). *The Mind Is Flat: The illusion of mental depth and the improvised mind*. Penguin Books.

24 The great pioneer of American psychology William James masterfully analyses the distinctions between the "I" of ego functioning and the "me" of what we understand about ourselves, in James, W. (1950). *The Principles of Psychology*, Vol 1. (1890–1950 edition Dover Books).

25 Graham subsequently did go to India – he jumped the plane on a stopover to Australia to hear the music, which subsequently became incorporated into his brilliant guitar music.

26 James, W., op. cit., and Seigel, J. E. (2005). *The Idea of the Self: Thought and experience in Western Europe since the seventeenth century*. Cambridge University Press.

27 Metzinger, T. (2003). *Being No One: The self-model theory of subjectivity*. MIT Press.

28 Implicated areas are the medial prefrontal cortex, the posterior cingulate cortex and precuneus, the inferior parietal lobule, the lateral temporal cortex, and the hippocampus (memory). See Raichle, M. E. (2015). The brain's default mode network. *Annual Review of Neuroscience*, 38: 433–447.

29 Trivers, R. L. (2000). The elements of a scientific theory of self-deception. *Annals of the New York Academy of Sciences*, 907: 114–192.

30 Discussed in Nicholson, N. (2000). *Executive Instinct: Managing the human animal in the information age*. Crown Business. (Published in Europe as *Managing the Human Animal*.)

31 Kurzban, R. (2010). *Why Everyone (Else) Is a Hypocrite: Evolution and the modular mind*. Princeton University Press.

32 To savour boosts serotonin, to signify is all dopamine driven, and to be seen calls on oxytocin amongst others; see Smith, G. (2021). *Overloaded: How every aspect of your life is influenced by your brain chemicals*. Bloomsbury Sigma.

33 Malonki, D. (2018). The storied self: Narrative construction in identity formation. *Journal of Personality*, 86: 321–335.

34 McAdams, D. (1985). The "imago": A key narrative component of identity. *Review of Personality and Social Psychology*, 6: 114–141.

35 Tiel, C., & Sudo, F. K. (2020). Personality changes in dementia: What is distressing to caregivers? *Journal of the American Medical Association*, 323: 1475–1483. For a graphic and moving fictional account, see McEwan, I. (2025). *What We Can Know*. Jonathan Cape.

36 Sacks, O. (1985). *The Man Who Mistook His Wife for a Hat*. Macmillan.

37 The idea that without memory we cannot have selves was first voiced by the philosopher John Locke in (1690/1975). *An Essay Concerning Human Understanding* (P. H. Nidditch, Ed.). Oxford University Press.

38 Tomasello, M. (1999). *The Cultural Origins of Human Cognition*. Harvard University Press.

39 Schulte, P. M., & Hall, J. G. (2019). Echoes across generations. In *Genetic and Epigenetic Influences on Health and Disease* (pp. 123–140). Springer; also, Nettle, D. (2006). The evolution of personality variation in humans and other animals. *American Psychologist*, 61: 622–631.

40 Yousafzai, M., & Lamb, C. (2013). *I Am Malala: The girl who stood up for education and was shot by the Taliban*. Little, Brown and Company.

41 Gandhi, M. (1957). *The Story of My Experiments with Truth: An autobiography*. Beacon Press.

42 In his autobiography, published in 1791, shortly after his death.

43 Flaim, M., & Blaisdell, A. P. (2020). The comparative analysis of intelligence. *Psychological Bulletin*, 146: 1174–1199.

44 For an authoritative account see, Mikhailov, N., & Yankov, G. (2024). *Personality: A User's Guide*. Robinson.

45 A thorough analysis can be found in David J Linden's excellent *Unique: The new science of human individuality*. (2020). Basic Books.

46 Allport, G. W. (1937). The functional autonomy of motives. *American Journal of Psychology*, 50: 141–156.

47 Symbolic interactionist sociologists coined this principle; see Thomas, W. I., & Thomas, D. S. (1928). *The Child in America: Behavior problems and programs*. Alfred A. Knopf.

48 Dweck, C. S. (2006). *Mindset: The new psychology of success*. Random House.

49 Attributed to Thomas Jefferson.

50 I discussed this at greater length in the context of leadership in my book *The "I" of Leadership: Strategies for seeing, being and doing*. Jossey-Bass/Wiley (2013).

51 The gold standard for these measures in academic research is the NEO-PI; see Costa, P. T., & McCrae, R. R. (1992). *Revised NEO Personality Inventory (NEO-PI-R) and NEO Five-Factor Inventory (NEO-FFI) Professional Manual*. Odessa, FL: Psychological Assessment Resources, and for business applications the suite of Hogan measures, see Hogan, R., & Hogan, J. (1992). *Hogan Personality Inventory Manual* (2nd ed.). Hogan Assessment Systems.

52 See Boyle, G. J. (2008). Critique of the five-factor model of personality. In G. J. Boyle, G. Matthews, & D. H. Saklofske (Eds.), *The SAGE Handbook of Personality Theory and Assessment: Volume 1 – Personality Theories and Models* (pp. 295–312). SAGE Publications Ltd.

53 See, for example, Rankins, E. M., & Wickens, C. L. (2020). A systematic review of equine personality. *Applied Animal Behaviour Science*, 231, Article 105076; and Svartberg, K., & Forkman, B. (2002). Personality traits in the domestic dog (Canis familiaris). *Applied Animal Behaviour Science*, 79: 133–155.

54 Jayawickreme, E., Infurna, F. J., Alajak, K., Blackie, L. E. R., Chopik, W. J., Chung, J. M., ... Zonneveld, R. (2021). Post-traumatic growth as positive personality change: Challenges, opportunities, and recommendations. *Journal of Personality*, 89: 145–165.

55 A similar estimate is recorded by Mueller, S. T., & Tan, Y.-Y. (2019). How many personality configurations exist? Clustering analysis produces a different answer than does factor analysis. *Psychology Today*, August 3.

56 For discussion of free traits, see Little, B. R. (2014). *Me, Myself, and Us: The science of personality and the art of well-being*. PublicAffairs; for metatraits, DeYoung, C. G. (2015). Cybernetic Big Five theory. *Journal of Research in Personality*, 56, 33–58.

57 Allport, G. W. (1937), op cit.

58 Harvey, A. (2023, June 18). How Bob Ross went from a drill sergeant to "The Joy of Painting." All That's Interesting. https://allthatsinteresting.com/bob-ross-military

59 Meyer, R. D., Kelly, E. D., & Bowling, N. A. (2020). Situational strength theory: A formalized conceptualization of a popular idea. In J. F. Rauthmann, R. A. Sherman, & D. C. Funder (Eds.), *The Oxford Handbook of Psychological Situations* (pp. 79–95). Oxford University Press.

60 Urminsky, O., & Bartels, D. M. (2019). Identity, personal continuity, and psychological connectedness across time and over transformation. In A. M. Reed II & M. Forehand (Eds.), *Handbook of Research on Identity Theory in Marketing* (pp. 225–239). Edward Elgar Publishing.

61 Khazan, O. (2025). *Me, But Better: The science and promise of personality change*. Simon Element.

62 Hopwood, C. J., & Bleidorn, W. (2020). Personality change in adulthood. *Current Opinion in Psychology*, 32: 1–5.

63 Nicholson, N. (1984). A theory of work role transitions. *Administrative Science Quarterly*, 29: 172–191.

64 Emre, M. (2018). *The Personality Brokers: The strange history of Myers-Briggs and the birth of personality testing*. Doubleday.

65 Capraro, R. M., & Capraro, M. M. (2002). Myers-Briggs type Indicator score reliability across studies: A meta-analytic reliability generalization study. *Educational and Psychological Measurement*, 62: 590–602.

66 Generally known as the Barnum effect, after the circus owner who reputedly said, "There's a sucker born every minute." See Furnham, A., & Schofield, S. (1987). Accepting personality test feedback: A review of the Barnum effect. *Current Psychology*, 6: 162–178.

67 Nicholson, N. (2000). *Executive Instinct: Managing the human animal in the information age*. Crown Business. (Published in UK under the title *Managing the Human Animal*. Texere.)

68 Hill, N. (2016). *The Nix*. Knopf.

69 Without getting mired in philosophical debate, the stance of this book is akin to evolutionist Daniel Dennett's view that we possess "evitability"—the ability to foresee and alter outcomes, a cognitive capacity that supports moral responsibility, even in a deterministic universe. See Dennett, D. C. (2003). *Freedom Evolves*. Viking Press.

70 Schwarzenegger, A. (2012). *Total Recall: My unbelievably true life story*. Simon & Schuster.

71 Aitkenhead, D. Arnold Schwarzenegger: On a mission to save the planet. *Sunday Times Magazine*, June 15, 2025.

72 Ciesla, J. A., & Roberts, J. E. (2007). Rumination, negative cognition, and their interactive effects on depressed mood. *Emotion*, 7: 555–565.

73 Inscribed at the Temple of Apollo at Delphi and a tenet of Socrates for his personal life and philosophy.

74 A metaphor used in Kurzban, R. (2010), op. cit.

75 A modified version of a pragmatist philosophical dictum, in Thomas, W. I., & Thomas, D. S. (1928). *The Child in America: Behavior problems and programs* (pp. 571–572). Alfred A. Knopf.

CHAPTER 4

1 Rilke, R. M. (1934). *Letters to a Young Poet*. Translated by M. D. Herter Norton, W. W. Norton & Company.
2 Nin, A. (1966). *The Diary of Anaïs Nin*, Vol. 1. Swallow.
3 Excerpted from Tagore's poem "This Dog." In *Arogya* (Poem No. 14). (1940).
4 Nagasawa, M., Mitsui, S., En, S., Ohtani, N., Ohta, M., Sakuma, Y., Onaka, T., Mogi, K., & Kikusui, T. (2015). Oxytocin-gaze positive loop and the coevolution of human–dog bonds. *Science*, 348: 333–336.
5 Polheber, J. P., & Matchock, R. L. (2014). The presence of a dog attenuates cortisol and heart rate in the Trier Social Stress Test compared to human friends. *Journal of Behavioral Medicine*, 37: 860–867; Brooks, H. L., Rushton, K., Lovell, K., Bee, P., Walker, L., Grant, L., & Rogers, A. (2018). The power of support from companion animals for people living with mental health problems: A systematic review and narrative synthesis of the evidence. *BMC Psychiatry*, 18: 31; Ein, N., Li, L., & Vickers, K. (2018). The effect of pet therapy on the physiological and subjective stress response: A meta-analysis. *Stress and Health*, 34: 477–489.
6 2014, written and directed by Spike Jonze.
7 See Chapter 11. For the many reasons AI cannot achieve anything like human sensibilities, see House, P. (2022). *Nineteen Ways of Looking at Consciousness*. St. Martin's Press.
8 Svartberg & Forkman (2022), op. cit.
9 Kumar, R. C. (1997). "Anybody's child": Severe disorders of mother-to-infant bonding. *The British Journal of Psychiatry*, 171: 175–181.
10 Dorahy, M. J., Brand, B. L., Şar, V., Krüger, C., Stavropoulos, P., Martínez-Taboas, A., & Middleton, W. (2014). Dissociative identity disorder: An empirical overview. *Australian & New Zealand Journal of Psychiatry*, 48: 402–417.
11 Jung, C. G. (1933). *Modern Man in Search of a Soul*. Kegan Paul, Trench, & Trubner.
12 Nicholson, N. (2014). Primal business: Evolution, kinship, and the family firm. In S. M. Colarelli & R. D. Arvey (Eds.), *Handbook of the Biological Foundations of Organizational Behavior*. University of Chicago Press.
13 Rohrer, J. M., Egloff, B., & Schmukle, S. C. (2015). Examining the effects of birth order on personality. *Proceedings of the National Academy of Sciences*, 112: 14224–14229.
14 Salmon, C., & Daly, M. (1998). Birth order and familial sentiment: Middleborns are different. *Evolution and Human Behavior*, 19: 299–312; Sulloway, F. J. (1996). *Born to Rebel: Birth order, family dynamics, and creative lives*. Pantheon Books.
15 Gordon, G., & Nicholson, N. (2008). *Family Wars: Classic conflicts in family business and how to deal with them*. Kogan Page.
16 Stasa Ouzký, M., & Machek, O. (2024). Family firm performance: The effects of organizational culture and organizational social capital. *Journal of Family Business Management*, 14: 353–373.
17 Haidt, J. (2006), op. cit.
18 The Looking-glass Self, first conceived in Cooley, C. H. (1902). *Human Nature and the Social Order*. Scribner's.
19 Gleason, T. R. (2002). Social provisions of real and imaginary relationships in early childhood. *Developmental Psychology*, 38: 979–992.
20 Li, C., & Bernoff, J. (2008). *Groundswell: Winning in a world transformed by social technologies*. Harvard Business Press.
21 King, M. (2021). *Social Chemistry: Decoding the patterns of human connection*. Dutton.
22 Cross, R., & Parker, A. (2004). *The Hidden Power of Social Networks: Understanding how work really gets done in organizations*. Harvard Business School Press
23 According to evolutionary biologist Robin Dunbar, the approximate number of people with whom we maintain regular contact. See Mac Carron, P., Kaski, K., & Dunbar, R. I. M. (2016). Calling Dunbar's numbers. *Social Networks*, 47: 151–155.
24 Snyder, M. (1974). Self-monitoring of expressive behavior. *Journal of Personality and Social Psychology*, 30: 526–537.
25 Lewis, M. A., & Neighbours, C. (2005). Self-determination and the use of self-presentation strategies. *The Journal of Social Psychology*. 145: 469–489.

26 Finkel, E. J. (2019). Complementing the sculpting metaphor: Reflections on how relationship partners elicit the best or the worst in each other. *Review of General Psychology*, 23: 127–132.

27 Abrams, Z. (2025, March 1). Social media and online civility. *Monitor on Psychology*, 56: 36.

28 Henrich, J. (2016), op. cit.

29 Cooley, C. F. (1902), op. cit.

30 Baumeister, R. F., & Leary, M. R. (1995). The need to belong: Desire for interpersonal attachments as a
fundamental human motivation. *Psychological Bulletin*, 117: 497–529.

31 Sociologist Erving Goffman analysed interaction rituals as co-creations of identity, though it may be
more a matter of planting images in each other's *umwelts*; see Goffman, E. (1959). *The Presentation of
Self in Everyday Life*. Doubleday; and Goffman, E. (1967). *Interaction Ritual: Essays on face-to-face behavior*.
Pantheon Books.

32 Asendorpf, J. B., & Wilpers, S. (1998). Personality effects on social relationships. *Journal of Personality
and Social Psychology*, 74: 1531–1544.

33 Hamilton, A. F. de C. (2020). Shared pleasure strengthens social bond: A neurocognitive perspective.
Nature Reviews Neuroscience. 21: 545–556; Boothby, E. J., Clark, M. S., & Bargh, J. A. (2014). Shared experiences are amplified. *Psychological Science*, 25: 2209–2216.

34 Dunbar, R. (1996). *Grooming, Gossip, and the Evolution of Language*. Harvard University Press.

35 Popularised by Malcolm Gladwell in *Blink: The power of thinking without thinking*. Little, Brown (2005).
See Ambady, N., & Rosenthal, R. (1992). Thin slices of expressive behavior as predictors of interpersonal consequences: A meta-analysis. *Psychological Bulletin*, 111: 256–274.

36 Brooks, D. (2023). *How to Know a Person: The art of seeing others deeply and being deeply seen* (p. 17). Penguin
Random House.

37 Byblow, D. (2020). The practice of levirate marriage: A cross-cultural comparison. *Agora Journal*, 11:
1–15.

38 In tribal contexts, see Boehm, C. (1999). *Hierarchy in the Forest: The Evolution of Egalitarian Behavior*.
Harvard University Press. In the modern context of personality research, see Hogan, R., & Blickle, G.
(2018). Socioanalytic theory: Basic concepts, supporting evidence and practical implications. In V.
Zeigler-Hill & T. K. Shackelford (Eds.), *The SAGE Handbook of Personality and Individual Differences: Volume
I – The Science of Personality and Individual Differences* (pp. 110–129). SAGE Publications.

39 Because of historical bottlenecks in human evolution, our genetic profile is much more uniform
than other great apes; Caspermeyer, J. (2014). Out of Eurasia, a great primate evolutionary bottle-
neck? *Molecular Biology and Evolution*, 31: 250.

40 Fromm, E. (1956). *The Art of Loving*. Harper & Brothers; Hatfield, E., & Rapson, R. L. (1993). *Love, Sex, and
Intimacy: Their psychology, biology, and history*. HarperCollins.

41 Contu, F., Kruglanski, A. W., Ellenberg, M., Yu, H., Lemay, E. P., & Pierro, A. (2025). Romantic relationships as a source of significance. *European Journal of Social Psychology*, 55: 17–36.

42 Emotions poured into his aptly named *Symphonie fantastique*. Berlioz, H. (1904). *The Memoirs of Hector
Berlioz* (E. F. Heron-Allen, Trans.). Macmillan.

43 Helen Fisher (2004). *Why We Love: The nature and chemistry of romantic love*. Henry Holt.

44 Psychologist Robert Sternberg says that this is the combination of intimacy and commitment,
after the passion has gone. Sternberg, R. J. (1986). A triangular theory of love. *Psychological Review*, 93:
119–135.

45 This concept is borrowed from the great sociologist Anselm Strauss, who used it to describe informal
role structures created by multifunctional working groups to accommodate their UI in talents and
personality. See Strauss, A. L. (1978). *Negotiations: Varieties, processes, contexts, and social order*. Jossey-
Bass.

46 Day, L. C., & Impett, E. A. (2016). For it is in giving that we receive: The benefits of sacrifice in relationships. In Knee & Reis (Eds.), *Positive Approaches to Optimal Relationship Development*. Cambridge University Press.

47 Found in unpublished research conducted in the 2010s by UC Berkeley scholar Charlene Nemeth
(personal communication).

48 Nongkynrih, A. K. (2018). Self-sacrifice: A philosophical analysis from the perspective of gender. *The
NEHU Journal*, XVI(2): 1–12.

49 Brodie, M. (2023, March 28). Why are caring roles often under-valued? A discussion in relation to
feminist perspectives (Part 2 of 3). *Everyday Society*. British Sociological Association.

50 A revolutionary institution for its time, founded in the UK in 1969, offering a free access multimedia platform to higher education for people without qualifications.
51 Tajfel, H., Billig, M. G., Bundy, R. P., & Flament, C. (1971). Social categorization and intergroup behaviour. *European Journal of Social Psychology*, 1: 149–178.
52 "Dining Across the Divide" feature, courtesy of Guardian News and Media Ltd.
53 This is the theme of most couples therapy; see Gutierrez Duarte, L. F. (2018). Witnessing in narrative couple and family therapy. In J. Lebow, A. Chambers, & D. Breunlin (Eds.), *Encyclopedia of Couple and Family Therapy*. Springer.

CHAPTER 5

1   Geertz, C. (1973). *The Interpretation of Cultures: Selected essays* (p. 5). Basic Books.
2   Russell, B. (1928). Dreams and facts. In *Sceptical Essays*. George Allen & Unwin.
3   Fernald, A., & Morikawa, H. (1993). Common themes and cultural variations in Japanese and American mothers' speech to infants. *Child Development*, 64: 637–656.
4   Bornstein, M. H., & Esposito, G. (2020). Cross-cultural perspectives on parent–infant interactions. In J. J. Lockman & C. S. Tamis-LeMonda (Eds.), *The Cambridge Handbook of Infant Development: Brain, behavior, and cultural context* (pp. 805–831). Cambridge University Press.
5   Yaffe, Y. (2023). Systematic review of the differences between mothers and fathers in parenting styles and practices. *Current Psychology*, 42, 16011–16024.
6   Hofstede, Geert. *Cultures and Organizations: Software of the mind*. McGraw-Hill, 1991.
7   Pinker, S. (2002). *The Blank Slate: The modern denial of human nature*. Viking.
8   Buscema, P. M., Lodwick, W. A., Massini, G., Sacco, P. L., Asadi-Zeydabadi, M., Newman, F., Petritoli, R., & Breda, M. (2025). The parallels between deep neural networks and modularity theories of brain function. In *AI: A broad and a different perspective* (pp. 1–7). Springer.
9   Pinker, S. (1994). *The Language Instinct*. William Morrow & Co.
10 Neill, A. S. (1960). *Summerhill: A radical approach to child rearing*. Hart Publishing Company.
11 Although the arrival of "cancel culture" on the campuses of Western universities seems to be contradicting my comfortable assumption.
12 Trommsdorff, G. (2009). Culture and development of self-regulation. *Social and Personality Psychology Compass*, 3: 687–701.
13 See Spickard, J. V. (1989). A guide to Mary Douglas's three versions of grid/group theory. *Sociological Analysis*, 50: 151–170.
14 Björnberg, A., & Nicholson, N. (2007). The family climate scales: development of a new measure for use in family business research. *Family Business Review*, 20: 229–246.
15 Nicholson, N., & Imaizumi, A. (1993). The adjustment of Japanese expatriates to living and working in Britain. *British Journal of Management*, 4: 119–134.
16 Hofstede, G. (2001). *Culture's Consequences: Comparing values, behaviors, institutions and organizations across nations* (2nd ed.). SAGE Publications; Trompenaars, F., & Hampden-Turner, C. (1997). *Riding the Waves of Culture: Understanding cultural diversity in business*. Nicholas Brealey Publishing.
17 Sloan Masters in Leadership & Strategy at London Business School.
18 However, the fact that they are here tells us they are bold, brave, and well-resourced enough to have crossed borders and continents – a welcome sample bias for our exploration of UI.
19 Greenfield, P. M., Keller, H., Fuligni, A., & Maynard, A. (2003). Cultural pathways through universal development. *Annual Review of Psychology*, 54: 461–490.
20 Odling-Smee, F. J., Laland, K. N., & Feldman, M. W. (2003). *Niche Construction: The neglected process in evolution*. Princeton University Press. Applied to the field of leadership by Spisak, B. R., O'Brien, M. J., Nicholson, N., & van Vugt, M. (2015). Niche construction and the evolution of leadership. *Academy of Management Review*, 40: 291–306.
21 Shaw, G. B. (1903). *Man and Superman: A comedy and a philosophy*. Archibald Constable & Co.
22 Ramstead, M. J. D., Veissière, S. P. L., & Kirmayer, L. J. (2016). Cultural affordances: Scaffolding local worlds through shared intentionality and regimes of attention. *Frontiers in Psychology*, 7: Article 1090.

The same idea is used by David Brooks in his book *How to Know a Person: The art of seeing others deeply and being deeply seen*. Random House, (2023).

23 Sunstein, C. (2019). *On Freedom*. Princeton University Press.

24 Sperber, D. (1996). *Explaining Culture: A naturalistic approach*. Blackwell; Richerson, P. J., & Boyd, R. (2005). *Not by Genes Alone: How culture transformed human evolution*. University of Chicago Press.

25 Eldredge, N., & Gould, S. J. (1972). Punctuated equilibria: An alternative to phyletic gradualism. In T. J. M. Schopf (Ed.), *Models in Paleobiology* (pp. 82–115). Freeman, Cooper.

26 Grant, A. (2016), op. cit.

27 Kunst, J. R., & Mesoudi, A. (2024). Decoding the dynamics of cultural change: A cultural evolution approach to the psychology of acculturation. *Personality and Social Psychology Review*, 29: 111–144.

28 Richerson & Boyd, (2005) op. cit.

29 Dartnell, L. (2019). *Origins: How the earth shaped human history*. Bodley Head.

30 Hill, N. (2006), op. cit.

31 Brooks, D. (2023), op. cit.

32 Stephenson, P. (2001). *Billy*. HarperCollins. See Chapters 1–2, pp. 45–86.

33 Sharansky, N., & Troy, G. (2021, October 25). The doublethinkers. *Tablet Magazine*.

34 Peterson, J. B. (1999). *Maps of Meaning: The architecture of belief*. Routledge.

35 Jessica Hagen-Zanker, J., Hennessey, G., & Mazzilli, C. (2023). Subjective and intangible factors in migration decision-making: A review of side-lined literature. *Migration Studies*, 11: 349–359.

36 Mesquita, B., & Frijda, N. H. (1992). Cultural variations in emotions: A review. *Psychological Bulletin*, 112: 179–204.

37 West-Eberhard, M. J. (2003). *Developmental Plasticity and Evolution*. Oxford University Press.

38 Kosic, A. (2025). Individual factors in acculturation: An overview of key dimensions. *Behavioral Sciences*, 15: 827.

39 Borriello, G. (2023). Chasing possible futures: Refugee entrepreneurs navigating uncertainty. *Journal of the Anthropological Society of Oxford*, 15: 218–242.

40 Agius Vallejo, J., & Keister, L. A. (2020). Immigrants and wealth attainment: Migration, inequality, and integration. *Journal of Ethnic and Migration Studies*, 46: 3745–3761.

41 Morris, M. (2024). *Tribal: How the cultural instincts that divide us can help bring us together*. Penguin Random House.

42 Filtzer, D. (2013). Privilege and inequality in communist society. In S. Smith (Ed.), *The Oxford Handbook of the History of Communism* (pp. 505–521). Oxford University Press.

43 Baudrillard, J. (1994). *Simulacra and Simulation* (S. Glaser, Trans.). University of Michigan Press. (Original work published 1981); Lacan, J. (2007). *Écrits* (B. Fink, Trans.). W. W. Norton. (Original work published 1966)

44 Lindeman, M. (1997). Ingroup bias, self-enhancement and group identification. *European Journal of Social Psychology*, 27: 337–355.

45 This technique was introduced to me by multi-talented, best-selling novelist and corporate storytelling consultant Preethi Nair, whose *Kiss the Frog* practice helps leaders find and express their UI.

46 Zurcher, L. A. (1977). *The Mutable Self: A self-concept for social change*. SAGE Publications.

47 Published by Random House. See Sheoran, S. (2024). The visibility of racism: A critical exploration of marginalization and identity in Ralph Ellison's "Invisible Man." *International Journal of English Literature & Social Sciences*, 9: 106–110.

48 Bate, E. (2020, Dec. 1). Billie Eilish opened up about having an "identity crisis" when she got famous. BuzzFeed News, and interview with *Vanity Fair*. (2020, November 30).

49 Tajfel, H., & Turner, J. C. (1986). The social identity theory of intergroup behavior. In S. Worchel & W. G. Austin (Eds.), *Psychology of Intergroup Relations* (pp. 7–24). Nelson-Hall.

50 Post, J. M. (2005). *The Mind of the Terrorist: The psychology of terrorism from the IRA to al-Qaeda*. Palgrave Macmillan.

51 Ibarra, H. (1999). Provisional selves: Experimenting with image and identity in professional adaptation. *Administrative Science Quarterly*, 44: 764–791.

52 Fukuyama, F. (2018). *Identity: The demand for dignity and the politics of resentment*. Farrar, Straus and Giroux.

CHAPTER 6

1   Jung, C. (1933). *Modern Man in Search of a Soul*. Harcourt, Brace & World.
2   From his song "Anthem," released in 1992 on his album *The Future*.
3   Note that psychologists have measured the so-called "Dark Triad" in personality testing of machiavellianism, narcissism, and psychopathy, which relate to several of the syndromes discussed here. See, Douglas, H., Bore, M., & Munro, D. (2012). Distinguishing the dark triad: Evidence from the five-factor model and the Hogan Development Survey. *Psychology*, 3: 237–242.
4   Wehr, G. (1987). *Jung: A biography* (D. M. Weeks, Trans.). Shambhala Publications; and Jung, C. G. (1989). *Memories, Dreams, Reflections* (A. Jaffé, Ed.). Vintage Books.
5   Najjar, S., Pearlman, D. M., Alper, K., Najjar, A., & Devinsky, O. (2013). Neuroinflammation and psychiatric illness. *Journal of Neuroinflammation*, 10: 43.
6   Dantzer, R., O'Connor, J. C., Freund, G. G., Johnson, R. W., & Kelley, K. W. (2008). From inflammation to sickness and depression: When the immune system subjugates the brain. *Nature Reviews Neuroscience*, 9: 46–56.
7   Van Reedt Dortland, A. K. B., et al. (2012). Metabolic syndrome and psychiatric disorders: A systematic review. *Psychosomatic Medicine*, 74: 453–464.
8   Caspi, A., Sugden, K., Moffitt, T. E., Taylor, A., Craig, I. W., Harrington, H., McClay, J., Mill, J., Martin, J., Braithwaite, A., & Poulton, R. (2003). Influence of life stress on depression: Moderation by a polymorphism in the 5-HTT gene. *Science*, 301: 386–389.
9   Haidt, J. (2012). *The Righteous Mind: Why good people are divided by politics and religion*. Pantheon Books.
10 American Psychiatric Association. (2022). *Diagnostic and Statistical Manual of Mental Disorders* (5th ed.).
11 Arendt, H. (1963). *Eichmann in Jerusalem: A report on the banality of evil*. Viking Press.
12 Milgram, S. (1963). Behavioral study of obedience. *Journal of Abnormal and Social Psychology*, 67: 371–378.
13 Haney, C., Banks, W. C., & Zimbardo, P. G. (1973). Interpersonal dynamics in a simulated prison. *International Journal of Criminology and Penology*, 1: 69–97.
14 Haslam, S. A., & Reicher, S. D. (2012). Contesting the "nature" of conformity: What Milgram and Zimbardo's studies really show. *PLoS Biology*, 10: e1001426.
15 Dieckman, J. (n.d.). Murder vs. suicide: What the numbers show. Alternative considerations of Jonestown & Peoples Temple. https://jonestown.sdsu.edu/?page_id=31969
16 Erich Fromm. (1942). *Fear of Freedom*. Routledge & Kegan Paul.
17 Allport, G. W. (1955), op. cit.
18 Nicholson, N. (2013). *The 'I' of Leadership: Strategies for seeing, being and doing*. Wiley/Jossey-Bass.
19 In his novel *Armadillo*, Boyd defines Zemblanity as the opposite of serendipity: "the faculty of making unhappy, unlucky, and expected discoveries by design." The term is derived from the fictional northern land of Zembla, which contrasts with the southern land of Serendip, known for its warmth and spice.
20 The success of narcissists. Boyd, W. (1998). *Armadillo* (p. 228). Hamish Hamilton.
21 Caspi, A., et al. (2003), op. cit.
22 Plath, S. (2000). *The Unabridged Journals of Sylvia Plath* (K. V. Kukil, Ed.). Anchor Books.
23 McClure, D. J., & Cleghorn, R. A. (1980). Hormone imbalance in depressive states. In F. G. Worden (Ed.), *The Future of the Brain Sciences* (pp. 525–553). Springer.
24 Nesse, R. M. (2019) *Good Reasons for Bad Feelings: Insights from the frontier of evolutionary psychiatry*. Dutton.
25 Seligman, M. (2011). *Flourish: A new understanding of happiness and well-being and how to achieve them*. Nicholas Brealey Publishing.
26 Dalí, S. (1942). *The Secret Life of Salvador Dalí* (H. M. Chevalier, Trans.) (p. 1). Dial Press.
27 Kennedy, A., & Panton, J. (Eds.). (2019). *From Self to Selfie: A critique of contemporary forms of alienation*. Springer.
28 The Wherry School in Norfolk England; interviews with Principal Rachel Quick and specialist teacher Imogen Sanchez-Harvey.
29 D. Bravata et al., (2020). Prevalence, predictors, and treatment of impostor syndrome: A systematic review. *Journal of Internal Medicine*, 35: 1252–1275.

30 Various sources including Wikipedia, Britannica, and miscellaneous journalism.
31 Represented in Hogan's socioanalytic theory of personality as "dark side traits," see Hogan, J., Hogan, R., & Kaiser, R. K. (2011). Management derailment. In S. Zedeck (Ed.), *APA Handbook of Industrial and Organizational Psychology: Vol. 2. Selecting and Developing Members for the Organization* (pp. 555–575).
32 Jane Fonda (2006). *My Life So Far*. Random House; See also Mason, D. (2023, November 16). Henry Fonda's dark life was Hollywood's biggest secret. *Factinate*.
33 Goodwin, R., Hou, W. K., Sun, S., Ben-Ezra, M., & Li, L. (2022). Love in the time of COVID-19: A multinational study. *Journal of Social and Personal Relationships*, 39(5): 1293–1312.
34 Cigna Corporation. (2021). *Cigna 2021 U.S. Loneliness Index: A deeper look at the impact of COVID-19 on loneliness and social isolation*. Cigna.
35 US census data; see Ausubel, J. (2020). Older people are more likely to live alone in the U.S. than elsewhere in the world. Pew Research Center, March 10, 2020; European data: Eurostat (2019). Eurostat, October 2019.
36 Smith, K. J., & Victor, C. R. (2018). Typologies of loneliness, living alone and social isolation, and their associations with physical and mental health. *Ageing & Society*, 39: 1709–1730.
37 Bate, J. (2003). *John Clare: A biography*. Farrar, Straus and Giroux.
38 *Macbeth*, Act 5, Scene 5.
39 Gemar, A. (2024). Religion and loneliness: Investigating different aspects of religion and dimensions of loneliness. *Religions*, 15(4): 488. His use of telic and paratelic corresponds to what neuroscience now calls Task Positive Network (TPN) vs. Default Mode Network functioning (DMN).
40 Nagel, T. (1979). *Mortal Questions*. Cambridge University Press.
41 Apter, M. J. (2001). An introduction to reversal theory. In M. J. Apter (Ed.), *Motivational Styles in Everyday Life: A guide to reversal theory* (pp. 3–35). American Psychological Association.
42 Lieberman, D. Z., & Long, M. E. (2018). *The Molecule of More: How a single chemical in your brain drives love, sex, and creativity—and will determine the fate of the human race*. BenBella Books.
43 American Psychiatric Association. (2022), op. cit.
44 Laertius, D. (1925). *Lives of Eminent Philosophers* (R. D. Hicks, Trans.). Loeb Classical Library. Harvard University Press.
45 Strobbe, S., & Kurtz, E. (2012). Narratives for recovery: Personal stories in the 'big book' of Alcoholics Anonymous. *Journal of Groups in Addiction & Recovery*, 7: 29–52.
46 Garnett, M. F., & Miniño, A. M. (2024). *Drug Overdose Deaths in the United States, 2003–2023* (NCHS Data Brief No. 522). National Center for Health Statistics, Centers for Disease Control and Prevention.

CHAPTER 7

1 Eliot, T. S. (1943). *The Four Quartets*. Harcourt, Brace and Co.
2 Douglas Adams (1988). *The Long Dark Tea-Time of the Soul*. Heinemann.
3 *As You Like It* (Act 2, Scene 7).
4 Erikson, E. H. (1980). *Identity and the Life Cycle*. W. W. Norton.
5 Vaillant, G. E. (1977). *Adaptation to Life*. Little, Brown.
6 Sheehy, G. (1976). *Passages: Predictable crises of adult life*. Dutton; Levinson, D. J. (1978). *The Seasons of a Man's Life*. Random House.
7 Loevinger, J. (1997). Stages of personality development. In R. Hogan, J. A. Johnson, & S. R. Briggs (Eds.), *Handbook of Personality Psychology* (pp. 199–208). Academic Press and Kegan, R. (1982). *The Evolving Self: Problem and process in human development*. Harvard University Press.
8 Piaget, J., & Inhelder, B. (1972). *The Psychology of the Child*. Basic Books.
9 Kohlberg, L. (1981). *The Philosophy of Moral Development: Moral stages and the idea of justice*. Harper & Row.
10 Mousley, A., Kuta, S., Lewsey, F., & colleagues. (2025). Topological turning points across the human lifespan. *Nature Communications*, 16, Article 12345.
11 See Eldredge, N., & Gould, S. J. (1972), op. cit.
12 Babakr, Z. H., Mohamedamin, P., & Kakamad, K. (2019). Piaget's cognitive developmental theory: A critical review. *Education Quarterly Reviews*, 2: 517–524.

13 Gratton, L., & Scott, A. (2016). *The 100-Year Life: Living and working in an age of longevity.* Bloomsbury Publishing; Scott, A. J. (2024). *The Longevity Imperative: How to build a healthier and more productive society to support our longer lives.* Basic Books.

14 Brockmeier, J., & Carbaugh, D. (2001). Narrative identity. *Theory & Psychology*, 11: 557–563.

15 More consistent with the UI perspective of this book is the insightful work of Dan McAdams, who describes three levels of personality: dispositional traits, characteristic adaptations, and life story – the narrative formed by autobiographical memory. See McAdams, D. P. (1993). *The Stories We Live By: Personal myths and the making of the self.* William Morrow.

16 Ibarra, H. (2023). *Working Identity: Unconventional strategies for reinventing your career* (2nd ed.). Harvard Business Review Press.

17 Symbolic interactionist sociologists coined this principle; see Thomas, W. I., & Thomas, D. S. (1928). *The Child in America: Behavior problems and programs.* Alfred A. Knopf.

18 Petriglieri, J., & Sheprow, E. (2025). Uprooting loneliness: A theory of continuity-breaking self-narrative change. *Academy of Management Journal*, 68: in press.

19 Wolynn, M. (2016). *It Didn't Start with You: How inherited family trauma shapes who we are and how to end the cycle.* Viking.

20 Guralnick, P. (1994). *Last Train to Memphis: The rise of Elvis Presley.* Little, Brown and Company.

21 Saigal, S., & Doyle, L. W. (2008). An overview of long-term outcomes of extremely preterm and very low birth weight infants. *Developmental and Behavioral Pediatrics*, 29: 373–381; Pattinson, R. C., & Pillay, S. (2007). Emotional and behavioural outcomes of premature birth. *Journal of Child Psychology and Psychiatry*, 48: 1012–1018.

22 *The Sunday Times Magazine.* (2024, June 9). Taylor Swift: [Feature article]. pp. 7–13.

23 Tomalin, C. (2021). *The Young H. G. Wells: Changing the world.* Viking.

24 McAdams, D. P. (2006). *The Redemptive Self: Stories Americans live by.* Oxford University Press.

25 Larkin, P. (1971). This be the verse. In "High Windows" (p. 62). Faber & Faber.

26 In his novel *The Beautiful and the Damned* (Charles Scribner's Sons, 1922).

27 Yousafzai, M., & Lamb, C. (2013). *I Am Malala: The girl who stood up for education and was shot by the Taliban.* Little, Brown and Company.

28 Novelist William Boyd's useful invented concept; see Chapter 6 note.

29 Lucy Foulkes says we look back on these as "reminiscence bumps," in *Coming of Age: How adolescence shapes us.* Bodley Head (2024).

30 The speaker was Richard Buzzard, director of the National Institute of Industrial Psychology, describing the legendary Tavistock Studies, conducted by Eric Trist and Ken Bamforth: Trist, E. L., & Bamforth, K. W. (1951). Some social and psychological consequences of the Longwall method of coal-getting. *Human Relations*, 4: 3–38.

31 Nicholson, N. (1984), op. cit.

32 Little, B. R. (2020). How are you doing, really? Personal project pursuit and human flourishing. *Canadian Psychology*, 61: 140–152.

33 2014, based on the memoir of Cheryl Strayed, *Wild: From lost to found on the Pacific Crest Trail.* Alfred A. Knopf, 2012.

34 *Life Reimagined: The science, art, and opportunity of midlife.* Riverhead Books (2016).

35 What Daniel Levinson calls "the Dream," op. cit., when in later life people have revived memories of abandoned ideas.

36 Kewell, H. (2024). *Midlife: Stories of crisis and growth from the counselling room.* Pinter & Martin.

37 Nicholson, N., & West, M. A. (1989). *Managerial Job Change: Men and women in transition.* Cambridge: Cambridge University Press.

38 Nicholson, N. (1984), op. cit.

39 Van Gennep, A. (1960). *The Rites of Passage.* (M. B. Vizedom & G. L. Caffee, Trans.) Routledge & Kegan Paul. (Original work published 1909)

40 Ibarra, H., & Obodaru, O. (2020). The liminal playground: Identity play and the creative potential of liminal experiences. In A. P. Kozlowski (Ed.), *The Oxford Handbook of Identities in Organizations* (pp. 471–485). Oxford University Press.

41 Matt Morgan (2014). *A Second Act: What nearly dying teaches us about really living.* Simon & Schuster.

42 *USA Today*, October 21, 2025.

43 Bonanno, G. A. (2004). Loss, trauma, and human resilience: Have we underestimated the human capacity to thrive after extremely aversive events? *American Psychologist*, 59: 20–28.

44 Galatzer-Levy, I. R., Huang, S. H., & Bonanno, G. A. (2018). Trajectories of resilience and dysfunction following potential trauma: A review and statistical evaluation. *Clinical Psychology Review*, 63: 41–55.
45 Logan, G. (2024). *The\ Midpoint\ Plan*. Piatkus.
46 Jamieson, A. (2022). *Midlife: Humanity's secret weapon*. Notting Hill Editions.
47 Barbara Olive Collard published four novels, all out of print, *Honey Out of the Rock* (1953), *A Point of Balance* (1954), *Gaster's House* (1955), *Daphne* (1956), plus an unpublished memoir, *Living in the Wilderness*.
48 Gratton, L., & Scott, A. (2016), op. cit.
49 Mousley et al. (2025), op. cit.
50 Ware, B. (2012). *The Top Five Regrets of the Dying: A life transformed by the dearly departing*. Hay House.
51 Pink, D. H. (2022). *The Power of Regret: How looking backward moves us forward*. Riverhead Books.
52 Silva, T. O., Ribeiro, H. G., & Moreira-Almeida, A. (2024). End-of-life experiences in the dying process: Scoping and mixed-methods systematic review. *BMJ Supportive & Palliative Care*, 13: 624–632.

CHAPTER 8

1 Commonly misattributed to Friedrich Nietzsche.
2 *The Soul of Man under Socialism*. Essay, 1891.
3 Sawyer, R. K. (2012). *Explaining Creativity: The science of human* innovation (2nd ed.). Oxford University Press; Amabile, T. M. (1983). The social psychology of creativity: A componential conceptualization. *Journal of Personality and Social Psychology*, 45: 357–376.
4 Tomalin, C. (1997). *Jane Austen: A life*. Viking.
5 Notably, Howe, M. J. A. (1999). *Genius Explained*. Cambridge University Press; Gladwell, M. (2005), op cit.; and Lewis, H. (2025). *The Genius Myth: The dangerous allure of rebels, monsters and rule-breakers*. Penguin Random House.
6 Frankl, V. E. (2006). *Man's Search for Meaning* (I. Lasch, Trans.; 4th ed., p. 109). Beacon Press. (Original work published 1946)
7 Kaplan, D. E. (2019). Creativity in education: Teaching for creativity development. *Psychology*, 10(2): 140–147.
8 Prospero in *The Tempest* channelling Shakespeare.
9 Goodman, J. (1984). The Playboy Interview: Paul McCartney. *Playboy Magazine*; McCartney, P. (2021). *The Lyrics: 1956 to the present*. London: Allen Lane; and Cross, C. (2005). *The Beatles: Day-by-day, song-by-song, record-by-record*. iUniverse, Inc.
10 Irving, Z. C., McGrath, C., Flynn, L., Glasser, A., & Mills, C. (2024). The shower effect: Mind wandering facilitates creative incubation during moderately engaging activities. *Psychology of Aesthetics, Creativity, and the Arts*, 18: 1096–1107.
11 Gilbert, E. (2025). *All the Way to the River*. Riverhead Books.
12 Cameron, J. (1992). *The Artist's Way: A spiritual path to higher creativity*. Tarcher/Putnam.
13 Zander, B. (2002). *The Art of Possibility*. Penguin Books.
14 Vanderbilt, T. (2016), *You May Also Like: Taste in an age of endless choice*. Simon & Schuster.
15 Funch, B. S. (2021). Art, emotion, and existential well-being. *Journal of Theoretical and Philosophical Psychology*, 41: 5–17.
16 Blier, S. P. (2019). *Picasso's Demoiselles: The untold origins of a modern masterpiece*. Duke University Press.
17 Prideaux, S. (2024). *Wild Thing: A life of Paul Gauguin*. Norton.
18 Vasari, G. (1903). *The Life of Leonardo da Vinci* (H. P. Horne, Trans. & Ed.). At the Sign of the Unicorn. (Original work published 1550)
19 Johnson, P. (2003). *Art: A new history* (p. 276). Harper Collins.
20 Isaacson, W. (2007). *Einstein: His life and universe*. Simon & Schuster.
21 Einstein, A. (1931). *Living Philosophies* (C. Fadiman, Ed.). Simon & Schuster.
22 Einstein, A. (2010). *The Ultimate Quotable Einstein* (A. Calaprice, Ed.). Princeton University Press.
23 Wright, R. (1994), op. cit.
24 van Wyhe, J. (2013). *Dispelling the Darkness: Voyage in the Malay Archipelago and the discovery of evolution by Wallace and Darwin*. World Scientific.

25 Nicholson, N. (2005). Meeting the Maasai: Messages for management. *Journal of Management Inquiry*, 14: 255–267.
26 Boehm, C. (1999), op. cit.
27 On the outskirts of Vence on the French Riviera.
28 Interview with *Guitar Player* magazine, 1999.
29 Csikszentmihalyi, M. (1990). *Flow: The psychology of optimal experience*. Harper & Row.
30 Maslow, A. H. (1954). *Motivation and Personality* (p. 150). Harper & Row.
31 Kaufman, S. B. (2022). *Transcend: The new science of self-actualization*. Sheldon Press.
32 Maslow, A. H. (1990), op. cit., p. 93.
33 Cardeña, E., Berkovich-Ohana, A., Valli, K., Barttfeld, P., Gomez-Marin, A., Greyson, B., . . . & Yaden, D. (2025). A consensus taxonomy of altered (nonordinary) states of consciousness: Bringing order to disarray. *PsycARTICLES*. https://psycnet.apa.org/fulltext/2026-28269-001
34 Solms, M. (2021). *The Hidden Spring: A journey to the source of consciousness*. W. W. Norton & Company.
35 Leary, M. R. (2004). *The Curse of the Self: Self-awareness, egotism, and the quality of human life*. Oxford University Press.
36 Leary, M. R., Diebels, K. J., Jongman-Sereno, K. P., & Hawkins, A. (2016). Perspectives on hypo-egoic phenomena from social and personality psychology. In K. W. Brown & M. R. Leary (Eds.), *The Oxford Handbook of Hypo-egoic Phenomena* (pp. 47–62). Oxford University Press.
37 Baumann, N. (2012). Autotelic personality. In S. Engeser (Ed.), *Advances in Flow Research* (pp. 165–186). Springer Science + Business Media.
38 Dederer, C. (2023). *Monsters: A fan's dilemma*. Alfred A. Knopf.
39 Strachey, L. (1967). *The Letters of Lytton Strachey* (M. Holroyd, Ed.). Chatto & Windus.
40 Munch, E. (n.d.). *Edvard Munch's Writings*. Digital archive, Munch Museum.
41 Dąbrowski, K., & Piechowski, M. M. (1977). *Theory of levels of emotional development* (Vol. 2). Dabor Science Publications; Piechowski, M. M. (1991). Inner growth and transformation in the life of the gifted. *Advanced Development*, 1: 1–16.
42 Landesman, F. (2015). *The Collected Poems*. The Permanent Press.
43 Maddi, S. R. (2006). Hardiness: The courage to grow from stresses. *The Journal of Positive Psychology*, 1: 160–168.
44 The answer my son Oliver, aged 10, gave me when I musingly asked him, "Who do you think has done more to change the world, artists or scientists?"

CHAPTER 9

1 Letter to friend and editor Sol Stein in early 1957. See Stein's 2004 memoir *Native Sons: A friendship that created one of the greatest works of the 20th century*.
2 Mill, J. S. (1859). *On Liberty* (Chapter III). London: John W. Parker and Son.
3 Cable, D. M., Gino, F., & Staats, B. R. (2013). Breaking them in or building them up? The role of organizational socialization in the emergence of newcomers' authentic best selves. *Administrative Science Quarterly*, 58: 1–36.
4 Baruch, Y., & Nicholson, N. (1997). Home, sweet work: Requirements for effective home working. *Journal of General Management*, 23: 15–30.
5 McPhail, R., Chan, X. W. C., May, R., & Wilkinson, A. (2023). Post-COVID remote working and its impact on people, productivity, and the planet: An exploratory scoping review. *The International Journal of Human Resource Management*, 35: 154–182.
6 Ashford, S. J., Caza, B. B., & Reid, E. M. (2018). From surviving to thriving in the gig economy: A research agenda for individuals in the new world of work. *Research in Organizational Behavior*, 38: 23–41.
7 Little, B. R. (2014). *Me, Myself, and Us: The science of personality and the art of well-being*. PublicAffairs.
8 Called "grid" and "group" in Mary Douglas's cultural anthropology. See Spickard, J. V. (1989), op. cit.
9 Ashikali, T., Groeneveld, S., & Ritz, A. (2021). Managing a diverse workforce. In P. Leisink et al. (Ed.), *Managing for Public Service Performance: How people and values make a difference* (pp. 182–198). Oxford University Press.

10 These criteria are central to the Gallup polling organisation's workplace survey; Gallup, Inc. (2017). *State of the American Workplace Report* drawing upon research such as, Harter, J. K., Schmidt, F. L., & Hayes, T. L. (2002). Business-unit-level relationship between employee satisfaction, employee engagement, and business outcomes: A meta-analysis. *Journal of Applied Psychology*, 87: 268–279.

11 Starbuck, W. H. (1993). Keeping a butterfly and an elephant in a house of cards: The elements of exceptional success. *Journal of Management Studies*, 30: 885–921. See also Nanda, A., & Cross, M. (2020). *Wachtell Lipton: Focused excellence* (HBS No. 720–396). Harvard Business School.

12 Schneider, B. (1987). The people make the place. *Personnel Psychology*, 40: 437–453.

13 Lewis, D. G., et al. (2022), op. cit.

14 Hutchinson, A. M., Troth, A. C., Caza, A., & Wilson, M. E. (2013). Discretion: What is it, and how is it useful? In M. A. Paludi (Ed.), *Psychology for Business Success* (Vol. 3, pp. 57–73). Praeger/ABC-CLIO.

15 Mainly the requirement to excel in teaching demanding adult populations and publishing in top-flight journals in a highly competitive context.

16 Nicholson, N. (1984), op. cit.

17 Frese, M., & Fay, D. (2001). Personal initiative: An active performance concept for work in the 21st century. *Research in Organizational Behavior*, 23: 133–187.

18 Nicholson, N. (1987). The transition cycle: A conceptual framework for the analysis of change and human resource management. In K. M. Rowland & G. R. Ferris (Eds.), *Research in Personnel and Human Resources Management* (Vol. 5, pp. 167–222). JAI Press.

19 Söderlund, J. (2008). Competence dynamics and learning processes in project-based firms: Exploring the role of project sequences. *International Journal of Project Management*, 26: 532–538.

20 Heath, C., & Heath, D. (2019). *The Power of Moments: Why certain experiences have extraordinary impact.* Corgi.

21 Puranam, P. (2025). *Re-Humanize: How to build human-centric organizations in the age of algorithms.* Penguin Books.

22 Toby Velte, technology author and consultant, the only identified person from my case book, was also an informant for Chapter 11. He is the founder of Probility AI and Budscout AI, author of multiple books on technology. See https://www.london.edu/faculty-and-research/contributors/toby-velte.

23 Microsoft. (n.d.). Empowering our employees. Microsoft Corporate Social Responsibility. https://www.microsoft.com/en-us/corporate-responsibility/empowering-employees

24 In my book *The "I" of Leadership* (2013), I used the case study of bandleader Duke Ellington, who inspired tremendous love and loyalty by many means, including giving musicians their "place in the sun" – a number in the repertoire showcasing their talents.

25 Kanter, R. M. (2013, January 16). Nine rules for stifling innovation. *Harvard Business Review.*

26 James Dyson (2021). *Invention: A lifetime of learning through failure* (p. 47). Simon & Schuster.

27 Follett, M. P. (1941). The giving of orders. In H. C. Metcalf & L. Urwick (Eds.), *Dynamic Administration: The collected papers of Mary Parker Follett* (pp. 149–158). Harper & Brothers.

28 The Nomadic Business School (see Chapter 10).

29 Boyd, W. (1998), op. cit.

30 Trivers, R. (2000), op. cit.

31 A theme prominent in *The "I" of Leadership*, op cit. Also Goffee, R., & Jones, G. (2015). *Why Should Anyone Be Led by You?* Harvard Business Review Press.

32 From the foreword to her album, *Lover* (2019).

33 *Nicholas Nickleby* (Dickens); *Portrait of the Artists as a Young Man* (Joyce); *It* (King).

34 Hill, A. (2023). *Centennials: The surprising strategy of the world's most enduring companies.* Penguin Business.

35 This is not a benign process, identified by Goffman as "mortification of the self," followed by the transformative process of "resocialisation" – a kind of brainwashing in effect. See Goffman, E. (1961), *Asylums: Essays on the social situation of mental patients and other inmates.* Anchor Books; and Becker, H. S., Geer, B., Hughes, E. C., & Strauss, A. L. (1961). *Boys in White: Student culture in medical school.* University of Chicago Press.

36 For help with this, see Ibarra, H. (2015). *Act Like a Leader, Think Like a Leader.* Harvard Business Review Press.

37 What I call "Critical Leader Relationships." See Nicholson, N. (2013), op. cit.

38 Interview conducted on a field trip to South Africa, in 2017. See also, Brand, C., & Mulholland, B. (2014). *Mandela: My prisoner, my friend.* John Blake.

CHAPTER 10

1 Angelou, M. (1970). *I Know Why the Caged Bird Sings*. Random House.
2 From Plato's *Apology* – an account of Socrates's trial and death.
3 Shakur, T. (1999). *The Rose that Grew from Concrete*. Pocket Books.
4 Watkins & Roberts, (2020), op. cit.
5 Gilbert, D. (2006). *Stumbling on Happiness*. Alfred A. Knopf.
6 Probably misattributed and anonymous, but it is certainly in the character of Twain.
7 This is a hardwired aspect of consciousness, as Dan Gilbert points out, op. cit.
8 One of the findings in Nicholson, N., & West, M. A. (1988). *Managerial Job Change: Men and women in transition*. Cambridge University Press.
9 To find more about the tactics and strategies of these; see Nicholson (1987), op. cit., and Nicholson, N., & West, M. A. (1988), op. cit.
10 Storr, W. (2020). *The Science of Storytelling: Why stories make us human and how to tell them better*. William Collins.
11 Maurois, A. (1939). *The Art of Living* (E. W. Dickes, Trans.). Harper & Brothers.
12 The NEO and the Hogan scales are among the most robust in the field, but there are many others measuring the same dimensions.
13 Rees, A., & Nicholson, N. (1994). The Twenty Statements Test. In C. Cassell & G. Symon (Eds.), *Qualitative Methods in Organizational and Occupational Psychology: A practical guide*. SAGE Publications. See also Zurcher, L. A. (1977), op. cit.
14 See endnote about Preethi's work in Chapter 4.
15 See Chapter 4 and Cooley, op. cit.
16 For a more detailed exposition, see Nicholson, N. (2003). How to motivate your problem people. *Harvard Business Review*, 81: 56–65.
17 Called in a weaker form, "perspective-taking" in social psychology. See Erle, T. M., & Topolinski, S. (2017). The grounded nature of psychological perspective-taking. *Journal of Personality and Social Psychology*, 112: 683–695.
18 Gottman, J. M., & Gottman, J. S. (2017). *The Science of Couples and Family Therapy: Behind the scenes at the Love Lab*. W. W. Norton & Company.
19 Hersch, E. (2014). Fact and value. In T. Teo (Ed.). *Encyclopedia of Critical Psychology* (pp. 665–673). Springer.
20 Evolutionary psychologist Stephen Pinker shows how difficult it is to escape the entanglement of our own assumptions in Pinker, S. (2025). *When Everyone Knows That Everyone Knows …: Common knowledge and the mysteries of money, power, and everyday life*. Scribner.
21 Rogerian "unconditional regard," the central pillar of his client-centred therapy embodies this principle; see Rogers, C. R. (1959). A theory of therapy, personality, and interpersonal relationships as developed in the client-centred framework. In S. Koch (Ed.), *Psychology: A Study of a Science* (Vol. 3, pp. 184–256). McGraw Hill.
22 Ibarra, H. (2023), op. cit., uses this idea to denote investments in areas where you might plant seeds for future development.
23 Nicholson, N. (2005). Meeting the Maasai: Messages for management. *Journal of Management Inquiry*, 14: 255–267.
24 To see and use these materials, apply to Anthony Willoughby, Anthony@nomadicschoolofbusiness.com.
25 Keating, C. F. (2016). The developmental arc of nonverbal communication: Capacity and consequence for human social bonds. In D. Matsumoto, H. C. Wang, & M. G. Franks (Eds.). *APA Handbook or Nonverbal Communication* (pp. 103–122). American Psychological Association; Malchiodi, C. A. (2013). *Art Therapy and Health Care*. Guilford Press.
26 In evolutionary biology, what are called "fitness peaks"; see Mehra, P., & Hintze, A. (2025). From valleys to peaks: The role of evolvability in fitness landscape navigation. *PNAS Nexus*, 4: pgaf221.
27 Allport, G. W. (1955). *Becoming: Basic considerations for a psychology of personality*. Yale University Press.
28 Kierkegaard, S. (1938). *Purity of Heart Is to Will One Thing: Spiritual preparation for the office of confession* (D. V. Steere, Trans.). Harper & Brothers. (Original work published 1847)

CHAPTER 11

1   Wiener, N. (1950). *The Human Use of Human Beings: Cybernetics and society*. Houghton Mifflin.
2   Gee, H. (2025). *The Decline and Fall of the Human Empire: Why our species is on the edge of extinction*. Picador.
3   It never was true – this was never a principle of evolutionary theory, but a phrase coined by Social Darwinist Herbert Spencer. Spencer, H. (1864). *Principles of Biology* (Vol. 1). Williams and Norgate. The concept of "reproductive fitness" is now accepted as the criterion for the viability of species' members.
4   Richerson & Boyd (2005), op. cit.
5   Nicholson, N. (1998). How hardwired is human behavior? *Harvard Business Review*, 76: 134–147.
6   Yakushko, O. (2023). Predicting, controlling, and engineering humans: Eugenic sciences in American psychology. In C. L. Frisby, R. E. Redding, W. T. O'Donohue, & S. O. Lilienfeld (Eds.), *Ideological and Political Bias in Psychology: Nature, scope, and solutions* (pp. 625–639). Springer Nature Switzerland AG.
7   ChatGPT (various iterations), Copilot, DeepSeek, Claude, and Gemini.
8   Principal among them Patrick Dixon of Global Change, Toby Velte of Probility AI and Spike AT, and Keith Coates of TomorrowToday Global.
9   See his website, GlobalChange.com, and best-selling book, Dixon, P. (2024). *How AI Will Change Your Life*. Profile Books.
10 Rogers, S. L., Branson, I., Hollett, R. C., Speelman, C. P., & Fraser, A. D. (2022). Realistic motion avatars are the future for social interaction in virtual reality. *Frontiers in Virtual Reality*, 3: 981400.
11 Personal communication, June 19, 2025.
12 Suleyman, N. (2025, August 20). Chatbots risk fuelling psychosis, warns Microsoft AI chief. *The Telegraph*.
13 Ponterotto, J. G. (2025). *The Psychobiographer's Handbook: A practical guide to research and ethics*. American Psychological Association.
14 Davies, S. (2004). *The Great Horse-Manure Crisis of 1894*. Institute of Economic Affairs.
15 Kahneman, D., & Tversky, A. (1979). Prospect theory: An analysis of decision under risk. *Econometrica*, 47: 263–291.
16 McGorry, P. D., Mei, C., Dalal, N., Alvarez-Jimenez, M., Blakemore, S.-J., Browne, V., Dooley, B., Hickie, I. B., Jones, P. B., McDaid, D., Mihalopoulos, C., Wood, S. J., El Azzouzi, F. A., Fazio, J., Gow, E., Hanjabam, S., Hayes, A., Morris, A., Pang, E., . . . Killackey, E. (2024). The Lancet Psychiatry Commission on Youth Mental Health. *The Lancet Psychiatry*: 1: 731–774.
17 Gupta, S. K. (2022). Meditation, mindfulness, and mental health: Opportunities, issues, and challenges. In S. K. Gupta (Ed.), *Handbook of Research on Clinical Applications of Meditation and Mindfulness-based Interventions in Mental health* (pp. 1–14). Medical Information Science Reference.

CHAPTER 12

1   Schweitzer, A. (1929). *Civilisation and Ethics*. (C. T. Campion, Trans.). A. & C. Black.
2   Marcus Aurelius. (2nd century CE/2002). *Meditations* (G. Hays. Trans). Modern Library.
3   Jules Goddard, private communication. See Goddard, J. (2024). *Letting Go of Logic*. Ethics International Press. Reynolds, A., Goddard, J., Houlder, D., & Lewis, D. G. (2019). *What Philosophy Can Teach You About Being a Better Leader*. Kogan Page.
4   This is one of the aphorisms in Sheldon Kopp's "eschatological laundry list," which captures many of the ideas in this book. See Kopp, S. (1974). *If You Meet the Buddha on the Road, Kill Him!* (pp. 161–163). Science and Behavior Books.
5   A paraphrase of Bai, Z. (2025). Forgetting: Its meaning in Zhuangzi's philosophy of self-cultivation. *Religions*, 16(8): 1037.